innerQuest

ALSO BY PANDIT RAJMANI TIGUNAIT, PH.D.

Books

At the Eleventh Hour: The Biography of Swami Rama
Tantra Unveiled: Seducing the Forces of Matter and Spirit
Swami Rama of the Himalayas: His Life and Mission
Shakti: The Power in Tantra (A Scholarly Approach)
From Death to Birth: Understanding Karma and Reincarnation
The Power of Mantra and the Mystery of Initiation
Shakti Sadhana: Steps to Samadhi
(A Translation of the Tripura Rahasya)
The Tradition of the Himalayan Masters
Yoga on War and Peace
Seven Systems of Indian Philosophy

Audio & Video

The Spirit of the Upanishads
The Spirit of the Vedas
Pulsation of the Maha Kumbha Mela
In the Footsteps of the Sages
Living Tantra™ Series:
- Tantric Traditions and Techniques
- The Secret of Tantric Rituals
- Forbidden Tantra
- Tantra and Kundalini
- Sri Chakra: The Highest Tantric Practice
- Sri Vidya: The Embodiment of Tantra

Eight Steps to Self-Transformation
Nine Steps to Disarming the Mind

innerQuest

YOGA'S ANSWERS TO LIFE'S QUESTIONS

Second Edition

By Pandit Rajmani Tigunait, Ph.D.

Himalayan Institute Press
Honesdale, Pennsylvania

The Himalayan Institute Press
RR 1, Box 1129
Honesdale, Pennsylvania 18431

www.HimalayanInstitute.org

Second edition 2002. First printing

Cover design by Janet Cerretani and Jeanette Robertson
Creative direction and design by Jeanette Robertson
Electronic design and production by Julia A. Valenza

The paper used in this publication meets the minimum requirements of American
National Standard for Information Sciences—Permanence of Paper for Printed
Library Materials, ANSI Z39.48-1984.

Library of Congress Cataloging-in-Publication Data

Tigunait, Pandit Rajmani.
Inner quest : yoga's answers to life's questions / Pandit Rajmani Tigunait.
p. cm.
ISBN 0-89389-222-X (pbk. : alk. paper)
1. Yoga. I. Title

B132.Y6 T57 2002
294.5'436--dc21

2001058337

Dedicated to my gurudeva,
Swami Rama of the Himalayas

Contents

Introduction *by Deborah Willoughby* 1

Starting Out 5

WHAT IS SPIRITUALITY? 5

YOGA AND RELIGION 12

YOGA AND GOD 24

Establishing a Personal Practice 33

TEACHER AND STUDENT 33

CHOOSING A PATH 40

PREPARING FOR THE JOURNEY 47

CREATING A SPIRITUAL ENVIRONMENT 57

Roadblocks Along the Way 75

TAMING THE MIND AND SENSES 75

PURIFYING THE EGO 81

OVERCOMING OBSTACLES 86

The Science of Life 101

REJUVENATION TECHNIQUES 101

HERBS 109

Working with Body and Breath 119

HATHA YOGA 119

ASANA AND PRANAYAMA 130

Turning Inward 141
THE PRACTICE OF MEDITATION 141
THE SACRED SOUND 159

Our True Nature 177
FREEDOM FROM MISERY 177
KARMA, THE MAKER OF DESTINY 186
TRANSCENDING DEATH 194

Staying on the Path 213
MAKING PROGRESS 213
PILGRIMAGE AND RITUAL 231
THE DAWNING OF ENLIGHTENMENT 239

The Journey's End 243

Glossary 249

About the Author 257

Introduction

There comes a time when the rewards and pleasures of the world around us lose their charm. It can happen in a flash: at a moment of achievement when a long-sought prize turns to dust in our hands, or when catastrophe strikes. But for most of us it begins with a wisp of unease, an indefinable sense of something missing that grows more insistent with time. Try as we might to stifle it, our disquiet grows—and grows again. Can it be that life has no meaning? And more urgent still, what is the meaning of *my* life? This is where the inner quest begins.

There are many routes to take once we start looking beneath the surface. Religious organizations, bookstores, websites, and workshops offer a maze of directions: astrology, *pancha karma,* yoga classes, church membership, flower remedies, psychotherapy, rituals, Reiki, chanting—the list goes on. Many of these routes seem to take us out of ourselves, at least for a time, but then the trail peters out and we wander on, finding a quick fix here, the glimmer of a real answer there. But the hollowness abides.

This isn't surprising when you think about it. It's as if we are trying to reach the Grand Canyon by flying from New York to Vancouver, then drifting off to Paris, embarking from Orly for a trip up the Nile, and flitting from there to the Yucatan before wandering up to Pittsburgh. At the end of all this exploring we're a few hundred miles closer to the Grand Canyon than we were when we set out, but the bulk of the journey still lies ahead. Similarly, taking a few yoga classes, dropping them to join a self-esteem therapy group, then spending a month in a Zen monastery before going off to a retreat to free the inner child might give us some insight into the vast potential locked within us, but it will not bring us much closer to unlocking it. The meaning and purpose of our lives is still out of reach.

The spiritual quest is often likened to a journey. And any journey, whether across the globe or into the depths of the spirit, unfolds in stages. If you live in Colorado, for instance, you cannot trek to a hidden valley in the Himalayas until you have found your way to an airport, flown to Asia, and hired a vehicle to convey you into the mountains. If you are smart you will have talked to people who have made similar treks, located your route on a map, purchased a reliable guidebook, and spent some time hiking in the Rockies, acclimating your body and breath to high-altitude exertion. The spiritual journey is no different: to reach your goal you need some idea of the terrain that lies between you and your destination and a plan for crossing it. Like any traveler, you will want an accurate map, the best information you can get from those who have made the trip before you, and a reliable guidebook.

This volume offers all three. Written by an experienced traveler in the spiritual realm, *Inner Quest* maps out the journey and provides systematic guidelines for recognizing and overcoming the obstacles that lie ahead. In a quarter of a century of working with students around the world, Pandit Rajmani Tigunait has found that those who embark on the spiritual quest have the same basic questions, regardless of age, culture, or ethnicity. So he has collected our inquiries and arranged them to address the issues that arise as a seeker journeys inward. They run the gamut from straightforward questions about diet and exercise to metaphysical queries about the nature of reality and how we shape our destiny. The first edition of *Inner Quest,* published in 1995, was drawn from columns by the same name that appeared in *Yoga International;* this second edition is more than twice as long and incorporates the columns that appeared in the magazine in the next six years.

If you start at the beginning and read this volume straight through to the end, you will come away with a clear picture of what the spiritual journey entails and how to find your way to the heart of the inner realm. On the other hand, you may prefer to consult the Table of Contents and go directly to the questions that address your most pressing concerns. Or you may choose to browse, leafing through the chapters and reading the answers to the questions that catch your eye. However you first approach it, you will reach for this book again and again. And as your inward journey deepens and you begin to master your body, breath, and mind, you will find yourself rereading it, finding answers to questions you didn't know you had.

Like any first-rate guidebook, *Inner Quest* can be used in whatever way suits you—as a comprehensive guide, a quick reference, or an inexhaustible treasury. Spiritual travelers will find it invaluable.

Deborah Willoughby
Editor, *Yoga International*

Starting out

WHAT IS SPIRITUALITY?

Q There is considerable confusion about spirituality. What exactly is spirituality?

Spirituality is a complete science that entails a comprehensive study of the intrinsic nature of the soul and its relationship both to the external world and to Universal Consciousness. When this science is not coupled with contemplative or meditative techniques for attaining the actual experience of higher reality, it is philosophy or metaphysics. When it is based on faith alone and is accompanied by superstition, dogma, customs, and cultural activities, it is religion. When it is accompanied by practices which, although difficult to grasp intellectually, have the power to unveil subtle and often indescribable realms of inner experience, it is mysticism. Only when this science rests firmly on a philosophy of life, incorporates ethical and moral values that are indispensable to health and well-being, and provides a workable system of self-training leading to self-transformation can it correctly be called spirituality.

Practically speaking, spirituality has two integral parts: theories and practices for removing obstacles to the inward journey, and theories and practices that elucidate the inner core of reality and lead an aspirant there, step by step. The goal of spirituality is direct realization of the true self and its relationship with the Universal Self. The body and mind are the most efficient tools for achieving that goal. Keeping the body and mind in good health, creating a balance between the two, and, finally, directing all one's resources toward spiritual unfoldment are the steps needed in spiritual practice.

A spiritual practice that fails to eliminate the conditions of illness, procrastination, doubt, laziness, hopelessness, indulgence in sense pleasures, confusion, instability, and inability to concentrate is like a body without breath; such a practice is lifeless. Involving yourself in spiritual practices, even those that are valid and potent, while disregarding the process of purification is like drinking pure water from a grimy cup.

The first step in spiritual practice is to address the health of the body. A healthy mind can dwell only in a healthy body. Because a confused mind is not fit for any kind of practice, the next step is to work with the mind. Systematically working with the body, breath, and mind introduces you to various levels of yourself and helps you overcome the obstacles to attaining direct, experiential knowledge of Truth. When these obstacles have been overcome, you will have more time and energy for your actual practice, which involves gaining access to the vast potentials that lie dormant within your body and mind.

Thus a holistic approach to spirituality involves working with your body by practicing *asana, pranayama,* and *mudras*—the subtle yogic techniques for unlocking pranic forces and rechanneling them toward the center of your being. You unfold the power of the mind by practicing the techniques of concentration and meditation, which enable you to collect the forces of the mind and direct them toward your center of consciousness, known as *atman,* your spirit or pure self. Only a properly trained and one-pointed mind can go beyond the realm of ordinary, sense-bound consciousness. Attaining a direct experience of the pure self is ultimately what is meant by "spiritual enlightenment," but those primary and secondary practices that help you reach this sublime goal are also an intrinsic part of spirituality.

What is spiritual practice?

Its definition changes depending on our understanding of life. In general, when people are trying to achieve something intangible and there is no direct connection between the means and the goal, they call it "spirituality." In this sense, spiritual practice takes different forms, depending on the culture and the end result being sought. For example, members of a tribal community may perform rituals involving herbs, ceremonial fires, dancing, and chanting. For them, these are spiritual practices. In a modern European community, people may go to a church and listen to a minister or priest say prayers, bow before an altar, sing hymns, and observe special holidays. Both communities believe these practices are a means of contacting "spirit" or "the center of consciousness" or "the core of being." When we set out to reach the core of our being, when we try to know the essence of our existence, we are said to be embarking on a spiritual path.

In relation to yoga, I have known people who consider their hatha yoga routine a spiritual practice. They do some yogic stretching exercises in the morning, a few rounds of alternate nostril breathing, a relaxation exercise, and consider that they have completed their spiritual practice for the day. But according to another standard, spirituality is the attainment of pure knowledge, which leads to the realization of the inner self, or atman. Those who hold this belief would tell you that only methods which help in attaining, retaining, and applying knowledge of that inner self can truly be called spiritual practices.

How can I attain spiritual knowledge?

The word "spiritual" is derived from "spirit"; spiritual knowledge refers to the core of our being, the pure self. Spiritual practices are those that help us gain the direct experience of this self. In the modern world we identify people by their level of education or by what position they hold, rather than by who they are. That is why we have difficulty distinguishing a truly spiritual person from one who merely holds a spiritual office. Spiritual knowledge is totally different from information about spirituality.

There are two sources of knowledge: direct, and indirect. Direct knowledge comes from within; it is a matter of revelation or personal experience. Only the knowledge that flows from the realm of direct experience has the capacity to guide us and help us in time of need. Indirect knowledge comes from books and other external sources, and when we are in need it is simply a burden on the brain. Revealed knowledge clears our mind; knowledge that we gather in the form of information clutters it. No matter how educated we are, or how many books we have written, if our own learning is not connected to the realm of the inner self, it is of little value when our emotions are in turmoil.

I have met saints with no formal schooling who had great spiritual knowledge. For example, I once knew a saint who could not even sign his name, and if you asked him about worldly matters he would smile and say nothing. Yet very learned people would come to sit at his feet and ask him spiritual questions, and he would answer them simply and clearly.

For a long time I wondered how this saint could have attained the profound peace that was always apparent on his face. Then one day in the course of my own self-study and contemplation I found the answer in the scripture *Tripura Rahasya:* Once you gain direct knowledge of your spiritual self, you begin to see things in the light of that experience. You spontaneously distinguish the pure self from the non-self, the real from the non-real, the eternal from the non-eternal. And because of your self-realization you no longer identify with the objects of the external world, including your body, mind, thoughts, and emotions. Non-attachment to this mundane world is a spontaneous outcome of self-realization. It is what the scriptures call *vairagya,* non-attachment. In fact these texts tell us that the highest state of knowledge is non-attachment, and they use the terms for "knowledge" and "non-attachment" interchangeably. More clearly, the knowledge that does not lead you to vairagya is simply information; it is not true knowledge.

If you have real knowledge, you know you are on a journey. On your way to your final destination, you pause at various rest areas. You are entitled to use the tables and other facilities there, but they are not yours. You can park your car and stay for a while, but you cannot build a house there—you have to move on. And while you are using a rest area you must follow the rules that have been established. You cannot claim that the place is yours, and before you leave you must clean up any mess you make.

That is what life is like. Use the objects that you encounter in your journey, and move on. But use them in the proper manner. They are not yours. Everything belongs to Nature. Whether you have achieved something through hard work or by chance, it is only a temporary gift. To know this, and to remain aware of it without losing that awareness for even a split second—that is spiritual knowledge.

People say they work hard. But, whose hard work is it? Is it the hard work of the body, breath, mind, or intellect? Where did you get all that energy? Energy comes from Nature. If you're an inventor, how were you able to invent? It is because of your *buddhi,* your intellect, and if something goes wrong with it you will become unbalanced: you might suffer from Alzheimer's or become schizophrenic; then all your intelligence will be gone. That means that the ability of your intelligence was not yours.

No matter what you have accomplished through your intellect, it was not your accomplishment, but the accomplishment of Nature. It has been given to you as a gift. Enjoy the gift with full awareness that it is a privilege to have it, and use it properly. And when that gift is passed on to the next hand, don't feel bad. When you achieve something, it's okay; when you lose something, it's equally okay. That is called spiritual knowledge.

Q **How do I know if I am practicing yoga properly?**

The essential technique of yoga is to bring your mind to a state of balance—to attain control over its modifications. You become the master of your mind when you attain the ability to guide it so that it works the way you want it to work. *Chitta vritti nirodha yogaha.*

Controlling the mind does not mean suppressing the mind. It's like driving your car. Having control over the car means driving it the way you want and to the extent you want. It also means that you are able to stop it when you wish and turn it when you want. Similarly, control over the mind means having the ability to let it work when it is needed, and to stop it from running when it is time to rest.

Any technique that helps you gain mastery over your mind is a part of yoga: your diet, exercise, and breathing, as well as your thinking process and your philosophy of life. But with any practice you do, see whether it is helping you become clearer, more concentrated, more organized, and more cheerful. Are you having fewer doubts, fears, attachments, and complications in your life? Is your life becoming simpler and more straightforward? If you are moving in that direction, you are practicing yoga. If not, there is something wrong either in the practice itself or in the way you are doing it. No matter how glorious a practice seems to be, no matter how popular it is, or how much others seem to admire it, if you do not notice a positive effect on your mind then such a practice does not qualify as yoga.

Q I work hard and am financially successful and happily married, yet life seems pointless. No one around me shares my sense of emptiness, but I can't seem to shake it.

Unless you understand the purpose of life and you work toward attaining that purpose, life will remain pointless. This lack of understanding creates a vacuum. And according to the enlightened ones, this vacuum becomes the source of perpetual loneliness. Financial success and a happy marriage are not enough, in themselves, to cope with this loneliness, so we busy ourselves with all kinds of activities.

The majority of people in the world work hard, yet find no real purpose or meaning in life. In the lives of such people a deep paralytic cynicism eventually sets in, and when it does, some begin to blame God, while others attribute their problems to their karma. Some search for a remedy in temples, churches, mosques, and synagogues, or place their faith in swamis, pandits, priests, astrologers, and fortune-tellers. Others place their faith in the modern scriptures—TV, the Internet, movies, novels, self-help books, magazines, and so on—but the answer continues to elude them.

A few people finally realize that the answer does not lie in the external world, and they turn their attention inward. And if they are patient and persistent, they eventually attain freedom from fear and doubt. They overcome their confusion and see the light within, and when they do, they become a light to themselves and a light to others. This is what it really means to live a successful life. All forms of worldly success are simply pacifiers, and it is not possible to banish your emptiness by clinging to them. Therefore, look within and find within.

Q **I don't have a clear idea of what it means to look within. When I turn inward, all I find is more emptiness. Do you mean I should try to know God?**

I don't mean to sound like Jesse Ventura—but the truth is, the popular concept of what it means to believe in God is for weak people. Many people claim that they have found God and yet you can see a great deal of emptiness in their lives. The sages' injunction, "Look within and find within," involves more than conceptualizing God, worshipping this concept of God, and expecting God to take care of all your problems. In the beginning stages of your search, when you do not yet know what God is or what the means are of knowing God, you will be disappointed if you try to focus your heart and mind on God.

It seems to me that you should start your inward journey by focusing your mind on your most immediate goal. Sit down quietly and reflect on yourself. What do you want in life? How can you be peaceful and happy? Try to discover whether your ultimate goal really is to know God or if you are actually more interested in achieving freedom from those thoughts, feelings, and problems that are keeping you from finding peace and happiness. What is your immediate goal: knowledge of God, or freedom from misery? Isn't it true that you want to know God because you have an underlying expectation that God-realization will bring your miseries to an end? If that is the case, then consider: What really is the goal? What are the means?

Once you understand that your first priority is to find peace and happiness, try to see what obstacles stand in your way. You will see that your peace and happiness are associated with many factors both in and around you: your physical health, your relationships, your emotional state, your habit patterns, and so on. Through self-reflection and self-observation, identify the trash both inside and outside you that needs to be cleared away. Which of your habits are draining your vitality? Which cravings are destroying your peace? Which negative thoughts rob your happiness? Are you master of your worldly possessions, or a slave to them? Are you enjoying the objects of pleasure, or are they actually consuming you? During this process of self-reflection and self-observation, be honest with yourself. Acknowledge the facts and unflinchingly make choices and decisions that will clear away the obstacles to your peace and happiness. This is called turning your mind inward, searching within and finding within.

On this inward journey you will come to see that your peace and happiness are not dependent on worldly objects and worldly relationships. It is your decision to remain happy in all circumstances in life that enables you to be happy. The realization that you have both the capacity to make such a decision and the capacity to remain unaffected by the charms and temptations of the world is called self-realization. And on the ground of this self-realization you will eventually come to know that the indomitable will that enabled you to search for and find happiness within is actually due to the Lord of Life who lies within you. In the scriptures this level of realization is called God-realization. And knowing and experiencing this God is the highest goal of life. Once you find this truth, you are free from emptiness forever.

YOGA AND RELIGION

Q What is the difference between spiritual practice and religion?

Spirituality encourages people to come to an understanding of right and wrong, truth and untruth, through personal exploration. Religion imposes a definition of right and wrong. In a spiritual tradition the heart is allowed to sense what is right and wrong, and the *buddhi* (intellect) is given the freedom to evaluate the ideas of right and wrong that have come to us from great masters in the past. If the heart and the intellect are not allowed to come forward and help us find our path, the life goes out of spirituality and it becomes a religion.

In other words, the moment a spiritual tradition begins to discourage people from seeking God independently, it turns into a religion. When the heart and brain are suppressed, when we are forced or manipulated to think along the lines of somebody else's thinking, spiritual wisdom declines and the process of inner transformation slows and stops. Transformation comes only when we put the teachings into practice in our own life.

Q **What would it take for yoga to spread and become as popular as the religions of today?**

It will never happen, because yoga demands that you practice and experience, rather than simply believe. Yoga requires you to find out for yourself, and most people are not interested in doing that; they are looking for someone to lean on. Religion has a hold on those who suffer from dependency, while those who are drawn to yoga are aware that they have to gather the wick, oil, and matches and light their own lamp. Such people suffer less from fear and doubt than those who are dependent. They know that they can reach somewhere higher only when they themselves move from here to there, and they know that this requires self-effort.

Every journey is a personal journey. It never happens that someone else undertakes the journey and you reach the destination. It is not enough to understand that someone else has walked the path—but unfortunately many will not accept that: they want others to walk the path for them. And because yoga will never pretend to do that, it will remain unpalatable to most people. Those seeking independence and personal freedom will be drawn to this path; others will not.

When people say that Jesus was a yogi, what do they mean? What makes a person a yogi?

A yogi is one who is in union with God or one who aspires to such union. Fearlessness is the clearest sign that one has attained that state of experience. After knowing the Truth and one's eternal relationship with that Truth, one is no longer affected by loss and gain, honor and insult, success and failure. The phenomenon of birth and death is of no more significance to such a one than putting on a set of clothes and taking them off again.

Evidently Jesus was such an accomplished master. He was fully established in his true self and was not affected by either honor or insult. He knew his relationship with Truth, which in Christian terminology is called "Almighty God." Death had no meaning for him. The willingness with which he gave his body can be seen in the account of the Last Supper ("Take, eat; this is my body." Matt. 26:26). As the yoga tradition has it, his resurrection is a purely yogic feat, known as *parakaya pravesha* (casting off the body and re-entering the same or another body at will). According to the yoga tradition, yogis of this caliber are immortal. They continue serving and guiding aspirants forever.

Did Jesus intend for his message to become a religion? If not, how did it happen?

As a representative of yoga, my answer is "no." No master wants his teachings, knowledge, or services to be confined to a limited group. Saints and spiritual masters understand the higher purpose and goal of life, and that is why their underlying message is always love all, embrace all; hate none and exclude none.

The teachings of all these masters are universal. They are grounded in deep spiritual knowledge and experience. But when a master passes away, their followers often become possessive of both the teacher and the teachings, claiming that they are the only ones who truly understand the master's teachings. They insist that they alone are entitled to carry on the master's mission. Further, to magnify the importance of both themselves and their teacher, they attempt to undermine other teachers and teachings. This is how a religion is created.

The Christian religion is not alone in shutting the door on other teachers; it happens in all religions. The Hindus, for example, have closed their eyes to Christ as well as to many other saints and sages. And within Hinduism there are hundreds of sects and hundreds of swamis, most of whom ignore or undermine all teachers but their own. In most ashrams, students are forbidden to practice any form of meditation other than that taught by the founder of that ashram.

Furthermore, when a spiritual path becomes a religion it also becomes a business, and in business you do not want to help your competitors. What had been a group of spiritual seekers becomes an institutionalized community, building a solid wall around the teachings of the master. When that happens, the message of the master has a hard time spreading beyond that wall.

Q **It is unlikely that Christ is the only master whose teachings have been distorted. Has the same thing happened with the teachings of Buddha?**

Yes. Christ and Buddha were great masters who offered their wisdom to all humankind. Think of the sacrifices they made, the forbearance they showed, what great hearts they had, and how willingly they subjected themselves to pain and insult in service of the teachings. It is by remembering these characteristics and attempting to manifest them in our own life that we become Christian or Buddhist.

It is simple: A Christian is one who follows the footprints of Christ; a Buddhist is one who follows the footprints of Buddha. Instead of walking in the footprints of these great masters, however, we redesign their footprints until they begin to resemble our own. Then we claim they are the footprints of Christ or of Buddha. If you examine Buddhism you will see that many of the teachings now delivered in his name were not taught by Buddha at all. In fact much of what passes as Buddhism goes against his teachings. For example, Buddha taught that our immediate concern is not with gods and goddesses, but with understanding that there is both pain and a cause of pain. He encouraged those around him to find a path that leads to the state beyond pain and misery and begin practicing that. He taught that our immediate goal is to achieve nirvana, the state where pain is extinguished forever, and when we have done that, we will not need to figure out whether God exists or not, or whether God lives in heaven or within ourselves. All this will become apparent once the mind is free from misery, hatred, loneliness, anger, and pain.

Until then, Buddha advised, "Do not waste your time trying to understand the subtler issues of life, and do not waste my time asking questions about God." He avoided the subject of the existence of God, and when pushed he said, "Forget God. What is clear is that misery exists and there is a need for happiness." Buddha never gave a straight answer to questions about the existence of God, and yet today Buddhism has one of the most elaborate mythologies and theologies ever conceived. This has nothing to do with Buddha or his teachings.

Q **I am struggling to reconcile some of the teachings of yoga with my Christian faith. Specifically, how can we strive toward the realization of our own divinity in light of the story of Adam and Eve? I can accept that I am created in the image of God, but I cannot accept that I am God or that I should want to possess the power of God. I'm afraid that doing so would lead me to the same mistake that caused our exile from paradise.**

There is no conflict between yoga and biblical doctrine. The source of your trouble lies in the concepts "All this is Brahman," "I am Brahman," "Individual souls and the Supreme Consciousness are one," and "I and my Father are one." These concepts are the intrinsic theme of non-dualism known as *advaita.* Yoga as a system of philosophy is purely dualistic. According to yoga philosophy, God is a unique category of reality. Individual souls can come closer to God or even merge in God, but they cannot become God.

However, many other streams of philosophy have joined and become an integral part of yoga philosophy and practice. Advaita is one such stream. To compound the confusion, teachers often introduce just one or two aspects of yoga, but to stress the importance of what they are teaching they give the impression that what they teach represents the totality of yoga. That is a mistake.

A person who has been born and raised in a dualistic faith like Christianity, as you have, can practice *raja yoga* without embracing the non-dualistic (advaita) philosophy, which comes from the Vedanta tradition and has intermingled with the yoga tradition. The practice of the *yamas* and *niyamas*—the ethical and moral observances of raja yoga (non-violence, truthfulness, non-stealing, non-sensuality, non-possessiveness, cleanliness, contentment, self-discipline, self-study, and surrender to God)—does not require that you change your personal belief in a God who is completely separate from you. The practice of postures, breathing exercises, relaxation, concentration, and meditation does not require a change in your faith either. In other words, if you are not comfortable with the non-dualistic element of yoga, do not embrace it.

Beyond the realm of raja yoga, however, we enter a realm of yoga practice that is supported by non-dualistic philosophy. All religions, Eastern and Western, have to some extent inflicted us with guilt, fear, and self-condemnation. The usual tendency of religious dogma is to stress that we are sinners and to teach us that the mistakes we have made—even the mistakes our ancestors made—are irreversible and that we must live with the guilt. Quite often self-proclaimed holy men use this concept to exploit us. On the other hand Vedanta, the philosophy of non-dualism, says that in reality we are divine. God created us in his own image, and therefore we are fully equipped to experience God if we can see our own image without any distortion. That is why yoga emphasizes self-realization rather than God-realization.

The particular aspect of the image of the self you realize in the course of practice determines your understanding of God. Some of the saints experienced a significant gap between God and themselves, and a dualistic philosophy *(dvaita)* emerged, grounded in their personal realization. Other saints perceived only a tiny gap between God and themselves; God and the individual self were sometimes experienced as separate, and sometimes as united. From the perspective of such saints God is both separate and not separate from us, and in the yogic tradition this level of experience and this relationship between God and individual souls is called *dvaita-advaita.*

In still other cases, saints became so intensely absorbed in the beauty and glory of the Almighty that they no longer had any sense of a separate existence. They saw only the reflection of God through the eye of God. Their realization was so pure that they saw neither themselves nor the world as separate from God—they experienced neither their own existence nor the existence of the world. This intense realization wiped out any notion of evil, devils, Satan, hell, heaven, bondage, liberation, birth, and death. This realization is immortality. Those who achieve it rise above the brief life of mortals by merging into the Eternal Being. It is from the perspective of such blessed ones that both the Upanishads and the New Testament say "I and my Father are one."

So as long as you are afraid of making the mistake that caused Adam and Eve to be expelled from the Garden, you should follow the rules and laws which give a clear direction to the petty ego, the little self. In total surrender to God, love alone becomes the guiding force. If you know that the whole universe is pervaded by God, exists in God, and is guided by God, and that God has no intention of separating you from himself and causing you pain, then you will have no fear of being expelled from paradise.

Non-dualistic philosophy has great merit if it is understood properly. If not and if it is used to fuel our petty ego, we may fall into the snare of confusing ourselves with the Almighty. We can avoid this trap by incorporating the principle of *bhakti* (love and devotion) into our practice. Had Adam and Eve had faith in God and reverence for his words they would not have been beguiled by the serpent nor become the victims of their own curiosity. They would have plucked the fruits for God as a gardener does, in the service of his master.

Q Does prayer have a place in the practice of yoga?

Yes. Prayer is a means of connecting your heart with the Divine, thereby allowing grace to flow and touch your heart. The heart is the seat of absolute, transcendental Truth. A prayer that truly comes from the heart transcends all boundaries and has the power to destroy all bondage.

The power of prayer is so immense that it has an unfailing effect on the mind and heart. Prayer changes intellectual dialogue into spiritual contemplation, transforming our normal emotions into devotion. Because it quiets our mental chatter and calms emotional turmoil, prayer creates the environment for the inward journey. One of the biggest problems that meditators face is preparing the proper mood. It is true that meditation makes the mind one-pointed and tranquil, but when we are already in a bad mood it is difficult to sit down and meditate. That is where prayer comes in.

Prayers can be repeated aloud, which does not require a great deal of concentration. The meaning of the prayer helps us organize our emotions, calm them, and turn our attention toward the Divine, the object of our prayer. Thus prayer is a technique for making the transition from mundane to divine awareness. But this is true only when the prayer comes from the heart. Prayers should not be said in a perfunctory manner. Prayer can be a complete path in and of itself, leading to the highest level of realization, provided it is genuine and not a mechanical regurgitation of some lines we have committed to memory.

Yet even the act of memorizing prayers and repeating them mechanically has some value if the prayers are authentic—that is, if they are prayers which were revealed to the saints and sages. Revealed prayers came directly from the Source, and because of this, they retain the power to transform and heal. This power is further intensified when such a prayer has been used and passed down for a long period of time. For example, people have been using the prayer of Saint Francis of Assisi for several centuries and so it has gathered immense energy. When you say this prayer from the heart you are repeating words that have touched the lives of countless people and allowing yourself to become part of an ever-flowing stream that reaches its destination by its own virtue. A prayer composed by an ordinary mind may induce a pleasant feeling, but it will not have the same effect as the prayers of saints such as Francis, Narada, and Tulsidasa.

When we repeat an authentic prayer our mind and heart are purified, and eventually the higher virtues of love, devotion, and faith begin to unfold within us. When these prayers fill the deepest recesses of our heart, the mind automatically travels inward to enjoy their subtle vibrations, and meditation begins spontaneously. The spiritual history of both the East and the West is replete with examples of saints who had never heard of meditation but, due to their intense practice of prayer, were blessed with meditative minds.

Q **Does prayer have the power to heal? What is your opinion about "remote healing"?**

Prayer has an immense power to heal. Through prayer we can heal both ourselves and others, but there is one condition: the prayer must be selfless.

Healing at a distance through what is called remote prayer is possible. The prayer acts in much the same way that a remote control device acts in operating a television set. We may not see the connection between the remote control and the television, but the energy being emitted from the source (the remote control device) is being received by the television. If the battery is dead, the remote control will not work. It is the same with remote prayer. Selflessness and unconditional love are the batteries. Without them, the prayer has no power.

According to the *Yoga Sutra* the energy emitted from prayer is eternal and cannot be sent forth in vain. This is also the secret of a blessing. Both intense prayer and blessing are at work in the process of an authentic spiritual initiation. You may pick up a mantra from a book and practice it for a long time without seeing much result—but if you receive the same mantra through initiation you will perceive a distinct difference. Initiation must be accompanied by intense prayer and unconditional love. If either of these components is missing, the initiation loses its power.

Q I am having some doubts about the transforming power of prayer closer to home—I pray regularly but see little sign of transformation in myself. Where does the problem lie?

For a long time I struggled with this question myself. Remember: to be effective, prayer needs to be selfless. Only after meeting a number of blessed saints did I realize that I did not really understand this about prayer. Most often my prayers were full of conditions. By that I mean they were not God-oriented prayers, but rather self-oriented. I said those prayers to achieve worldly goals—good grades, a good job, or the favor of influential people. Most of the books that inspired me to undertake the practice of prayer, as well as the people I knew, encouraged this attitude.

Once when I noticed that things were not working out as I desired, I decided to make a concrete deal with God. Inspired by worldly minded prayer experts, I began saying this prayer: "O Divine Mother, if I become a professor at the University of Allahabad I will do a hundred recitations of the scripture *Durga Saptashati* at thy shrine, Vindhya Vasani." Deep in my heart I was not fully convinced that prayers alone could help me achieve this goal, so during the period I was saying this prayer I also visited the university authorities I thought would help me get the job. Yet long before the selection committee met, I heard that someone else would be chosen.

While puzzling over why my prayers were not heard, I met someone who helped me realize that the highest kind of prayer has nothing to do with worldly goals. God is not a petty-minded merchant with whom we can negotiate. The will of the Divine is unfailing and ever-auspicious, I discovered, and that is why the heart of real prayer is surrender. When we surrender to divine will, we rise above the realm of desire and attachment; our desires and goals are no longer our own. Then we are no longer concerned with whether or not our prayers are effective. We understand that everything that happens happens through the will of the Divine. We come to accept everything as divine will and find delight in it. A person familiar with the secrets of divine will and self-surrender knows that even loss and failure are manifestations of divine grace.

Then why pray at all? If the divine will is unfailing and unalterable, then what effect can prayer have?

Prayer is a means of unfolding our own willpower and connecting ourselves with the Divine within. It is an invisible thread of sounds connecting the individual with the Supreme, and it is strengthened when spun with feelings of faith, love, and total surrender.

Prayers that burst from us when we are confronted with life's calamities are too weak to connect our heart with the Supreme. The same is true of the prayers we say by rote or as part of a ceremony. The formal practice of prayer involves choosing a specific prayer and focusing our mind on that—but when we do so, the selection of the right kind of prayer is of the utmost importance. The best prayers are those that have been revealed to the saints and sages, and because they have their origin in divine experience, such prayers are capable of leading the mind and heart to that experience. These prayers are always accompanied by *anahata nada,* the eternal music that is always playing in the interior of our being.

There are countless prayers written in books. According to the authors, many of them were revealed to saints. How do I choose the right one?

To make sure that the answer to this question is clear and unforgettable, the scriptures make a very strong statement: "The difference between a prayer you receive from a teacher and one you choose yourself is like the difference between your wife and a prostitute."

A true teacher is one who has practiced according to the injunctions laid down by previous teachers, and there is a definite system for saying the prayer that such a teacher imparts. I came to realize the importance of receiving a prayer directly from a qualified teacher as the result of two experiences. The first took place when I was a student in Allahabad; the second years later, after I had come to the United States.

There is a set of prayers in the *Ramayana* known as *aditya hridaya,* which according to this and other scriptures is one of the most potent set of prayers for healing purposes. Although I had no personal experience of its results, I was impressed with this set of prayers because I had great faith in the scriptures. Thus I said the *aditya hridaya* thousands of times for general health and well-being and was satisfied simply with the act of saying the prayers. Then my mother began to suffer severe headaches. I did these prayers for her again and again, yet she did not improve. I was disheartened, so to cope with my own disappointment I took refuge in philosophy, with the thought that I must have lots of bad karmas, which were counteracting the results of *aditya hridaya.* Yet in spite of this rationalization, deep down I began to harbor doubt and skepticism about the true power of these prayers.

Then one day I received the news that my mother's headaches had become constant and excruciating. Even worse, she had lost her eyesight, and her health had become so poor that her doctors had given up. With a heavy heart I went to see a saint I often visited, Swami Sadananda, and told him about my mother. With a compassionate look he said, "During your twilight meditation *[sandhya upasana],* after you have finished offering water to the sun and have done *japa* of the *gayatri* mantra, pray to the Sun, the source of life and longevity, by reciting *aditya hridaya.* Repeat that prayer once a day and soon your mother will be healthy." Although I had done this prayer for her many times while her health continued to decline, I followed the instructions of this saint. Within three days my mother's headache disappeared, and within twelve days her eyesight was fully restored.

Later I asked Swamiji why this miraculous effect had taken place on this occasion and not when I had repeated this same set of prayers for my mother earlier. His answer was that while I had originally collected these prayers from a book, this time they were given to me in their awakened form. That is why they invoked the healing power of the Sun, which in turn awakened the healing force in my mother.

My second lesson in the power of an awakened prayer came when a friend who was an initiate of my gurudeva, Sri Swami Rama, asked me to teach him a prayer of the Divine Mother. So I taught him one from the scripture *Durga Saptashati.* Several years later Swamiji asked my friend what practice he was doing, and when he told Swamiji about the prayer that I had taught him, Swamiji instantly replied, "How can he teach you this prayer if he himself does not have it?" Putting his hand on my friend's head, he said, "Now I am giving it to you. You should do this prayer every day."

After hearing what Swamiji had said and what my friend experienced after Swamiji gave him that prayer, I realized that prayers and mantras collected from books are of very little value. A prayer must be received from one who has received it properly and practiced it faithfully. Only then does it display its power.

YOGA AND GOD

Q I have always associated gods and goddesses with myths and paganism. The Greek god Zeus and the goddess Athena spring to mind. Yet the Hindu gods and goddesses are often mentioned in conjunction with yoga, especially tantra yoga. Can you explain?

The concept of gods and goddesses in yoga can be understood only if we understand tantric metaphysics. According to tantra there is only one reality, known as *chit,* pure consciousness. It is all-pervading, eternal, and endowed with all powers and potentials—both those we can imagine and those that are outside the scope of our imagination. The relationship between consciousness and its intrinsic power is like the relationship between the Sun and its light, or fire and its heat. Although Sun and sunlight are one and the same, these two terms are used for the sake of reference. Similarly, in tantra, consciousness is referred to as Shiva and the power of consciousness as Shakti.

The Hindu religion treats Shiva and Shakti as god and goddess, but in the yoga tradition the concept of Shiva and Shakti (along with terms referring to other gods and goddesses) has an entirely different meaning. In Hindu religious literature Shiva is believed to reside in Banaras or on Mount Kailas, Krishna was born and lived in Mathura, and many other gods live in the celestial realm. But according to the yoga tradition, gods or goddesses are not individual celestial entities; rather, they are manifestations of consciousness. In this, they are like all other forms of matter and energy that constitute the universe, including humans. Gods and goddesses are superior forms of the manifestation of consciousness only because the divine powers of consciousness—such as omniscience, omnipresence, and omnipotence—are less veiled in them than they are in us.

We humans are born, and one day we die; the gods and goddesses, however, are not born and therefore they do not die. They come into existence from a non-material, immortal source, which yogis call *mantra shakti* or *spanda shakti*, the divine word or the divine vibration. Mantra shakti is the imperceptible, eternal pulsation of consciousness which materializes in the form of gods and goddesses. In a sense, therefore, gods and goddesses are the children of mantra shakti—mantra shakti is the mother, and the seers to whom the mantras are revealed are the fathers. Through its own revelation mantra shakti transforms the sages and blesses them with divine vision; thus they become "seers."

As mantra shakti dawns in their hearts, the seers *become* mantra shakti: the veil of duality between the seers and the knowledge revealed to them is lifted, and the seer and the seen become one. The relationship between the seer and the mantra is identical to the relationship between Sun and sunlight. According to the *bhava* (the inner feeling) and *samskara* (the subtle tendencies of the personality) of the seer, mantra shakti materializes itself by emerging from the sage's field of intuition, descending into the mind-field, and taking a personified form—literally appearing in front of the sage. Thus a god or goddess is born. This is why the gods and goddesses are called the children of the sages in Indian spiritual literature.

For those of us with religious backgrounds, this is hard to comprehend; it is almost inconceivable to us that a god or a group of gods could be the offspring of the sages. Religion teaches us that a god or goddess is a being beyond our reach, that a person may become a saint by praying to the deity, and in rare cases may even be blessed with a vision of the deity. But according to the yoga tradition, having a vision of a god or goddess is not as important and spiritually illuminating as receiving and retaining mantra shakti and rejoicing in it.

Q What relevance, if any, do these deities have for a student who is seeking self-transformation through yoga practice?

For those of us who do not know how to comprehend and establish a personal relationship with an impersonal, transcendent, divine being (pure consciousness), a personified form of the deity is the best way to advance on the spiritual path. But for those who understand the eternity and omniscience of consciousness, mantra shakti itself is the deity, for there is no difference between consciousness and this imperceptible, eternal pulsation. All scriptures, whether they are classified as yogic or non-yogic, hold the mantra (the word) in the highest regard. Like the Bible, yoga scriptures repeatedly state, "In the beginning was the Word...and the Word was God."

But even after intellectually knowing the divine nature of the Word, people still fail to cultivate faith in the mantra. In its manifest form, we feel that a mantra is just a sound or a set of words, and in our normal life it never occurs to us that a sound can be a living entity. Thus, despite the fact that scriptures of almost all spiritual traditions of the world tell us about the oneness of the Word with God, we still want God to be more tangible. Our attraction to shape, color, size, and texture induces us to imagine God in a personified form.

Long before the birth of modern physics, the yogis understood that sound and light are simply two forms of the same energy, and further, that matter and energy are interchangeable. Constant repetition of mantric sound creates an extraordinary energy field within our body and mind. And as this energy field is intensified, it begins to form a reality of its own; at some point it may take a visible form and become perceptible to our naked eyes. This is called *darshana,* having direct experience of a deity corresponding to a particular mantra. This level of darshana, which entails a face-to-face vision of the personified form of the mantra, requires intense and prolonged meditation on the mantra. The intensity in the practice is the fruit of an unshakable faith in the mantra.

Such faith can come only from direct experience—but direct experience can come only from prolonged practice. To bypass this chicken-and-egg dilemma, the adepts introduced the concept of *Ishta Devata,* the most concrete form of the deity. A teacher with a direct vision of the Ishta Devata can describe its features and characteristics and recount the circumstances in which he or she received that vision. After hearing about the Ishta Devata and the transformation that has taken place in the teacher, we develop faith in the deity, and this faith serves as an anchor for our mind. While holding on to the image of the Ishta Devata we can meditate on a mantra with greater concentration than we can without that image. Thus the Ishta Devata, which represents only one aspect of the totality of the Absolute, helps us reach our goal more easily and quickly. The form of the deity we began to meditate on merely on the basis of a description given by our teacher soon becomes the object of our own personal experience. That is when we realize the oneness of the mantra and the deity, the god or goddess.

Q I don't quite understand this concept of Ishta Devata that you are referring to. Would you explain it more clearly?

God is nameless, formless, transcendental, Absolute Reality, although this concept is difficult for most people to grasp. We say God is the One Whose Name Cannot Be Spoken, yet we still use the word "God." What do we mean by this word? Generally, when we say "God" we mean the divine force whose sheer will allows this universe to manifest, the force that rules and regulates all subtle and gross forces in existence. It is the ultimate source of security, protection, happiness, and ever-lasting fulfillment. Our intuition tells us that this force was there before the beginning of existence and will continue to be there after this phenomenal world is destroyed.

We have a natural urge to hold on to this invisible divine force, yet we do not know how, because it is formless, nameless, and intangible. So to comprehend it, we give it a name and form. That is what the Ishta Devata is: our chosen name or form for God. In this way the impersonal Absolute Reality becomes personal, at least from our standpoint.

The philosophy and metaphysics underlying the concept of Ishta Devata refers to the Absolute, transcendent and formless, but we often forget the philosophy and fight over our individual concepts, which we call God. This is the root of religious wars. In this regard we are like little children in a large family who sometimes fight over the parents: "She's *my* mom!" "He's not your dad, he's mine!"

This tendency is destructive—and absurd. There was a guru, for example, who had two somewhat dull students. They were both massaging his feet when one grabbed the foot the other student was massaging. The other student said, "Don't touch *my* foot!" and jerked it away. "What do you mean? This is *my* foot!" said the first student, jerking the guru's foot back. The guru, who was in some pain, said, "It's okay, it's okay!" But the students paid no attention. "No, no, it's *not* okay," said the other, jerking the guru's foot toward him—"he's grasping *my* foot." And so the poor guru got mangled by his students because neither realized that the foot belonged not to either of them but to the guru.

That's what happens. God is God, but we come up with the concept of "*our* God," our personal God. And that is fine. That is how we all start our spiritual journey.

Q Why is it said that the Ishta Devata keeps changing as our understanding matures? How can God change?

God—the Ishta Devata—does not change; it is our understanding of God that changes. As we grow into adulthood our understanding of the world and the basic principles of spirituality matures, and our concept of Ishta Devata expands accordingly. Knowledge and understanding should grow as we go through life. It is only in the realm of religious fanaticism that a person's concept of God, once formed, remains fixed. If that happens, we are not growing, we are not gaining knowledge, and we are not trying to refine our understanding of God.

There was a time when my Ishta Devata was Hanuman. In the village where I grew up there were small tornadoes in May and June. It is terribly hot at that time of year, and these little tornadoes swirl around, picking up dust and dry leaves which makes them look quite big, although they are really not very powerful. The villagers believed that ghosts lived in the eye of these small tornadoes.

Every day when I was coming back from school I would see these ghost-carrying tornadoes. When I told my mother how scared I was, she told me not to worry and taught me a prayer. "All you have to do is recite this prayer when you see a tornado, and none of these ghosts can come close to you," she told me. "When you see one, never run away. Just stand and recite this prayer. If the tornado comes near to you anyway, lie down and think that your head is at the feet of Hanuman. Hanuman is the mightiest among all the gods. Nobody can stand in front of Hanuman. If the ghost tries to attack you, Hanuman will crush it with his mace!"

I did what she said, it worked, and my faith in Hanuman grew. Then, after reading the *Ramayana* I thought, "Hanuman is a devotee of Rama and is in his service. If the servant has that much power, how much more power the master must have! I should worship and meditate on Rama."

This interest in Rama did not lessen my love and respect for Hanuman, but it did broaden my understanding of God. I came to understand God as one all-pervading, omniscient divine being which, for the sake of *lila* (the divine game) and to satisfy our personal needs, assumes different names and forms.

Q **How do we decide which particular form or manifestation of God we should choose as our Ishta Devata?**

Just as the teacher initiates you into a mantra, he or she introduces the Ishta Devata to you. A teacher with direct knowledge and vision knows the form of the deity corresponding to the mantra in which you are initiated. However, no one can give a precise description of the Ishta Devata corresponding to a particular mantra, because the experience of the Ishta Devata varies with the individual. Ten people practicing the same mantra often gain different results because each has unique characteristics, personality traits, desires, and expectations. Not only is it likely that each will gain slightly different visions of the same Ishta Devata, but the degree of spiritual transformation engendered by such visions will also vary.

The descriptions of gods and goddesses found in the scriptures simply give us a general idea; the details are the unique properties of our own *bhava* (feelings). Thus just as God is one and his manifestations are many, similarly, depending on our bhava, even one Ishta Devata can manifest in manifold forms. For instance, let's say you and I both call our Ishta Devata "Krishna." Your Krishna will not be exactly like my Krishna. For me, Krishna is Parabrahman, the Absolute Reality, whose physical body was an illusory veil that it carried around in a certain point of time and space. For you and others, Krishna might be the son of Yashoda—the divine being who manifested in the flesh—and you may see him as a radiant baby or a mischievous child, while others may see him as a brilliant adolescent or a mighty king.

Q **Does everyone have an Ishta Devata? What about atheists?**

Every living being has an Ishta Devata, even an atheist. If a person does not believe in anything, he or she believes in "nothing." Thus Shunya ("nothing" is only an approximate translation) could be considered the Ishta Devata for those Buddhists who practice Shunyavada. Nobody can live without a belief in something; having no conviction in anything is having conviction in nothing. At the very least you have conviction in yourself, and therefore your own personality is your Ishta Devata.

In whatever form, in whatever manner, in whatever time and place your conviction and faith become condensed and concentrated, that concentrated form of your own *shraddha* (faith) and conviction is your Ishta Devata. It is a deeply personal form and name of the impersonal Reality—so personal that you may not be able to formulate it in words. Everybody and everything is searching for something—there is a force that pulls everything toward the goal of its search. For example, the Earth is constantly circling the Sun, held in orbit by the gravitational force of the Sun. There is only one goal of that journey: to become one with the source, the Sun. Thus, the Sun is the Earth's Ishta Devata. Similarly, there is a force that pulls every human toward the goal of our search, and that force is the Ishta Devata.

So whether we know it or not, the Ishta Devata is there. Both those who are enlightened and those who are not have an Ishta Devata. The difference is that the enlightened ones know it and the others don't. But even if we know it, we must keep refining our understanding of our Ishta Devata so that we don't get stuck with an inferior concept of God. Our convictions become an integral part of our psyche. From the depths of the psyche these convictions shape our thoughts and feelings, and thus determine how we behave. This becomes obvious at the time of death, when the conscious mind is subdued and the unconscious becomes dominant. Our convictions, hidden deep in the unconscious, come forward as we die. That is why the scriptures say that the worshippers of ghosts go to the realm of ghosts, while the worshippers of the gods go to the realm of the gods.

establishing a Personal practice

TEACHER AND STUDENT

Q Can a person attain enlightenment without the help of a teacher?

Anything, including enlightenment, can be obtained without anyone's help. But help really helps! In any field of knowledge, mentors are needed to help the novice grow systematically and become more focused. A mentor (or teacher) is someone who has assimilated the experiences of previous seekers and explorers and has made good use of these experiences.

A proven system of education is of the utmost importance, whether it aims to give training in the external or the internal world. Such a system develops after a series of experiments has established the validity of a method of teaching and when this method has been applied repeatedly and been found to yield similar results, time after time. It is needlessly time-consuming to chart your own path when a map of the area is available; setting out on an uncharted path is often fruitless and can even be perilous. Those walking such a path are beset with doubts and uncertainty. Many seekers who begin on their own and get no help from a teacher search here and there, trying different methods. Often, by the time they stumble on a system of practice that works for them, their lives are almost over, and no time is left for the practice itself.

An authentic teacher has received clear instructions from his or her own mentor, has traveled the path, and has integrated the wisdom gleaned along the way. Such a person is qualified to help us find and follow the most appropriate path.

Q How can I find a teacher?

You will find what you look for. The Bible says, "Ask, and it shall be given you; seek, and ye shall find; knock, and it shall be opened unto you" (Matt. 7:7). The tricky part is that the Bible never tells you how many times to knock, or even where to find the door!

Our instinct, intuition, destiny, karma (or whatever word you want to use) guides us toward the door. That is the law. In the natural course of events, we begin wondering: What is the purpose of life? Where have I come from? Where am I going? As these questions become stronger and more persistent, worldly charms begin to lose their luster, and we become seekers. We find the time and energy to search for the door—a spiritual teacher, an organization, a center, or an ashram.

You won't necessarily find the right place or the right person in your first attempt. Even if you are fortunate enough to meet the right teacher immediately, he or she may not give you what you expected. The teacher is not bound to fulfill your expectations. In fact, a teacher who has undergone training with a competent master knows the importance of teaching only what is best for you, regardless of what you expect. Even though your immediate expectations may not be met, your first encounter with your teacher makes an enormous impression on your mind and heart. Intellectually you may think that you didn't get anything, but deep down you feel blessed by his or her company. This kindles a desire to learn something from that person.

The first meeting between teacher and student is crucial. In the first instant, you recognize each other—not with your eyes or through a formal introduction, but with your hearts. Two hearts meet and know each other at the level of feeling. Catch hold of that moment of recognition and cherish it so that, later on, your undisciplined and argumentative mind doesn't confuse you.

Q **If the teacher within is the real teacher, then why is an external teacher necessary?**

Just as God is within and yet is unknown, so too the teacher within remains unknown until our intuitive eyes are opened. According to yoga, God—the Supreme Consciousness—is the primordial master. The teacher in the external world shows the student how to go within and find the Truth that abides there. If you can introduce yourself to the teacher within, you do not need to be bothered with a teacher outside, but unfortunately, few people have that ability.

Remember, even those great, blessed ones—such as Krishna, Rama, and Buddha—who perhaps had the ability to achieve the goal without an external teacher, searched for their teachers, underwent the disciplines given by their teachers, and gave the entire credit for their *sadhana* (spiritual practice) to their teachers. The example of these great ones warns us not to disregard the teacher outside while waiting for everything to be unveiled by the teacher within.

Q **Much has been written about the responsibility of the teacher to the student. Does the student have a responsibility to the teacher?**

The responsibilities are mutual. The closer you come, the more you learn. The more the student learns and understands, the finer and more subtle is the bond that develops between teacher and student. The subtler the bond between the two, the greater the commitment. It is the degree of commitment from both sides that determines the degree of responsibility on both sides.

In the beginning, there is little commitment on either side. You enroll in a seminar, the teacher gives a lecture, you listen, the session is over, you leave, and that's that. At this stage, the teacher is simply an instructor. Her or his responsibilities are simple: to teach only what she or he has actually learned and practiced, to refrain from making too many promises, and to teach only that which is healthy and useful. If it's a spiritually oriented seminar, the fee must not be the teacher's prime motivation. A student's responsibility at this stage is almost nothing. So long as a student doesn't deliberately create problems for the instructor, the student's duty is discharged.

Later on, when personal interactions begin, the teacher's responsibilities grow. The teacher must take the student's physical capacity, intellectual grasp, and emotional maturity into consideration. On the student's side, there are also obligations. A student is expected to be honest with the teacher and to be open when the teacher speaks unpleasant truths, although at this stage a responsible teacher doesn't examine the personal details of a student's life. Doing so before there is clear understanding and communication creates an uncomfortable situation. It is only when a student realizes that all the other fine people whom he or she has met in the past were simply instructors, while this particular person is the final spiritual guide, that the teacher begins to behave like a master and treat the student as a disciple.

When a master/disciple relationship is established, the responsibilities of both parties change dramatically. When a student is committed to this extent, it becomes the master's responsibility to gather all the resources necessary for that disciple's ultimate spiritual unfoldment. At this stage, the master does everything to bring the disciple to the highest level. The master's greatest delight comes when the disciple reaches the summit.

From the perspective of the disciple the responsibilities grow enormously, but subtly. The disciple has the duty to serve the master, but whatever he or she does is little compared to what the teacher is doing. From the perspective of the master, the disciple's duty is simply to do the practices sincerely and to be happy. If the master expects anything other than spiritual growth from the student, then she or he did not receive the proper training from the tradition. However, a master might use some unpleasant methods to foster the disciple's spiritual unfoldment. The disciple must be ready to accept this treatment gratefully. Not every disciple will have this experience—it comes only to a few fortunate, qualified students, and the fruit is beautiful and blissful.

In many ways this relationship must be experienced to be understood. Confusion regarding the responsibilities of teacher and student arises only when high standards of duty and responsibility are established too early in the relationship. The responsibilities are not based on a set of rules; rather, they grow naturally and spontaneously. There is no greater delight than experiencing the spontaneous unfoldment of this unique relationship. The very question "What is whose responsibility?" shows either that the relationship has not yet been fully established or that there is fear of establishing such a relationship.

Q **What are the obstacles to establishing a master/disciple relationship? How can a student overcome them?**

Fear and doubt are the greatest obstacles. Study yourself carefully, and find out what you are afraid of losing in that relationship. What is the exact nature of your fear? What makes you feel threatened and prevents you from coming close to your teacher and receiving guidance without hindrance?

If you analyze yourself, you will find that the major obstacle is the petty ego. Your ego has a hard time accepting anyone's supremacy. Tell your ego that it's not a matter of accepting someone as superior to yourself; it's simply a matter of allowing someone who is selfless to guide you on the path.

The second problem is doubt. In the past, you may have been deceived and misguided by others. If that's the case, tell yourself that you will not allow one failure to halt your progress on the path, and that you will not permit even a hundred failures to stop you. Overcome your skepticism. Your previous negative experiences were at least partially due to your blind faith, your unclear perception, and most importantly, your lack of a definite goal. Remove these conditions, search for a teacher, and you will find one. And once you have met your teacher, let that relationship take its natural course; follow it and meet your responsibilities in a loving, selfless, and relaxed manner.

Q Isn't another pitfall the tendency to use a teacher as a crutch?

While skepticism and fear of being absorbed into a group can be obstacles to spiritual unfoldment, the opposite tendency is equally a barrier—that is, using a teacher as a crutch. This obstacle is more subtle than the other two. Most people are accustomed to leaning on others. This tendency lingers in the mind even when one begins the spiritual search. Meditation is the path of liberation, the path on which a student attains freedom from all external crutches. A spiritual teacher should never be taken as a replacement for a counselor, therapist, or priest.

On the path of meditation, you are responsible for meditating. A teacher can guide you but cannot meditate for you. Beware of teachers who promise they will take care of all your spiritual needs, whether you practice or not. Students who are looking for such panaceas are the ones who will fall into the hands of false teachers.

Q My guru claims to be a master, yet he engages in what appear to be corrupt activities: charging exorbitant fees for common ayurvedic herbs (which are labeled with codes rather than their names), charging high fees for services, and even charging a fee to answer questions, among other shady activities. How much of this behavior should one tolerate before leaving such a guru?

If that's the kind of person you have as a guru, and you are expecting him to guide you on the path of enlightenment, you will be disappointed. In my opinion you'd better leave him as quickly as possible.

It seems that the relationship between you and that so-called guru is that of therapist/client, not that of teacher/student. In that case, as in any other commercial relationship, make your own experience the ground for deciding whether or not you should continue taking the herbs he prescribes, and paying him to answer your questions.

The guru/disciple relationship is pure and dignified. A thread of unconditional love always runs between guru and disciple, and if that is missing, then the spiritual bond between the two is lost. Once that bond is gone, you will find yourself harboring doubt and fear. That leads you nowhere.

Q **How can I tell whether my doubt about my teacher is a product of my resistance, skepticism, and limited vision, or whether it is a signal that I have involved myself with a charlatan?**

To find the answer to this question, you must first study yourself. Through self-analysis, find out what role you expect a teacher to play in your spiritual quest. Are you seeking a guide who can show you the path of total independence and freedom, or are you looking for someone you can lean on?

Most of us want someone who will take care of all our problems. This leads us to seek out psychics, astrologers, palm readers, numerologists, and priests. We believe their predictions and promises not because we are fully convinced but because accepting them gives momentary comfort to the mind. The trouble is that the mind does not want to confront its own problems; it is unwilling to do what is necessary to overcome them once and for all. This is the part of our mind that leads us to find and follow false gurus. (Here by "false gurus" I mean people who exploit our impulse toward dependency.) Such people make false promises; selfishness is one of their leading characteristics.

However, there is a brighter part within us that continually reminds us that such teachers, and the spiritual teachings imparted by them, cannot lead us very far. The unlit part of the mind, which loves to be lazy and dependent on others, cleverly tries to obscure the message coming from the brighter part within us. That is why we get confused.

If we have formed the habit of finding fault with others, including those who love and care for us, it is an additional obstacle. So you must analyze your tendencies and your motives. Try to uncover the source of your doubt and skepticism. Your own motives for drawing close to a teacher, and the force behind that motivation, will tell you whether you should doubt your doubt or doubt the teacher.

CHOOSING A PATH

Q How do I know which of the many paths of yoga is best for me?

Six months after you start practicing systematically, observe the degree to which you have overcome the problems and concerns you had at the beginning. Is your mind less scattered? Is your body stronger and more flexible? Do you have more energy? If you have been working systematically, you will find that your capacity has expanded. Make good use of that expanded capacity by seeking more advanced instruction.

If you have become enchanted with the sublime philosophy and metaphysics of yoga, and if you have come to find the charms and temptations of the world less alluring, then look for a master who can initiate you into mantra yoga. He or she may instruct you to undergo a serious and systematic practice of mantra meditation, which in the scriptures is known as *purash charana,* "the first step toward the divine experience."

If you have studied the authentic texts and are amazed by the powers and potentials that lie dormant within the human body, and if you are sure that your body is healthy and your mind sound, find a teacher who can instruct you in the path of kundalini yoga. But if you choose this path, remember that the authenticity of the teachings is purely experiential and is self-evident. Any experience that doesn't bring out previously unknown dimensions of knowledge and joy is not a spiritual experience. A spiritual experience is never bizarre or painful, nor will it harm your health. *Kundalini shakti* (the dormant force within) and problems simply do not go together. My personal warning: If any experience of so-called kundalini awakening causes a problem, then it is not a kundalini experience.

If instead of studying books you have studied yourself—your body, breath, mind, and your worldly circumstances—and realized that, to some degree, you are interested in mantra, kundalini shakti, and the immense power of the mind, then it's better to follow the path of raja yoga. On this path you will work with yourself simultaneously on every level of your personality in a gentle and progressive manner. An experienced teacher of raja yoga instantly knows which area of your life needs immediate attention—body, breath, mind, or lifestyle. He or she will help you focus on that particular area in such a way that the other areas of life are also addressed in an appropriate manner.

On the path of raja yoga you will develop healthy and harmonious relationships with others by practicing the five *yamas: ahimsa* (non-harmfulness), *satya* (non-lying), *asteya* (non-stealing), *brahmacharya* (walking in God), and *aparigraha* (non-possessiveness). As a means of disciplining yourself, you will practice the five *niyamas: shaucha* (purity), *santosha* (contentment), *tapas* (austerities), *svadhyaya* (self-study), and *Ishvara pranidhana* (surrender to God). For your body, you will practice *asana;* for your breath, *pranayama.* To gain control over your senses, you will practice *pratyahara* (withdrawal of the senses), and for your mind, you will practice *dharana* (concentration), *dhyana* (meditation), and *samadhi* (spiritual absorption). You can climb these eight rungs of yoga step by step, or you can embrace them simultaneously, depending on your needs, circumstances, problems, and capacities.

Regardless of what specific path you follow, you must organize your worldly life and your spiritual life so that one is not a source of disturbance to the other. This can be done by incorporating the basic principles of *karma, bhakti,* and *jñana* into your specific practice. Let's take a brief look at each one.

According to the school of karma yoga, a human being cannot live without performing actions. Attachment to the fruit of these actions is a source of bondage. When an action is performed selflessly, lovingly, and skillfully, then neither that action nor its fruit has any power to bind.

Bhakti means love and devotion. Without it, spiritual practice becomes dry and boring. Doubts seep in and you begin to wonder, "What's the point of doing all these practices?" Cultivating love for your practice will help you become devoted to it.

Jñana means knowledge. In this particular context, knowledge means understanding that nothing in this world really belongs to you. You can enjoy the objects of the world, but you have no right to own them mentally or become attached to them. Placing little value on the objects of the world and constantly remaining aware of the Truth within will strengthen your understanding of the world and enable you to stay on the path.

Q By nature I am emotional rather than intellectual. Does this mean that bhakti yoga is my path?

It is usually assumed that bhakti yoga (the path of love and devotion) is the most suitable path for emotional people, just as jñana yoga (the yoga of knowledge) is for those who are intellectual. Such notions are overly simplified. Bhakti yoga requires a great deal of knowledge—knowledge of self, knowledge of God, and a clear understanding of the relationship between the two. This knowledge is the ground for the true practice of bhakti yoga. Committing yourself to the path of bhakti without this knowledge, as people often do, may lead you into the trap of spiritual insanity.

In addition to knowledge, you need the virtue of positive emotions. There are certain ways of channeling and transforming emotions toward God that will strengthen the "bhakti bond," helping it to naturally and spontaneously unfold in the fertile soil of knowledge. It is these transformed emotions—together with love, faith, and surrender—that collectively constitute devotion.

Q Is chanting the main practice in bhakti yoga?

Chanting is one of the ways to open your heart and use devotion as a connecting thread between you and God, but it is just one of the many practices in this path. According to bhakti yogis and prominent bhakti scriptures, such as the *Bhakti Sutra,* the *Srimad Bhagavatam,* and the *Bhagavad Gita,* the practice of bhakti incorporates a number of elements.

The first and foremost is to see everything and everyone as a manifestation of God. The flower of love blossoms only after we have removed the subtle traces of negative emotions, such as hatred, jealousy, and animosity, from our mind and heart. If we do not actively consider all living beings, friendly or unfriendly, to be manifestations of God, these negative tendencies flare up and scorch the flower of love before it can blossom. Love and hatred do not go together; to embrace one, we must eliminate the other. To love God while living in the world, we must find God in all aspects of the world.

If we are on the path of bhakti we must also cultivate an unshakable conviction in divine protection and will. We must take any circumstance, pleasant or unpleasant, as the will of the Divine. This requires maintaining the awareness that nothing can happen unless God wills it to happen. There is something good in whatever is happening in our life, whether or not our present level of understanding permits us to perceive it. Never, ever doubt the Divine. This is the essence of faith. Just as love and hatred do not go together, neither do faith and doubt.

The bhakti yogi must always be in the circle of saints. Whenever—due to your previous *samskaras* or the memories related to your previous experiences—doubt and confusion are about to set in, the company of the saints will help you stay on the path. The problem for many of us is that we do not have enough knowledge and experience to recognize a saint should we come across one. And even if we do have enough knowledge and experience, in most cases circumstances don't permit us to be in the company of a saint for an extended period. But the advice of saints is documented in the scriptures, so we can study the scriptures and learn from the stories about them.

This particular component of bhakti is called self-study *(svadhyaya).* Listening to the spiritual deeds accomplished by the saints and relating them to your own life in the spirit of devotion is called *kirtana.* Chanting is a form of kirtana.

The scriptures describe a ninefold bhakti, as follows:

- Being in the company of saints.
- Taking delight in the stories of God.
- Serving your spiritual mentor and following their instructions.
- Contemplating divine qualities and the all-pervasiveness of God.
- Meditating on your mantra sincerely and faithfully.
- Practicing self-restraint and purity, as well as eliminating worldliness.
- Considering the world to be the manifestation of God, and regarding the saints as the way to God.
- Being content with whatever you have, and not finding fault with others.
- Cultivating simplicity, innocence, total reliance on God, and dispassion.

Q **After reading your book *Tantra Unveiled,* as well as several other books on tantra, I have the impression that the goal of tantra is to awaken kundalini. That is also the goal of kundalini yoga, so I'm wondering what the difference is between tantra yoga and kundalini yoga.**

It is true that both tantra and kundalini yoga aim at awakening kundalini shakti. They also share other characteristics. For example, both schools are based on a common philosophy: Shaktism, which holds that the Divine Mother is the highest reality. Further, according to both schools the human body is a living shrine, the repository of boundless energy, most of which remains dormant. This dormant energy is called kundalini shakti, and the relatively small amount of active energy is called prana. Yogis of both paths use their active energy to try to awaken their dormant energy. Yogis of both paths have a positive view of the world—they view it as a manifestation of the divine force. Thus, everything that exists is divine, beautiful, and a source of joy. The inability to experience the presence of the Divine within or without is called ignorance and is the source of bondage. Overcoming this ignorance and experiencing the beautiful and blissful Divine in every aspect of life is called liberation. How they lead you to liberation is what distinguishes the two paths.

Those on the path of kundalini yoga depend heavily on the techniques of hatha yoga. In this context hatha yoga means the practices related to *asana, pranayama, bandhas*, and *mudras*. Aspirants following the path of kundalini yoga believe that the body itself is the best tool to awaken the dormant energy of kundalini shakti. They describe kundalini as a sleeping serpent: snakes are cold-blooded creatures; as the temperature drops, snakes become stiff and cannot move. That is what has happened to kundalini shakti. Those on the path of kundalini yoga say that this serpent is hiding within us in the fireplace called the *muladhara chakra*, but the fire here is almost extinguished—all that exists is layers of ash covering a still-glowing coal. Before you can awaken this serpent, they tell us, you have to blow away the layers of ash and allow the heat to radiate until it warms the serpent and the serpent begins to move. As it emerges from hibernation it becomes conscious of itself and its surroundings. And because it has just awakened from its long slumber, it is hungry. So it devours sloth, inertia, hopelessness, and all other forms of darkness and heaviness. The result is spiritual awakening.

The layers of ash are blown away in kundalini yoga by practicing vigorous pranayama, and the prerequisite for practicing pranayama is mastering asana, especially the sitting postures. To strengthen and purify the nervous system you practice bandhas and mudras, advanced techniques developed in the tradition of hatha yoga. This method of awakening kundalini is purely physical and requires technical accuracy. If you are successful you will experience a surge of energy along your spinal column. And if the body (heart, lungs, kidneys, endocrine glands, and the nervous system) is in good health, you will experience this movement of energy as blissful. However, if your nervous system is blocked and your emotions are not stable, then this movement of energy may damage the nervous system or cause hallucinations. Even if you are physically and emotionally fit and do not experience any side effects from kundalini awakening, you still have a major task to accomplish, because this awakening causes you to become energetic. Your stamina and endurance will increase, and if you don't have a good understanding of the higher dimensions of life this energy will make you productive only at the physical level. Therefore the challenge in kundalini yoga is to learn how to channel that energy so that it becomes an instrument of spiritual awakening.

Tantric yogis also believe that the body is a living shrine. Even though the body's potential is infinite, tantra recognizes that individual bodies have their own limitations. Very few people in the world are perfectly free from fatigue, disease, and the tendency to procrastinate. Most of us are confronted with obstacles in one form or another. Tantrics therefore attempt to make the best use of all available means and resources—both internal and external—to remove these obstacles and make the body and mind healthy, strong, and happy. In addition to employing the techniques of hatha yoga, tantric yogis also include the techniques of meditation, visualization, rituals, mantra recitation, and prayer.

Tantrics do not treat kundalini as mere energy; they view it as the Divine Mother herself, and from the beginning of their quest they cultivate an attitude of love and devotion toward kundalini shakti. They may do an intensive practice, but that practice is always accompanied by the sense of self-surrender. Unlike the practitioners of kundalini yoga, tantrics are gentle. They attempt to awaken kundalini shakti like a hungry baby lovingly attempts to awaken its mother. Thus the distinction between kundalini yoga and tantric yoga is that the former is more physical, vigorous, gross, technical, and has no component of love and devotion, while the latter is more spiritual, gentle, and subtle, and is always accompanied by love and devotion. In hatha-based kundalini yoga there is a sense of victory; in tantra yoga there is a sense of surrender.

PREPARING FOR THE JOURNEY

Q How can I prepare myself to establish a personal practice?

The first and most important step in preparing for the spiritual journey is knowing why we are undertaking it. We must come to a clear understanding of why our inner peace and spiritual prosperity can no longer be ignored. We develop this understanding when we realize that something precious is missing in our life. Think about it. Has what you have achieved so far given you complete satisfaction? Have you found the real meaning of your life?

Most of us have been working all our life to make ourselves secure and comfortable. We are also seeking emotional satisfaction. But instead we find only fatigue and disappointment. We spend our entire life meeting the demands of the body and mind—yet even those who have been the most successful in attaining material comfort are not satisfied. Everyone wants more, but most people do not quite know what it is that they want more of.

If we listen, we can hear the voice of the soul from deep within asking, "What about me?" If we heed it, we realize we have not been attending to the needs of the soul. That is when we start thinking about spirituality. Not knowing exactly how to undertake our spiritual search, we begin browsing in bookstores; attending lectures; listening to tapes; visiting holy shrines; or searching for swamis, pandits, medicine men, kung fu teachers, or tai chi masters. In the beginning it is hard for us to know why one path is more appropriate than another, why certain practices are more fruitful than others, and most importantly, which practice is most suitable for us at this stage in our spiritual development.

We can successfully begin our quest only if we know where we stand, physically, mentally, and spiritually. Therefore, we must first look at our life as a whole and understand that we are neither body alone nor mind alone. Neither can function smoothly without the help of the other. It is also important to understand the force connecting the body with the mind. This is the vital force, the life-sustaining energy known as prana, chi, or hara. A person whose pranic energy is depleted cannot maintain either physical or psychological health. A person with an unhealthy body and a confused mind is not fit to follow any path. Such a person is always dependent on others, whereas spirituality is a quest for freedom on every level. Therefore, no matter which path we eventually choose, the second step is learning how to balance the body, breath, and mind.

Once we have begun working with the techniques of bringing the body, breath, and mind into a state of harmony, the next step is learning how to recognize and heed the voice of the soul. Because it is not possible to be happy unless our life has spiritual meaning, the forces of our body, breath, and mind have to be brought into the service of the soul. To be complete, a spiritual path must encompass techniques for creating harmony among the body, breath, and mind, and ultimately connecting them with the soul. Once this connection has been made and our actions are guided by the light of the soul, our relationships are no longer complicated or difficult. Our vision of life becomes clearer and we are able to choose the appropriate path, the one that will lead us to our goal. Unless our vision is clear, we are in danger of choosing a path at random and staying on it only until we meet obstacles and become frustrated—at which point we switch to whatever path next presents itself, and stay on it until our excitement again peters out; and so on and on.

Q How can I decide which part of myself to work on first?

The task of choosing the right path and following it consistently until we reach the goal requires an assessment of our physical, pranic, and mental capacities. We can avoid wasting our time if we get a complete picture of our life before deciding where to begin the process of self-transformation.

All of us have strengths and weaknesses. Take the time to consider whether it will be more fruitful for you to overcome your weaknesses by enhancing the stronger parts of yourself, or whether you can best strengthen yourself by overcoming your weaknesses. The tendency is to identify with the weak and messy parts of yourself, but this leads to self-condemnation, which damages your willpower. Usually it is better to invest your energy in further cultivating the strong, healthy, and beautiful parts of your personality. By doing so you will eventually create such a reservoir of self-confidence, self-trust, and inner strength that working with the weaker parts of yourself will be much easier.

However, there are instances where the weak and dark parts of the self have put down such deep roots that each time you attempt to work toward self-transformation, you run into a wall of obstacles—illness, procrastination, doubt, laziness, lack of motivation, and so on. In such cases it's better to work on eliminating the weaknesses that are the source of these impediments. With the help of self-analysis and self-observation, and under the guidance of a competent teacher, you can discover where you are stuck and identify the weaknesses that are at the root of your frustration.

Once you have found out where you are stuck and have decided whether it's best to begin working with the stronger or the weaker parts of yourself, you must take charge of your body and mind. No one else can walk the path of spiritual unfoldment for you. This is the path of self-mastery and self-discovery. Unless you find yourself you will remain lost, so you must learn to resolve your fears, insecurities, and other psychological complaints by yourself. In the beginning you may seek help from therapists, counselors, teachers, and gurus, but ultimately what counts is your own commitment to help yourself and to turn your mind inward.

If you think about it, you will realize that you have been searching for happiness all your life. You have tried everything—fine clothes, gourmet food, various sensual gratifications, exercise classes, stress-management techniques, counseling, and so on. But your mind has remained filled with anxiety and negative thoughts. At some point you will discover that transformation takes place only when you work with yourself and that happiness comes only from within. Remind yourself of the moment when you realized how important it was to heal your body, to protect your nervous system, and to nourish and revitalize your senses. This reminder will inspire you to withdraw your mind from the stressful activities of the world and to turn it inward to find the peace which cannot be found anywhere else.

Remember, too, how painful and frustrating it is to be caught up in the worldly mess. Remind yourself of all the disappointments you have suffered trying to find lasting peace and happiness in the external world. A mind that does not have a firm understanding of the unsatisfactory nature of the so-called pleasures of the world falls prey to disturbing thoughts, emotions, memories, and anxieties during its inward journey. Such a mind tends to go back to its old grooves. Turning your mind inward requires firm knowledge that this is the only way you will find peace and joy.

Q How can I turn my mind inward?

Meditation is possible only when the mind is one-pointed, organized, calm, and tranquil. A fragmented mind cannot be turned inward, and so the first step is to collect the fragments by training the mind to concentrate. This is tricky in the beginning because concentrating a scattered mind is like collecting droplets of mercury—they slip away when you try to pick them up. Similarly when you try to collect and concentrate your scattered mind, it slips away and you cannot get a good grip on all those hundreds of pieces.

A mind that is in the habit of running from one object to another cannot concentrate on one object for a prolonged period, and if you attempt to force it, it will make excuses and play tricks. While you are concentrating on one object—your breath, for example—another object flashes before your mind and the mind runs after it. When you notice that the mind is no longer trained on the breath, you bring it back, but before long it is distracted again. You bring it back, it runs off again. Eventually you give up in frustration.

That is why in the beginning it is not advisable to force your mind to focus on one object for a long time. A gradual approach is required. Asking a mind that is used to thinking of thirty things in ten minutes to think of only one thing for ten minutes is asking too much. Compromise by creating a situation in which you are neither forcing your mind to focus on one object for a long period of time nor letting it run constantly from one object to another. Provide the mind with a series of objects; focus it on one object for a short time, and then allow it to move to the next object in the series before it becomes rebellious.

Training the mind to travel from one point to another point according to your plan is the basis of all systematic relaxation exercises. This technique provides an environment where the mind can slow down as it moves from one point to the next in your body, so that instead of suffocating the undisciplined, scattered mind, you are training it. It can still move from one place to another, but instead of jumping from Florida to Las Vegas, from a phone conversation to what you are planning for supper, you are allowing it to travel from your forehead to your eyebrows, moving systematically through the body to the fingertips and toes and back to the forehead. In the ten minutes it takes for the mind to move from point to point through the body, it becomes concentrated. In this way a systematic and gentle mental training has begun.

Q **If slowing down the movement of the mind is the goal, then why not simply ask the mind to attend to a series of thoughts at a slow pace? Is there a specific reason for confining the mind to the body and asking it to travel from one point to the next?**

The relationship between the mind and the body is like the relationship between master and servant: mind is master and body is servant. When the servant sees that the master is dull and careless, the servant becomes careless too; thus the body does not receive any guidance or motivation from a careless and scattered mind. But when the servant knows that the master is attentive and vigilant, the servant becomes alert and active. For example, all the activities of the body are dependent on decisions made by the mind. The organs and bodily systems of an absent-minded person or a person with a disturbed and distracted mind are sluggish. But when the body notices that the mind is making its rounds, checking all departments—the brain, nervous system, circulatory system, respiratory system, and so on—it becomes alert and active.

This is because the mind is a flow of energy. When it is moving from one place to another throughout the nervous system and the energy channels, it automatically notes toxins and impurities that impede its flow, and the bodily systems involved in the cleansing process usually rush to begin removing them. Thus in the course of this self-guided journey of the mind from one point to another the energy channels are unblocked, impurities are removed, and a deeper level of cleansing begins.

What is more, after practicing systematic relaxation over a period of time, the mind gradually begins to sense that turning inward leads to a delightful sense of ease and stillness. Searching for happiness, it has been running in the external world, often finding only disappointment and frustration. But once it turns inward and slows down, it encounters the centers of peace and tranquility within—for example, at the heart center or at the eyebrow center. This encounter leads it to wonder why it is wasting time running here and there in the external world when the best joy is within. And this dawning awareness causes the mind to become less interested in running after the objects of the world, which in turn allows the mind to go back to that restful place voluntarily, without repressing a desire for worldly objects. The delight that it finds inside overshadows the charms and temptations of the external world. The natural and almost effortless process of meditation begins at this point.

Q How can I begin to practice meditation?

The first step is to acknowledge that you want to be happy and healthy. Learn to distinguish temporary pleasure from real happiness, and then decide that you are going to attain happiness, maintain it, and enjoy it. When you have made that decision, examine your body and explore your physical strengths and weaknesses. This will give you some idea of where you need to work on yourself.

In the beginning you may search for some support or instruction from others, but ultimately you must do the work by yourself. On the path of meditation you must not lean on others, not even your teacher. Meditation is self-therapy, and the aspirant must attain freedom from the teacher right from the start.

Once you begin to overcome your body's stiffness and learn to relax, you will notice that your breathing pattern is irregular. So the first step is to work with your breath and replace shallow chest breathing with deep diaphragmatic breathing. Deep diaphragmatic breathing will relax and soothe your body, because regulating the motion of your diaphragm regulates the function of your lungs. This in turn affects the function of the heart and the entire circulatory system. Ultimately, diaphragmatic breathing will bring the functions of the sympathetic and parasympathetic nervous systems and the left and right hemispheres of the brain into harmony.

When you have mastered diaphragmatic breathing, your body may still be stiff in places, but this discomfort will not disturb your breath. Rather, the disturbances in your breath can be traced directly to your mind. Every single ripple of thought that arises in the mind-field creates a jerk in the breathing pattern. When your awareness becomes refined enough to notice this, it is time to begin to learn the more subtle aspects of meditation—that is, how to deal with the mind and its modifications.

Before jumping into the practice of sitting in meditation, it is advisable to learn a systematic method of relaxation. Lie on the floor. Survey your body and relax it one point at a time. For example, first think of your forehead. Notice the tension you are holding there; relax and release it. If you are unaware of the tension or don't know how to release it, deliberately create tension in your forehead, notice how it feels, and then release the tension and observe the contrast.

Using this technique go from your forehead to your jaw, throat, shoulders, arms, chest, stomach, hips, thighs, calves, ankles, and toes, and then reverse the direction and bring your awareness back to your forehead, point by point, beginning with your toes. Then bring your attention to your navel center and notice your abdominal muscles rise and fall as you inhale and exhale. When your breath has become completely calm and tranquil, come into a seated position slowly and gently.

You will notice that the effort of sitting up has disturbed the calmness of your breath to some degree. Reestablish that calmness by again watching your abdomen move in response to your breath. Continuing to maintain that tranquility, be aware of your spinal column, and keep your head, neck, and trunk straight. If you are sitting on the floor, arrange your legs so that you are comfortable and rest your hands on your knees. If you are sitting in a chair, be sure to sit forward on the chair, rather than leaning against the back. Place your hands palms-down on your thighs and allow both feet to rest flat on the floor.

To withdraw your mind from unwelcome thoughts, simply resolve to watch your breath. Observe your breath as it flows from your nostrils to your heart center and from your heart center back to your nostrils. This is called breath-awareness meditation. It is the simplest and most effective method of meditation in the initial stages of practice and will help you calm your mind and balance the active and passive energies in your body.

Beyond this point of practice, it is important that you receive instructions from an experienced teacher to reduce the chances that you will be wasting your time.

Q What is the best kind of exercise to include in my daily routine to ensure my physical well-being?

According to the science of yoga, exercises that stimulate the whole body, rather than just one particular muscle group, are best. Yoga postures stretch and stimulate the muscles, ligaments, and joints, restoring elasticity and tone to the body. They stimulate circulation and revitalize the internal organs, the brain, and the nervous system. Practicing these postures also enables the respiratory system to perform more efficiently, taking in greater amounts of oxygen and eliminating more toxins. The postures also increase stamina and relieve tension. Yoga asanas are designed to balance exertion with rest and relaxation.

Because they don't affect the normal functioning of the lungs and heart, yoga postures are not a substitute for aerobic exercise. The effectiveness of asanas lies in the coordination between breath and movement. These postures can be practiced by the strong and the weak, the healthy and the relatively unhealthy. The basic goals of these postures are to create and maintain a healthy body and a peaceful mind.

What is the key to a fruitful practice of yoga postures?

There are four primary points to keep in mind when practicing:

1. Watch your breath. Coordinate your movements with your breath. Pay attention to your breath and make sure that your physical movements do not interfere with your breathing pattern, and vice versa. Inhale each time your torso expands in a posture and exhale when it contracts. Breathe deeply and smoothly.
2. Stay within your capacity. Be aware of your level of strength, flexibility, and stamina each time you practice. These may change from day to day. Stop before you feel fatigued. The object is to feel good while you are doing the postures and to feel refreshed and energized after you are done.
3. Follow a balanced practice. Any exertion of a particular limb, organ, or muscle group created by an exercise should be counterbalanced by another exercise. For example, the plow posture stretches the back of the neck and should be followed by the fish posture, which stretches the front of the neck.
4. Take time to relax. Begin and end each exercise session with a systematic relaxation.

My schedule is so hectic that I can't manage more than twenty or thirty minutes for exercise. Can you design an effective asana routine for me?

Yoga postures work with the entire body, including the internal organs. The effects are subtle, so be careful not to do too much at first. Spending twenty to thirty minutes doing simple asanas is plenty in the beginning. Watch how your body responds as you include more advanced exercises in your routine—your body and your sense of enjoyment are your best guides. Maintaining a regular, moderate practice and following it with a period of relaxation will enable you to expand your capacity in a delightful and amazing way.

Traditionally the morning is considered the best time for yoga postures, because the stomach is empty, the colon is clean, and the atmosphere is calm and soothing. But the stresses of modern life often make this impractical. Many people feel too stiff to practice in the morning or have such busy schedules that they do not have time for a relaxed session then and prefer to practice in the evening. Hunger and fatigue are the main drawbacks to practicing at the end of the day. You cannot do yoga postures on a full stomach, so you must either practice before dinner or eat a light meal and then wait for at least an hour and a half before doing your postures. Be sure to do a relaxation exercise to eliminate tension and fatigue before beginning the exercises themselves.

As for how to organize the routine itself, the following sequence of postures will prove beneficial:

1. Simple warm-up exercises, including upward stretching, forward and backward bending, and side bending.
2. Exercises for the wrist, shoulder, hip, knee, and ankle joints.
3. A spinal twist.
4. An abdominal lift.
5. Alternate nostril breathing.
6. Systematic relaxation.

On those days when you only have a few minutes to practice, a few repetitions of the sun salutation will stretch all the major muscle groups and leave you feeling relaxed and energized. Follow the sun salutation with a minute or two of *agni sara,* a technique for activating the solar plexus, strengthening the digestive system, and toning the internal organs in a minimum amount of time.

Q **There are many days when I can't manage to find more than five minutes for relaxation. What is the simplest, quickest relaxation exercise I can do?**

The word "relaxation" may be somewhat misleading. If you "try" to relax, you will fail. This is doubly true if you try to relax in a hurry. Relaxation is the art of letting go. It must be learned systematically and then allowed to progress naturally. There are many methods of yoga relaxation. The simplest one is to lie on your stomach in the crocodile pose for five minutes (see page 132 for complete instructions). In this pose you will naturally begin to breathe diaphragmatically. As you lie in the posture, observe your breathing. Let the breath become deep and smooth. While inhaling, feel the abdomen gently press against the floor; while exhaling, feel the abdomen contract. Let the body relax completely and keep your attention gently focused on your breath for the next five minutes.

CREATING A SPIRITUAL ENVIRONMENT

Q **No one around me supports my meditation. Their thoughts are scattered and their actions are so disruptive that I find being around them is disturbing. I need to live in a place where people will support my spiritual aspirations, share my meditation practice, and contribute to my sense of tranquility. Where should I go?**

No matter where you go this problem will follow, so it is better to solve it right where you are. You are expecting your family and friends to help you in your meditation and you want people to behave in a certain way so that you will not be disturbed. You do not realize that it is your own expectations, not the people around you, that are disturbing you. Close your door and don't carry those people in your mind, and you can meditate undisturbed.

Why do you care whether someone supports your practice or not? Can anybody really support your practice during the practice itself? If I arrange my legs properly, will it help you stay in a meditative pose? The same is true with your mind. How can the state of someone else's mind support your meditation? The truth is: Nobody can support you in anything. When you are injured no one can share your pain. No one can breathe for you. No one can die for you. Just as no one can share your pain, no one can share your joy, and no one can share your meditation and the peace derived from it. Both tranquility and disturbance are your own personal experiences.

Be practical. Do your meditation in a manner that does not inconvenience others. Furthermore, do not expect others to meditate in order to keep you company. Cultivate an attitude of neutrality toward everyone and everything. Consider both those who like you and those who do not like you to be equal. When you sit down for meditation with an attitude of equanimity, your mind will be at peace, and a peaceful mind cannot be disturbed by external causes.

If the world around you is noisy and displeasing, then behave like a turtle. Withdraw yourself not only physically but also mentally. The first step is to realize that you are an individual working on yourself. Remind yourself: "All relationships come and go; I existed and I lived my life before these people were part of it, and I will continue to exist when these people are gone." Why not get out of everybody's life for ten or fifteen minutes a day and see how wonderful it feels? The truth is that you are deliberately dragging the people around you into your mind and disturbing yourself.

Q **That doesn't make much sense. Being disturbed is unpleasant. Why would I deliberately disturb myself?**

The greatest obstacle in meditation is loneliness. The mind is not trained to enjoy solitude, and so it suffers from loneliness. To cope, the mind brings forward memories—both pleasant and unpleasant—to keep it company. Agitation and anger come at the invitation of your mind. Then it says, "These people are bothering me, these thoughts are bothering me." It is your mind—no one else's. How can anything take place in your mind unless you allow it to?

The mind is playing a game called "attachment" and is fooling itself by pretending that external forces are responsible for your happiness. Attachment is the root cause of all mental disturbances, and expectations play the biggest role. Your expectations breed likes and dislikes. Then you get attached to your likes and dislikes and cling to them. It is your expectations that create distractions and disturbances when you do your meditation practice—not the outside world and not the people around you.

Q It is hard to imagine being free of expectations—they seem to be such a big part of life. How can I use my meditation practice to overcome them?

Expectations cannot be overcome by meditation. When you are in the grip of expectations, the meditative techniques of yoga are useless unless they are supported by the philosophy of Vedanta. Pondering the principles of Vedanta is called contemplation. To free yourself of expectations, you need to practice contemplation.

The facts of life set forth in the Vedantic scriptures remind you of two facts. First, the objects of the world and worldly relationships are short-lived. They can make your life relatively comfortable, provided you know how to use them properly. But if you expect worldly objects and relationships to secure your happiness, you will be disappointed. Disappointment leads to misery. The second fact is that there is a higher force that is ever-existent, and omniscient. That and that alone is the source of genuine security and protection. This force accompanies us all the time.

By using these two simple facts as contemplative guidelines we can calm our mind and free it from all expectations. Let me give you an example.

Let's say that you had formulated an investment strategy that you expected would bring you peace and prosperity. For a long time your stocks were doing extraordinarily well and you were thrilled. But without warning, your stocks plummeted and you suffered a severe loss. This caused you to sink into an anxious depression. At the same time your spouse, who you thought was your soul mate, dumped you for someone else. Now this world, which seemed so rosy a few short weeks ago, seems like a terrible place. You do not feel motivated to do anything, including your meditation practice. Even when you do manage to force yourself to sit for meditation, all you do is brood about your losses. Instead of meditating, you are complaining, grieving, and intensifying your anger and despair.

Now is the time to turn to contemplation: "I had a fairly good life before I got into the stock market and before I got into a relationship with my spouse. Who was around in those days to keep me happy and healthy? When I was hanging upside down for nine months in my mother's womb, what kind of investments was I making then? Who was providing everything I needed to grow? How foolish I have been to forget that invisible, benevolent force that accompanies us always, protecting, guiding, and nurturing. Instead of remembering that force, I am complaining and worrying. Instead of brooding on the past, I will open my heart to receive guidance from that divine force."

As you go deeper in your contemplation you will notice that all of your expectations are being channeled toward the Divine, the ever-existent Reality who has been protecting and guiding you from the beginning of your life—and even before then. You will find yourself exploring the deeper dimensions of life, where peace and happiness are not dependent on transitory worldly success. This does not mean that you will become passive or withdrawn. On the contrary, you will find yourself inspired to be active in the world and to be kind and compassionate to those around you—but you will not expect anything from anyone but the Divine. This is pure faith, and once the virtue of pure faith begins to blossom in your heart you will no longer be dependent on the world and worldly relations to make you happy. Contentment will become your nature.

Q **That sounds great, but it's not how I feel. I've been a little lonely since yoga became part of my daily life. My friends and I don't have as much in common, and they seem put off by my new way of life. This sometimes makes me feel uncertain about the course I've chosen.**

Skillful action is one of the requirements of spiritual life. You may be creating unnecessary problems for yourself by talking too much about your spiritual path. This is common, especially in the beginning, before you have actually experienced the support that comes from the Truth and before the ground underneath you is solid.

When you are beginning your search, take care not to create conflicts with your friends and family members. Don't challenge their beliefs and lifestyles, as doing so would cause needless tension in your relationships. You don't have the time to argue with others. In fact, you don't yet have the strength to sustain your own assertions. Instead of clarifying your own ideas and strengthening your sense of purpose, wasting precious time in meaningless debates would serve no useful purpose and could actually increase your doubts.

Remember that in a war, each side can easily justify its actions. Don't expect to strengthen your position by using reason and logic to attack the position of others, and don't expect others to validate your position. The best logician in the world may also be the best liar. Intellectual understanding ultimately comes up short. Intuitive understanding is the only way to know what's right and wrong, what's good and bad for you.

You must find a way of living that makes the best use of your time and energy. Only then can you overcome self-condemnation and the fear of being abandoned. Every human being is always alone. You came into this world alone, and you will leave it alone. You will never get inner peace and satisfaction from external objects. You cannot share your inner life, not even with those who claim to love you and those you claim to love—in fact, they are the ones that make you lonely.

Even so, at this stage it is best not to become too adamant and say, "I don't care whether others like my way of life or not." Unless you go off to live in a forest or a mountain cave, you are at the mercy of the human community in which you live, at least to some degree. Remain a member in good standing. That is the best way to ensure that other people will create a minimum number of obstacles for you. Maintain harmony with the external world while finding your way internally.

Q Can you give me more practical advice about how to live in the world while growing spiritually?

Worldly and spiritual life cannot be completely separated. Because you cannot maintain your existence without the help of the material world, you must learn how to obtain sufficient worldly resources and how to use these resources as a means for obtaining spiritual wisdom. The trick is to expand your consciousness without losing yourself in the material world.

In relationship to the world, be vigilant like the hawk, which focuses on its prey while keeping an eye out for possible danger. The heron is another model of the right attitude toward the world: it stands still in the water, as if in deep meditation, but when the right moment comes, it catches the fish in a flash. Be still and patient when there is no need to be active. When it is time to act, perform your actions effectively and on time, and again return to a state of stillness. Learn how to relax like a dog relaxes. A dog falls asleep quickly, but if anything moves, it's awake in an instant and ready for action. When the moment has passed, the dog falls asleep again. Work hard, but take it lightly. Perform your duties to the best of your ability, but with as little attachment as possible.

Don't get lost in an endless round of worldly duties and obligations. No matter how skillful you are, or how selflessly you carry out your duties, there will still be an endless number of things left undone at the end of your life. If you don't learn how to balance duties and your personal spiritual practice, you will be lost.

Regulate your life. Go to sleep on time and get up on time. Maintain a schedule—when it's time to sleep, sleep; when it's time to get up, get up. After ten p.m., even a five-minute deviation from your schedule makes a difference. For example, a close friend calls you after ten p.m. and you feel you have to talk to her. Conversations with those who are close to us affect us deeply, so you may not be able to sleep for a while after the conversation is over. If your sleep is disrupted, it will be difficult to get up on time in the morning. If you sleep late, your schedule is in shambles. From the perspective of your practice, this conversation with your friend is not constructive.

When you are developing the habit of practice, everything counts. You have to consciously make a strong commitment to your practice and resolve that while you will not ignore the world, you will also not let it get in the way of your *sadhana.*

Q Does that mean I have to give up my close friends?

No. Skillful people act in such a way that they are not abandoned by others. But it's even more important not to abandon others. This is a subtle point. Don't think, "Now I have found the way, and to hell with everyone else." Rejecting others is a sign that you have an internal conflict and you feel abandoned. Never reject others because they are not living according to your standards. Instead, look at your own life and remember how long it took you to become firmly established on the path. Think how lucky you are to have gotten help along the way. Rather than focusing on what other people are doing wrong, think about how you can be a tiny lamp to light their way.

Most of us already know better than to be narrow-minded. We know that principles of right and wrong differ according to time and place. We know that God loves us all and that we should love one another. But somehow we forget. Why? Because we fail to remember the needs of the soul.

At the level of the soul, are we different? All of us have the same awareness or sense of I-ness. We all want to express ourselves. A seed pushes all obstructions away and sends a sprout to the surface when it receives water, warmth, and light. It's a miracle that a tender sprout can push pebbles and clods aside and make its way to the surface. It works hard and strives for life. Even if it doesn't get enough nourishment, it will often survive and struggle to bloom. The same is true with the life of the spirit. The tiny seed of consciousness is constantly trying to express itself, despite life's hardships. No matter how hard the journey, no matter how many obstacles it must overcome, it never stops.

Constant awareness helps us stay focused on our goal. A disorganized lifestyle is disruptive and distracts our awareness from the highest goal of life. That is why, in spite of knowing the value of the goal, we fail to practice sincerely and wholeheartedly—and thus the tiny seed of consciousness, which constantly tries to express itself, becomes weak and fails to blossom.

Yet attending to this process of inner unfoldment doesn't mean we have to abandon our family and friends. What happens is that when this process of unfoldment slows down, we feel sad and lost. That internal sadness manifests in feelings of abandonment. We feel that we have abandoned others or that others have abandoned us—whereas in truth these feelings are simply symptoms of loneliness for the eternal Friend within. It is a conflict that has little basis in external reality. During those periods when we notice that the process of inner unfoldment has slowed, we feel lost and project these feelings outward: we frantically begin to notice who else doesn't care for us.

We must shake off the tendency to be discouraged and must continue with our practice, working to refine our perception. Only after we have lit the lamp within can we walk safely on our own personal path. Then we can light the path for others at the same time. Spirituality involves the expansion of consciousness. As your consciousness expands, you embrace all and exclude none. Everyone becomes your friend, yet you remain undisturbed by the friendly or unfriendly activities of those around you.

Q I will be getting married in a few months. My fiancée follows a different teacher and her practices are different from the ones I've been given. Is it necessary for a married couple to have the same teacher and practice?

No. It is wonderful if a wife and husband have the same teacher and follow the same path; it will lessen the strains that inevitably come with marriage. But it is by no means necessary. However, in order to live a healthy and happy life, you must respect each other's path and honor each other's practices.

Always keep in mind that even though you have different teachers and different practices, you are both moving in the same direction. Your values are the same or similar—that is why you became close in the first place. Minimize your differences. If you felt a strong conflict regarding your spiritual values and practices and yet fell in love anyway, this was not pure love but rather an expression of physical attraction and emotional involvement. If that was the case, your marriage will be neither healthy nor happy and will eventually fall apart.

Whether or not we consider ourselves to be spiritual, spiritual values hold a very important place in our lives. When we marry, our spiritual values must marry too. If they don't, we end up living with loneliness. Spiritual loneliness is even more painful than loneliness at the physical and emotional levels. Therefore, as a married couple, either you must provide enough space for each other to grow independently, or one of you must adjust to the other's spiritual model. Either course requires understanding. The truth is, if you really love someone, you will love that person's teacher and practices too.

Q My husband and I are long-term practitioners of meditation. We are concerned that our son, now two, will be unduly influenced by the cultural emphasis on the external and the material. How can we nurture a love for spiritual values in our son? Should we adopt formal teaching methods or simply trust that he will pick them up from the atmosphere we create in our home?

You will create and nurture love for spirituality in your children when you allow your own spirituality to manifest effortlessly in your thoughts, speech, and actions. Your children expect love and affection from you; the last thing they will accept is the imposition of rigid discipline.

Make sure your method of inspiring and guiding your children in spiritual matters doesn't create a bad impression in their minds. Excessive preaching and lecturing and overt attempts to control their behavior will make a negative impression, and they may rebel. Instead, let them notice how much value you place on spiritual principles compared to all other components of your daily life. Through observation they will figure out the connection between the brighter and loving part of you and your spiritual practices.

Children are smart—their minds are like sponges, especially in the early years. They gather information by comparing and contrasting. They process this information and assimilate only that which makes sense. I have heard children talking about their homes, making astute comments about why their parents or their friends' parents talk and behave in a particular way. If you are maintaining a spiritual environment in your home, your children will automatically figure out why, compared with their friends' parents, you are so wonderful. That much realization will be enough.

Q What constitutes a spiritual environment and how can we maintain one in our home?

The foremost component of spirituality is love for inner truth. Creating a spiritual environment means working toward that inner truth, using all worldly objects and achievements as means. Meditation is a system through which we shift our search for truth from the external to the inner world.

To create a spiritual environment, therefore, you need only to maintain a regular schedule for your spiritual practice and let all your other schedules center around it. You may not be able to alter the time that you must leave for work or the time you get home, but leave for work only after you have attended to the core of your life: your formal meditation practice. It doesn't matter if your practice time is relatively short. Your children will come to understand that the ten minutes you spend in meditation are more important to you than the ten hours you spend at your job. This concept gradually sinks into their minds and, one day, they automatically find themselves drawn to spiritual practice.

If, as in your case, your child is quite young, simply sit down at the same time every day and do your practice. If possible, let your partner take care of the child during that time. If this isn't feasible, let the child occupy himself with some other activity while you meditate. But be warned: because you are quiet and not paying attention to your son, he will want your attention. To get it, he may cry. If that doesn't work, he may pull your hair or pinch you. If this happens, manage the situation by lovingly ignoring him. Let your son know that you love him very much, but that these ten minutes are very important to you and you will attend to him only when they are over. For a week or even a month, he will try his best to get you to acknowledge his right to your attention. But gradually he will see that you cannot be swayed and he will be trained. This childhood training is more important than any other spiritual training you may provide later on.

This is how I managed my practices while raising two children. I kept an extra pillow and blanket and a bottle of milk next to my meditation seat. When my son was two years old, he always woke up at exactly five a.m. and walked sleepily from the bedroom to the meditation room. He would cry if the door to the meditation room was closed, so I left the door open. I knew that he would be coming, so when he arrived I extended my hand and gently laid him on the pillow, put the bottle in his mouth, and covered him with the blanket. While he drank the milk, he fell asleep and I continued my practice.

My teacher used to tell me that a young child can be taught during his sleep. Before having children, I never knew how this was possible. Now I know that my son learned meditation while he was sleeping next to me as I did my practice.

Q The *Devi Mahatmya* states that "although there are bad children, there can never be a bad mother." Yet some mothers abuse, abandon, and even kill their children. How do we square this with the scriptural statement?

The *Devi Mahatmya* is a *Shakta* scripture, which means it comes from a tradition that regards the Divine Mother *(Shakti)* as the highest reality. The scripture is referring to the sublime form of motherhood that transcends the imperfection of human relationships. The mother spoken of is one who knows only how to give, love, and sacrifice herself for her children. These virtues do not grow in the contaminated soil of the four primitive urges (the desire for food, sex, sleep, and self-preservation), nor are they products of our biochemistry. These are divine virtues and they manifest more spontaneously in women than they do in men. That is why in the Vedic tradition a dwelling is considered to be a home only if a woman is at its nucleus. In her absence, it is merely a house.

The *Devi Mahatmya* is referring to a mother who loves her children unconditionally. She doesn't care how good or bad her children are, but only for what they need and what will make them happy. Thus, in the mythology of the Shakta tradition, the mother gladly severs her own head so that her children can drink her blood as wine and eat her body as bread. Such a courageous and compassionate mother is known as *Chinnamasta* and the followers of this branch of yoga say with confidence that Christ himself was a manifestation of Chinnamasta.

Because your question is specific to mothers, I will stick to mothers, but it should be understood that fathers also have these problems. The spiritual virtues of humankind have declined through the ages, along with many other virtues—such as moral strength, truthfulness, and selflessness. That is why the statement that there can never be a bad mother seems far-fetched and unrealistic today. Negligent and abusive mothering is a chronic problem that has been passed on from one generation to another. If a girl is not raised with wisdom, love, and attention, she will have a hard time spontaneously exhibiting these virtues toward her own children, and her children will have similar difficulties. But if this cycle can be broken by cultivating an awareness of the virtue of Divine Motherhood, a woman's inherited emotional injuries will be healed. As the pain she has undergone in childhood is eased, the positive virtues of Divine Motherhood will manifest in her, and she will give the best to her children without caring whether or not they are perfectly well-behaved or live up to her expectations for them.

The trauma visited on children by their parents is a hot topic these days. There are many, many counseling and therapeutic paradigms for healing this trauma, but so far one hundred percent effectiveness seems to be rare. The spiritual approach advocated by yoga's Shakta tradition is to forget what has happened in the past and focus instead on creating a bright future for ourselves. However, these old memories cannot simply be forgotten, for they are powerful and push their way into our mind-field. The only way to let the past be the past is to forgive our mothers. But forgiving implies that the mother was at fault, and as long as this thought remains in our mind we are simply acting out a drama of forgiveness. Thus yogis advise that even if we were abused in childhood, it is still important to develop the attitude that "there can never be a bad mother."

This can be done by contemplating on the truth that human nature is essentially divine—hurting others is not part of our intrinsic nature; no one deliberately sets out to harm others for the sake of harming them. This is especially true of mothers and their children. Mothers harm their children when their mind and emotions have been distorted by stress and their perceptions distorted by their own pain and confusion. People who do not realize that only those who have been hurt themselves can hurt others, yet still try to get help from a therapist or a spiritual teacher, usually are stuck struggling with the bitter image of a "bad" parent they are holding in their mind. Often such people see the therapist or teacher as that parent, and sooner or later they try to even the score. That is when they turn on the therapist or the teacher—an occurrence that is becoming quite common.

I am a police officer. How can I practice non-violence and still do my job?

The conflict you perceive between practicing non-violence and doing your duty as a police officer will disappear when you come to understand the relationship between truth, non-violence, and duty. These three always go together, and how they are defined depends on time and place. Take truth, for example. There are occasions when failing to speak up is the same as lying, just as there are occasions when it is best not to involve yourself in a situation by speaking the truth because it is none of your business. Remaining silent when it is not necessary to speak is practicing truth, just as failing to speak up when it is necessary is equivalent to lying. In either case, whether or not you are practicing truth depends on the situation in which you find yourself.

The same is true of non-violence. If you were a monk living in a monastery, your standard of non-violence would be different than it is as a police officer. The apparently violent action of a police officer—for example, physically subduing a criminal who is trying to escape arrest—is not a violent act because it is the ground for ensuring the safety of law-abiding citizens. You are doing your duty. The fear you inspire in certain people is the source of peace and tranquility for society at large. Criminals need to be afraid of you—it is one means of inducing them to refrain from violent acts that will disturb the peace of others.

If personal issues are involved, however, it is another matter. For example, if you are required to arrest someone with whom you have personal issues—someone you believe has hurt a friend or member of your family—and you treat that person roughly when it is not necessary, this is a form of violence. In this case you are letting violence manifest through you; you are not doing your duty.

Any time personal issues are involved, you have to be especially vigilant. If you act blindly, allowing your personal feelings to shape your actions, the fruit of these blind actions will create binding negative karmas. If you are simply doing your duty, you do not have to be concerned that you are creating negative karmas for yourself. If the act is fitting because it is your duty to do it, for you that act is not a base action. It is the time and place that defines an act as good or bad.

Q **It is the duty of police or military officers to follow the orders of their superiors, regardless of how painful the consequences. Are you saying that no action committed in the line of duty is a base action?**

The answer is both "yes" and "no," again depending on the situation. The hardest part is to be objective and clear in defining our duties. While it is true that time and place determine whether an act is good or bad, an impure mind can easily confuse the two and mistake right for wrong. The tricky part of the mind can skillfully and convincingly justify any action. If we are free from mental pollutants, such as desire, attachment, anger, hatred, jealousy, and greed, we can easily see our actions in their proper context with time and place and we can define our duties clearly and accurately. Then if duty dictates, we will follow the orders of our superiors even though by doing so we may create some degree of pain for ourselves and others.

If the situation is not clear or if you have no freedom to choose whether or not to take an unwholesome action, it means you are caught in a karmic web. In such a situation, act as skillfully as possible and surrender your actions to the Divine, who is the inner, eternal witness of your intent. Thus you are free from the fruits of such unwholesome actions. The scriptures call such a situation *dharma sankata* (a spiritual dilemma where you are caught, with no ability to go either forward or backward). You can face and conquer these circumstances by making the best use of whatever freedom of choice you do have and by ultimately surrendering yourself to the Divine.

Q Given the nature of rationalization, how do I know if I am letting violence manifest through me?

You will have to make use of your intellect, which is your decisive faculty. It is through the intellect, a most sophisticated instrument for making the right decisions, that the higher intelligence flows, illuminating all aspects of our being.

The problem is that if the instrument of the intellect is faulty, the flow of higher intelligence becomes distorted. Desire, attachment, anger, hatred, jealousy, greed, and ego pollute the intellect. And because of these pollutants the intellect loses its power of discrimination, diminishing its decisive capacity. We fall into confusion and are not able to distinguish whether we are letting violence manifest through us or whether we are using our strength to uphold the higher virtues.

Purification is the way to sharpen the decisive faculty, but it may take a long time to attain complete freedom from all these pollutants, so you must use your present level of intellectual purity and sharpness and decide the best course of action. Before you perform an action, think about it logically and consult your own inner counselor, the Divine within you. With real feeling in your heart, surrender both your action and the expected result of your action to the Divine. Bring life to the process of surrendering by mentally repeating this prayer: "I have tried my best to come to the right decision. My knowledge and my intellect are both limited. Whether this action is right or wrong, I surrender it and its fruits to you, the Lord and Inner Guide of all living beings."

Q **I feel it is my duty as a parent to be strict with my son and tell him he cannot do certain things. If he doesn't listen, I get so upset that I feel I am doing emotional violence both to myself and him. How can I make sure that I don't practice violence in these situations?**

If you are emotionally involved, then you will commit violence. If you are trying to vicariously fulfill those desires which you could not fulfill on your own through your son, you will commit violence. Do not try to see yourself in your son; let him grow as an independent and complete person. Offer your love, knowledge, and worldly resources so that the best of him will emerge. Children are intelligent and observant. They know why their parents are disciplining them, so make sure that you are not trying to get him to be good and well-disciplined for your convenience. And do not tell him to refrain from doing things which you do yourself—children follow examples, not commandments.

The habits you want your child to learn and practice as an adult are the habits you must have yourself. If you want him to value reading above watching television, he must see that you prefer reading; if you want him to value meditation, he must see that you practice it every day. Your sincere love for such things will have an indelible influence on your son's mind and heart. Let them become part of your lifestyle and they will eventually become part of his. Then there will be no room for violence to manifest in either of you, for frustration and the violence it breeds come from expectations. Your respect for that lifestyle and your love for your son are spontaneous and effective teachers.

Q Yoga philosophy seems to concentrate on individual transformation, but says little about the crucial issue of transforming the world around us. What about world peace and other pressing issues? Does yoga advocate withdrawing into meditation and ignoring the external world?

By no means. But yoga philosophy recognizes that communities evolve from individuals and that external peace evolves from internal peace. Any meaningful transformation of humanity must begin with the individual and proceed from there.

According to yoga, individuals are beings of light. If humankind is to live in peace and harmony, this light must manifest and radiate from a significant number of individuals. The relationship between individuals and humanity is like the relationship between the trees and the forest. Just as a large group of individual trees viewed collectively is a forest, groups of individuals form families, communities, societies, and, ultimately, humanity as a whole.

At first glance it might not be obvious how a forest deteriorates when individual trees are diseased, yet it is impossible to have a healthy forest without healthy trees. Likewise, it is impossible to have a wise and just society without wise and just individuals. That is why the sages, whose concern and compassion for humanity are boundless, have always emphasized the enlightenment and self-transformation of individuals. As the quality of each person's life improves, the lives of those around that person automatically improve, and this improves the quality of life for society as a whole.

roadblocks along the way

TAMING THE MIND AND SENSES

What should we do to understand life better and live happily?

You may try hundreds of things, but nothing will work unless you have control over your mind. It is the mind that creates a mess outside and inside, and it is the mind that finds a way to clean up the mess. All problems are created and solved by the mind, but surprisingly, the mind is not known to itself.

Mind is the greatest of all mysteries. It stands between an individual and the highest Truth and is the cause of both bondage and liberation. Properly trained, the mind can help you attain enlightenment, but a misguided mind can leave you stranded on the shoals of confusion and bondage. Peace is created by the mind. First, make the decision to be content in any circumstance. From that womb of contentment, peace is born. It is foolish to expect to achieve peace by retiring into the deep forest or departing for a distant galaxy. Ultimately we must all find peace within our own minds.

Why does the mind prefer to run to the external world rather than turning inward to find peace?

The mind has bound itself tightly to the senses. Driven by sense cravings, the mind runs to the external world. As long as you do not know how to withdraw the senses from the external world you have almost no choice but to let your mind remain a victim of sensory pleasure.

The objects of the senses, as well as the pleasure derived from them, are momentary. After experiencing a sensory pleasure, the mind realizes the emptiness of the experience. But it is always seeking satisfaction and, not knowing where else to find it, turns again to the external world. Thus dissatisfaction becomes a way of life. Dissatisfaction leads to frustration. Peace vanishes, and the inner world becomes chaotic. Inner discontent, frustration, and restlessness then manifest in a person's external life, and both internal and external worlds are full of misery.

How do we stop the mind from constantly turning to the external world?

Vairagya (non-attachment) is the only way. You will cultivate an attitude of non-attachment when you come to realize that all the objects of the world are transitory. The value of worldly objects is simply a creation of the mind. You arrived in this world with nothing, and you will depart with nothing. When you realize this, you will not be attached to the objects of the world.

Q I understand that worldly objects have no real value. I also know the value of practicing vairagya, but somehow I fail to maintain this knowledge, especially when it comes to interacting with the world. Why?

The mind is fully convinced that this world and its objects are real; this is called maya. Maya is a strong belief in the existence of that which does not exist. The following story illustrates this point:

Once a washerman asked his son to go to the barn and get his donkey. But when the son tried to fetch it, the donkey wouldn't budge. The boy went to his father and told him the donkey wouldn't move.

"Is the donkey tied up?" the washerman asked.

"No. That's what I don't understand," the son replied.

"Well then, slap him on the rump to get him moving!" the father replied in exasperation.

The son tried that, but the donkey still wouldn't move. He went back to his father and said, "Father, he must be sick. Please come and see for yourself."

This time, father and son went together to fetch the donkey. The father tried to get the donkey to move, but to no avail. Then suddenly he understood the problem: the donkey's rope was attached to his halter but not attached to the post. The washerman wound the rope around the post, then unwound it and began walking out of the barn. The donkey, realizing he was untied, followed him.

People whose minds are fully convinced of the reality of worldly objects and the bondage they create are like this donkey. This world is not capable of binding either the mind or soul; the mind is in bondage simply because it believes that it is in bondage.

How can the mind overcome the illusion that it is in bondage?

First, it must overcome the craving for worldly objects with the help of constant contemplation on the illusory nature of worldly pleasure. Second, the mind must recognize its true nature and learn to maintain that awareness constantly. Forgetfulness of the true nature of the self is what makes a human being subject to timidity, weakness, fear, and insecurity. It is this forgetfulness that causes us to keep searching for a haven in the external world. Once you realize your inner self you become free from the charms of the world, as well as the fear of death. In this context, ponder this ancient tale:

Once there was a lion cub who was separated from the pride at birth, before his eyes had opened. He never saw his real mother. He was helpless, but in a short while a flock of sheep happened by. He joined the flock and was raised with the lambs. As a result, he identified himself with the sheep and learned to behave like them. He learned to follow others blindly, to fear dogs, and to submit to the shepherd. He grew to adulthood, but his identification with the sheep around him was so complete that he never noticed his size or his sharp, powerful claws. He never discovered how fast he could run, how high he could jump, and how loud he could roar.

One day another lion crept up on the flock and let out a tremendous roar. The flock scattered. The young lion, who was as frightened as the other sheep, ran away too. He passed a pond in full flight and saw his reflection for the first time. To his astonishment, his reflection resembled the lion he was fleeing. Here was a puzzle: why didn't he look like the other sheep? As he examined this reflection, his disappointment at not seeing the reflection of a sheep quickly turned into curiosity. As an experiment he tried roaring like the lion he had just heard—and found that he could! This filled his mind with delight. He jumped and roared and relished the realization that he was truly a lion. He never returned to the flock, but joined the pride and lived as the king of the forest.

Like that lion cub, we create a self-image, and based on that we create a reality. If this identification is false, we become victims of falsehood. If the identification is correct, then we are fortunate to live in the light of Truth.

Q I want to practice non-attachment, but I am distracted by the world's pleasures. What can I do?

Learn to withdraw your senses and mind systematically before practicing non-attachment or committing yourself to an intense meditative practice. This process is called *pratyahara* (sense withdrawal). Through a systematic practice of pratyahara you can tame your senses and mind and bring them under your conscious control.

Practicing pratyahara requires a basic understanding of the nature of the external world so that while disciplining yourself, you don't feel that you are being deprived of sensory pleasure. The practice itself should be a source of joy rather than a dry discipline. You must realize that people who search for joy in the external world are always disappointed. Desires and cravings begin in the mind and motivate the senses to seek pleasure in the external world. That is why trying to control the senses without placing your discipline within a more comprehensive context will not be effective—you must first have understanding.

Q What is a systematic practice for taming the senses and the mind and turning them inward?

The first step is to convince the mind and senses that it is necessary to withdraw. If you are attentive, you will discover that the mind and senses busy themselves in the external world—or resort to sleep—in order to escape from reality, which is painful. This external search for peace is exhausting; sooner or later, the mind stops to rest. Rest feels good. If the mind can be made to see and acknowledge the effect of rest, it will begin developing a willingness to withdraw the senses and rest.

When we pull in the mind and senses voluntarily with the thread of knowledge, we experience true relaxation. After the mind experiences the joyful stillness in the body that results from sense withdrawal, it can be successfully instructed to look within for the true source of happiness.

There are three ways of practicing pratyahara. The first is to withdraw the senses and mind from the external world and then focus them consciously on a chosen object in the realm of the mind. Another approach is to see everything in the world as existing within the *atman* (the self). With this approach nothing is outside the atman, so there is no need to withdraw the senses. A third practice is to carry out all your activities as if they were sacred duties. In this way you bring sanctity to even the most mundane aspects of life. When a human being gives up all desires of the mind and delights in the self, then they are said to be a person of steady wisdom.

Q I have practiced some of these techniques successfully, but soon I find myself back in my old habits, driven by my old distractions and urges. Do you have any advice?

If you couldn't master your senses after a couple of attempts, don't be discouraged. Believe me, most of us are in the same boat. The process by which the senses move toward the objects in the external world is very subtle. It begins with thinking—you become attached to something just by thinking about it. Something becomes attractive because of an inner craving or because of latent impressions from the past that still exist in the mind. These latent impressions are called *samskaras* or *vasanas*. They are like living entities deep in the mindfield. Through the windows of the senses and the conscious mind, these samskaras peep out into the external world, looking for something similar to themselves. The moment the mind finds an object that corresponds to its previous memories, a great sense of joy arises. This joy comes from the mind's identification with the object rather than from the object itself. The mind ignorantly feels, "This is mine. I love it. It is so beautiful." Attachment arises immediately from this feeling.

Therefore, attachment arises merely from thinking about something. The desire to act is based on that attachment. If that action is impeded, we become angry. If the obstruction cannot be overcome we become depressed, and depression is itself a form of anger. From anger, delusion arises, and from delusion arises loss of memory. With loss of memory, the power of discrimination *(buddhi)* is lost. It is then impossible to decide anything appropriately and, at this point, a human being is doomed: spiritual practice is not possible.

Study yourself, because only then can you build the foundation that will enable you to withdraw your senses and mind. Examine the nature of pleasure and pain and determine for yourself the results of attachment to the world of names and forms. As a human being, you have freedom to create your world—and you have already done this. Mastering your senses and mind and employing them for true joy is your birthright. Therefore, practice pratyahara to conserve your energies; then concentrate and focus these energies one-pointedly in the direction of true peace and happiness.

PURIFYING THE EGO

Q **Isn't a strong ego a requirement for success in anything, including spiritual practice?**

Often people think they need a strong ego to live successfully in the world and to be successful in their spiritual endeavors. This is not true. We cannot be successful in either the external world or the internal world while we are tossed about by a powerful ego. What success in both realms requires is a strong will.

The difference between ego and will is that the ego is blind, while the will has vision. Will has its source in the pure self. Ego springs from a false sense of identification *(avidya)* with the external world, and is usually concerned with preserving self-image and self-identity. Ego is characterized by stubbornness, selfishness, and an unwillingness to compromise.

The ego is like a little pool. An egotistical person crouches in that little pool like a frog—his world is small, his borders insecure. He has only a vague awareness of the grove of trees surrounding his pool, and he cannot even imagine the frog-filled marshes just beyond. From his perspective, only his own feelings and voice are meaningful.

But the power of will is like a spring whose source is the Pure Being. It infuses the mind and body with enthusiasm, courage, curiosity, and the energy to act. In yogic literature this force—the intrinsic power of the soul—is called *iccha shakti,* and it is from this force that all the various aspects of our personality, including the ego, receive the energy to carry out their activities.

Achieving success in the world requires a strong will, and that strong will needs to be properly guided so that we may develop a strong personality rather than a trivial, egotistical one. A strong personality exhibits tolerance and endurance. It has the power to vanquish and punish an opponent, but forgives and forgets instead. When we are egotistical, on the other hand, we demonstrate our weakness by answering a pebble with a cannon. We lose our composure the moment our feelings receive even the mildest bruise. We have a hard time forgetting the injuries we have received from others, but an even harder time remembering how much we have hurt others.

All the problems in the world—at home, at work, everywhere—are caused by the collision of egos. These problems are overcome not by one ego dominating others but by a person of strong will and clear vision coming forward and overshadowing the trivial egos of those who are quarreling.

As for the question of whether you need a strong ego to do spiritual practice, the answer is "No, definitely not." The stronger the ego, the bigger the hurdle it will create. The solution, however, is not to kill the ego or even to weaken it. Rather, we should do our best to purify, transform, and guide it properly. We can do this by employing both our intelligence and our power of discrimination. In other words, when we meditate, practice contemplation, pray, study the scriptures, and seek the company of the wise we make our ego purer and less confined, and this in turn inspires us to move one step ahead. From here the purified ego, accompanied by a sharpened intellect, gets a glimpse of the next level of awareness, and naturally aspires to reach it. Thus the ego becomes the tool for purifying and expanding itself, and in this way the petty ego begins to be transformed into an expanded, more purified ego.

Along the way it becomes increasingly apparent that this transformation must end with the ego dissolving and becoming one with the pure self, experiencing its union with Universal Consciousness. As the ego of a dedicated seeker merges with the Infinite, all confusion disappears, the veil of duality lifts, and the purified ego sees the whole universe within itself and itself in the whole universe.

Q **That's a bit too philosophical for me. From a practical standpoint, how do you go about purifying your ego?**

As I've already mentioned, contemplation, meditation, prayer, study of the scriptures, and the company of the wise purify the ego. Any obstacle that arises again and again should be noted, and the student should focus on removing that particular obstacle. For example, if in the process of purification and inner expansion the student is constantly facing problems caused by stubbornness, then the student must find a meditative or contemplative practice that provides an antidote to stubbornness. If doubt, an inferiority complex, and vanity are the main hurdles, then a personal practice must be devised that will help the student overcome these obstacles.

Be honest with yourself, and gather the courage to face your own problems. Start working with yourself without hesitation. However, if you are not that strong or clear and, therefore, aren't sure that you will ever be able to identify your own problems, find a teacher. But here too there is an obstacle: you must be flexible and open to learning from a teacher, and those are characteristics you will have to engender by yourself.

How can I know if my actions are coming from my ego or from my will?

The tussle between ego and will occurs when we keep doing things that others oppose or refuse to do things that others are urging us to do. In such situations it is important to ask yourself if you are being driven by ego or by will.

The degree of fear involved in your actions—feelings of insecurity, the sense of tarnishing your self-image, your concern with the opinions of others—is a sign that you are acting from your ego. A defensive attitude is a symptom that your ego is being threatened. This impels you to take every possible measure to protect your position and defend your point of view. Also, seeking a reward for your actions is a sure sign that you are motivated by ego.

When you are operating from will your motivation is pure, unselfish, and free from the need to protect your self-image. Your actions are not influenced by your reactions. You are not affected by either positive or negative comments from others. You are pulled to do what you do purely by the voice of your heart. When you are pouring your mind and heart into your actions without seeking a reward, you can be sure that you are acting from the strength of your will.

What is the cause of fear? How can fear be overcome?

Fear is innate; anyone who is born is afflicted by fear. The greatest of all fears is the fear of death. This fear springs from the human tendency to cling to life without knowing what life actually is. We humans identify ourselves with our bodies and we are terrified by the knowledge that our bodies are subject to change, death, and decay. From the moment of birth to the moment of death we busy ourselves gathering external resources that might help us preserve our physical existence—yet all the while we know that ultimately all our efforts will be in vain and our bodies will perish. Because we think we are our bodies, this realization is terrifying and causes intense pain.

The desire for self-preservation springs from the ego. Ego is a psychological principle through which we identify with the body and the mind, thus confining our awareness to a limited range. We become attached to this confined sense of I-am-ness and are consumed with the desire to preserve this identification with the body and mind.

The ego does not want its boundaries to be breached, but at the same time it feels lonely when it finds itself isolated from others. The ego does not want its privacy disturbed, but at the same time it wants to receive love from the whole world. Even though isolation is painful, we nonetheless isolate ourselves, primarily because of our confined self-identity.

This tendency of the ego makes us fearful, selfish, greedy, and self-centered. Internally, we become misers—we do not want to give anything to anyone. At the same time, we expect others to give to us, but we do not want them to break through the wall of self-identity that our egos have built. This self-created misery cannot be cured by anyone else or by anything external. The only cure is to trace fear back to its roots in desire, attachment, and ego. Unless we treat the aspect of our personality that is actually sick—the ego itself—there is no hope of attaining freedom from fear.

The problem of ego arises from ignorance—mistaking the unreal for the real. A false identity is developed: "I am this body." So long as we do not know our immortal, eternal, blissful nature, we will always be afraid of losing this self-imposed identity. The body is not the soul; it is not immortal. The body dies. As long as we remain ignorant and cling to the belief "I am the body," we will be victims of fear. Knowing the atman, the real self, is the only way of attaining final freedom from fear.

Q Is it possible to become advanced in meditation practice and still have serious ego problems?

Yes, it's quite possible to develop an advanced meditation practice in spite of a big ego or other negative personality traits. If an egotistical student works hard and does the practices correctly, the student may develop willpower and achieve *siddhis* (extraordinary abilities), but an egotistical meditator can never become a sage.

As you develop your meditation practice you will come to understand why ego problems are serious. It is possible to use meditation as a means to overcome an ego problem, but if you have decided to love your ego and live with it, then meditation becomes a means of nourishing and strengthening your ego. In that case, meditation will help you nourish your ego problems. This kind of meditation cannot unfold the joy of the self.

Meditation is a powerful tool. Meditation with ego is like a flower with no fragrance. But meditation that is devoid of ego and nourished by devotion *(bhakti)* is like an eternal flower that yields the fragrance of the Divine. Egotistical meditators can harm themselves and others, whereas meditators who are free from ego and guided by devotion can be torchbearers for the human race.

OVERCOMING OBSTACLES

Q How can I tell the difference between temptation and something that's good for me?

No matter how glamorous and charming it seems, if an object or activity causes you to have second thoughts about your spiritual journey and the importance of reaching the goal, then it's a temptation. Nothing that distracts you from the path is good, no matter how good it appears. Nothing is more important than reaching your goal and gaining inner fulfillment. Anything that distracts you from your goal is a temptation and is to be avoided.

Q **The four greatest obstacles to spiritual life are said to be anger, hatred, jealousy, and greed. But knowing this doesn't help me get rid of these feelings. I don't want to be angry or jealous, but telling myself not to be doesn't work. How can I overcome these obstacles?**

Teachers describe many techniques for dealing with these problems. The most common suggestions are: witness these emotions as if from a distance and let them go; analyze the nature of these obstacles, understand their causes, then deal with them appropriately; cultivate a positive attitude, which automatically will counteract these negative feelings; meditate and pray more; avoid situations in which these obstacles arise; and so on. But in my experience, none of these solutions work in the long run. They sound good in theory, but when we are in the throes of these powerful feelings such advice is not very helpful. These solutions seem to work only as long as we are teaching them to others.

I will tell you what works for me, although I don't know how easy it is for others to cultivate and live with this concept. What works for me is maintaining the constant awareness of my *Ishta Devata* (the completely personal concept of God). To give you a clear understanding of what I mean, I will relate one of my experiences.

Once my *gurudeva* gave me a *japa* practice (repeating a mantra a specific number of times). I was supposed to complete the practice in thirty-six days and to observe certain disciplines during that time. But I broke the disciplines and had to start all over again. This happened several times. Frustrated, I finally decided to do the practice in solitude while observing silence. I also decided to triple the practice so that I could do it in twelve days rather than in thirty-six.

It was January and I had lectures scheduled every weekend. All but one were in cities distant from my home at the Himalayan Institute. During that one weekend, I was scheduled to lecture at a seminar at the Institute. I asked my colleagues if it was possible to schedule my lecture for an evening so I could walk quietly over to the main building, give my lecture, and resume my silence. They kindly scheduled me for Saturday night. I moved to a secluded cottage on the Institute grounds and began my practice.

On Thursday one of my colleagues heard that an ice storm was forecast for Saturday. Thinking it would be inconvenient for me to walk to the lecture hall in such conditions, she sent a note asking if I could lecture Friday evening instead of Saturday evening. I wrote "Yes" and sent it back. A day later, she sent another note, asking "Is it all right if you lecture Sunday morning?" Again, I wrote "Okay." But Saturday morning she sent yet another note saying "I think it would be better if you lecture tonight."

I lost my temper. Seething with fury, I thought, "She is deliberately trying to disturb me. She's a bad person. She doesn't like me…" The anger and hatred occupied my mind so strongly that I could not do the japa of my mantra. Usually it took three minutes to complete one round on my mala, but looking at my watch, I noticed that fifteen minutes had passed and I was only halfway through a single round. I got scared and thought, "If I can't overcome my emotions, how will I complete my practice?"

I took a shower to change my mood, but it didn't help. I went for a walk hoping the frigid air would cool me off, but that didn't help either. I didn't want to be angry, but I didn't know how not to be. I tried to witness my turmoil from a distance and let it go, but I couldn't get any distance. I tried my best to analyze the nature of my upheaval and understand its cause, but my mind was so unsteady and scattered that it failed to focus on the process of analysis and self-observation. I also told myself, "Hey, be positive. She must be doing this for a good reason." None of these techniques helped, probably because I was already in such a bad frame of mind that I could not apply them properly. I even went so far as to put into practice my childhood beliefs in purifying the meditation room, removing obstacles by reciting purifying and protective mantras, and drawing a line around my meditation seat with another set of mantras. Nothing helped.

Now my frustration was complete. With a deep sense of despondency I picked up my favorite scripture, the *Ramayana,* and begged for help: "You are a gift to seekers from the wise and compassionate sage Valmiki. You embody the noble deeds of Rama, who walked among humans in the flesh to uplift those who were stuck in the mud of affliction. Today I am stuck. Come forward, O light of the sages, and uplift me." So praying, I opened the book at random and saw the couplet in which Shiva is speaking to his wife. Roughly translated, it goes like this: "O Uma, how can one who has surrendered at the feet of Rama and consequently is free from ego, desire, anger, and greed, and who sees this world as though it is a manifestation of the Ishta Devata, maintain any anger or animosity toward anyone?"

The passage hit home. I realized that my faith in my Ishta Devata was not complete. My surrender was not complete. As a result, I was still under the influence of anger, hatred, jealousy, and greed. I was certainly unable to see this world, worldly objects, and people—including the friend writing those notes—as a manifestation of my Ishta Devata. What a low-grade aspirant I was! This realization lifted the veil from my ego and transported me to the realm where automatically I surrendered. My anger dissolved and I resumed my practice.

Only a person who has surrendered has the courage and ability to acknowledge their faults and still remain free from guilt. Only such an aspirant can pray with feeling, receive guidance, and overcome these four obstacles, which are otherwise indomitable.

Q **My biggest obstacle is procrastination. I can't seem to get around to establishing my practice the way I know I should. Why do I keep procrastinating?**

One of the causes of procrastination is lack of desire. Without a burning desire, people tend to put things off. Small discomforts get in the way. For example, you think, "I don't have a good room to do my practice in. Next month I'll move, and then I'll begin my practice." But next month you have to paint the new apartment. Then you think, "My daughter is visiting. Once she's gone, I'll begin my practice." These are all excuses, and excuses are endless.

Excuses are a form of guilt therapy. You collect reasons to justify your procrastination so you won't feel guilty about it. The underlying problem is that you have not yet come to understand that your spiritual goal is the most important part of your life. Everything else is left behind at death. Only knowledge—the *samskaras* stored in the mind—go with you. You have not yet grasped this and may not even believe it. That's why you continue to procrastinate.

Q Are there techniques that can help me overcome procrastination?

In our technological society we have come to believe that everything depends on technique. Techniques help smooth the way, but when it comes to penetrating your own inner being, they are of no avail. What you need are some principles and a philosophy of life that will prevent your mind from being disturbed by the external world. You must have sincerity; otherwise you will procrastinate and your practice will be irregular. When you are sincere you pour your whole heart into your practice, and when you do that your practice will be so rewarding you won't want to miss it. Your whole heart is in the practice only when you understand how crucial your practice is. If you believed that it is the most important part of your life—more important than your eight or ten hours at the office, for example—you would certainly do it.

Think about it. Why do you always get to the office on time? For one of two reasons: either because of fear (the fear of losing your job, the fear of losing out on a promotion, and so on) or because you love your work so much that you are eager to get started in the morning. If you really understand that you will lose your internal world if you neglect your practice, then you will put more emphasis on it. If you fall in love with your practice, skipping it will become unbearable. This is the role of knowledge. You must come to know what is important and eternal. Know which world you really dwell in, even in this life, even while you are in this body.

Q I value my meditation practice, but I like to have fun too. I go out to dinner and the movies several times a week and often stay up late partying with my friends. I miss these things when I don't do them, but I know they tire me out and disrupt my meditation practice. What shall I do?

The craving for sense pleasures is one of the strongest urges there is. Driven by these cravings, we continually change or postpone our spiritual practices, although at some level we know that a self-indulgent lifestyle is the breeding ground for sloth, inertia, fatigue, and procrastination. The problem lies in failing to understand the subtle line between enjoying sense pleasures and becoming the victim of our sense cravings. It is the failure to recognize this borderline that causes us to repeat activities that leave us feeling tired, dull, and undernourished, so that we have no energy for higher pursuits.

To overcome this problem we must come to realize that in living this way we are working for our senses, rather than disciplining our senses to work for us. Our eyes, ears, nostrils, tongue, and generative organs are tools for nourishing ourselves physically, emotionally, and spiritually. The senses gather data from the external world, and when coordinated with a properly trained mind they are a means of gaining knowledge and attaining victory over the primitive urges and cravings. The senses are also instruments through which we can express the infinite creative force that lies within us.

When we lose the ability to distinguish between enjoyment and indulgence, the forces of our senses make our life chaotic, pulling us in this direction and that every time a craving arises. This is a source of misery and it saps our energy. Constant awareness of the highest goal of life and proper understanding of sense pleasure are the keys to mastering our cravings and disciplining our senses to serve us.

Yogis advise us to enjoy the objects of the world in a manner that does not involve us in suppression and repression, but to refrain from indulging ourselves to the point where our energy is drained from our body and mind. If we adopt a balanced approach there will be no conflict between spiritual practice and enjoyment of the world's pleasures.

The key is to be vigilant in keeping track of our subtle urges toward sense pleasures. Only a trained mind and purified heart can tell us whether we are enjoying these pleasures within the limits of our natural urges or whether we are harming ourselves. If we learn to notice how we feel afterward, we will know whether we truly enjoyed a sensual experience or were being consumed by it.

Once we have developed the ability to make this distinction, the next step is contemplation. Whenever we find that we have allowed ourselves to be ordered around by our senses, we should take time to contemplate on how we are depleting our energy and weakening our ability to attend to our spiritual practices. Doing this will help prevent the memories and subtle impressions of those pleasures from causing us to remain at the mercy of our senses. This practice is called *pratyahara* (sense withdrawal) in the yogic tradition. In Vedanta, it is called *vichara* (contemplation).

Q **I meditate regularly. From time to time I feel like I've reached an expanded level of awareness. The problem is that I can't sustain it. I don't know how to reach firm ground so I won't be continually hampered by these setbacks.**

It is frustrating to practice without seeming to reach the goal, and it's even more frustrating to lose ground. When we take this problem to a teacher, they usually tell us to continue practicing or to have patience—things will work out. These directives might inspire us once or twice, but if the problem keeps recurring, such advice loses the power to inspire.

Overcoming this problem requires understanding the law of karma—the simple law that we reap what we sow: if we do something, there is bound to be a result. The law that every action bears fruit also applies to spiritual practice. If we do not see a result, it is because the time is not yet ripe. The fruit is not yet manifest, although it may already be there in its subtle form. We need a sophisticated and sensitive instrument to perceive it: the powerful microscope of the inner eyes. If we don't have inner eyes of our own, then we have to rely on those of an experienced teacher in whom we have faith. Such a person can tell us what is happening—although this is like borrowing a microscope that is too sophisticated for us to operate on our own and to which we don't have continual access. The other option is to develop our own inner eyes, the eyes of intuitive understanding. Intuition unfolds gradually as we continue meditating.

However, this does not answer the question of how to gain firm ground and progress from there. We are motivated to continue our meditation practice in spite of this experience of slipping backward only if we are fully convinced that we are moving in the right direction. We can discover whether or not we are moving in the right direction if we have a knowledge of the theory that supports our practice. It is this knowledge that engenders interest in the practice. The more we know of the philosophical and spiritual doctrines that stand behind the practice, the more we will be inspired to renew our efforts each time we slip from the summit. Knowing the philosophical and spiritual doctrines will not give us direct experience, but it acts as an antidote to discouragement, frustration, and waning motivation. That is why yoga texts and experienced teachers advise aspirants to incorporate the study of genuine scriptures into their daily practice. These include the *Bhagavad Gita*, the Upanishads, and the *Bhakti Sutras*, as well as books by saints and sages such as *Autobiography of a Yogi, Living with the Himalayan Masters, The Story of My Experiments with Truth,* and *In Woods of God-Realization.* In this way we will be inspired to continue to make efforts in our practice, which is the only way to solidify our attainments.

Q **Some texts say *svadhyaya*—self-study—is a complete path. How can it help me remove obstacles to my spiritual growth?**

The word *svadhyaya* means "study of the self by oneself, or by pondering on the scriptures." Practically speaking, it means doing *japa* (repetition) of the revealed mantras that we receive from a teacher through initiation and contemplating the instructions we receive from our teacher or those which are expounded in the authentic scriptures.

Often we commit ourselves to a spiritual discipline without having enough knowledge about ourselves, our goals, and the means by which we are trying to accomplish our goals. Because of this, when obstacles begin to surface during our practice we become discouraged. Because we lack sufficient knowledge, we often fail even to recognize the obstacles.

And once we have recognized them, we do not know how to overcome the obstacles because we do not know their cause. We become frustrated and disheartened, and blame the practice, the teacher, and ourselves. By incorporating svadhyaya into our daily practice we acquire the ability to detect the obstacles before they surface.

For example, by studying the experiences of previous aspirants as set forth in the scriptures and applying the lessons of these stories to ourselves, we learn to recognize our own strengths and weaknesses. Studying the scriptures helps us understand that the obstacles confronting us are the same obstacles that have confronted seekers through the ages. It may also help us detect obstacles that are lying in wait for us before they manifest, so we can avoid them altogether.

Furthermore the scriptures give us clear guidelines for self-analysis, self-observation, and self-reflection. They set forth a systematic way of looking at life and its circumstances and gaining a clear vision of spiritual goals. Those who practice svadhyaya come to know the trivial nature of worldly pleasures, and inspired by scriptural doctrines, they long for everlasting joy. Aspirants who do not practice svadhyaya, however, run the risk of developing a pessimistic attitude toward the world and living an empty and meaningless life even though they are engaged in spiritual practice. Svadhyaya works like a living counselor within.

Self-study also strengthens our conviction that the practice we have undertaken is noble and valid. Through self-study, as the *Yoga Sutra* tells us, we come closer to the Ishta Devata (the unique name and form of our chosen representative of the Divine), for svadhyaya infuses our practice with divine awareness. That is what helps our practice become spiritual. Without it, the practice of *japa,* for example, turns into a purely mental exercise. It is svadhyaya that opens the channel of *bhakti* (love and devotion) and thereby brings sweetness to the practice. Without this awareness the practice becomes dry and mechanical.

In the *Yoga Sutra,* svadhyaya has been placed between *tapas* and

Ishvara pranidhana. Tapas means "austerity or discipline." It consists of dietary observations, physical exercises, mental restraints, and exercising control over our thoughts and feelings. *Ishvara pranidhana* means "surrender to God, or offering the fruits of our actions to the Divine Being," the spiritual master of all subsequent masters. Unless the gap between tapas and Ishvara pranidhana is filled with svadhyaya, tapas is merely penance—physical and psychological torture—and Ishvara pranidhana is mere religious sentiment. Self-study gives meaning to both; it transforms tapas into self-commitment and Ishvara pranidhana into spiritual ecstasy.

Q **There are so many obstacles on the spiritual path that it seems like overcoming them one at a time will take forever. Is there an all-purpose remedy?**

Yes: the grace of God. We receive and retain this grace by Ishvara pranidhana, remembering the name of God and surrendering ourselves to it. From the practical standpoint, all great traditions of the world place a greater emphasis on the name of God than on God Itself.

Unless we know the profound metaphysics of the Divine Word, it is hard to understand how the name of God can cure our diseases, remove doubts, solve problems related to laziness and procrastination, and help us gain and maintain solid ground in our practice. But it works! This is not just an experience of one or two yogis or saints, but of everyone who has completed the spiritual journey. That is why prominent scriptures, such as the *Yoga Sutra,* clearly state that if someone takes this remedy wholeheartedly, then no other practice is needed. It is not merely a remedy, but a compassionate and omniscient vehicle that knows its own destination. You simply get into this vehicle—the name of God—and it will take you to the goal and help you remain there.

Because our minds are distracted and our hearts are polluted, we have a hard time comprehending and holding on to the name of God—the mantra—one-pointedly. That is why we do not see dramatic progress even when we do lots of *japa.* The scriptures tell us to have patience and assure us that success is certain if we continue our practice for an uninterrupted period of time.

Even more important than sustaining an unbroken practice is doing the practice with love and reverence. Do not allow the repetition of the mantra to become mechanical. Let it flow from the depths of your heart. Meditating successfully on the name of God requires a one-pointed mind and a pure heart. Try to understand why your mind becomes disturbed and your heart filled with impurities. If you look carefully, you will see that the causes are anger, hatred, jealousy, greed, and attachment. A person filled with these pollutants is like a temple filled with trash; the altar is obscured and the shrine buried. Clean the temple of your body and mind, let the altar of your heart be illumined with love and knowledge, and you will find the Divinity shining within. Thereafter, no obstacle will be able to stand against the brilliant, sweet smile of the indwelling Divinity.

•

Q **I have heard that *shaktipata* is the quickest and easiest way to remove obstacles. I have received shaktipata from two famous teachers, and even though I had complete faith in them, nothing happened. Some of my friends shook and saw bright lights or experienced other symptoms of kundalini awakening. What is wrong with me?**

Nothing. Much of the fascination with shaktipata comes from the faulty premise that there is an easy way to enlightenment. As you have found, many books these days talk about shaktipata as an effortless way to spiritual attainment: someone gives you shaktipata, your kundalini shakti is aroused, and you are in bliss; forever after everything is fine and divine. But it doesn't really happen that way.

Shaktipata is the descent or transmission of spiritual energy. *Shakti* means "energy"; *pata* means "descent or transmission." Shaktipata is the process of transferring energy from one point to another—in the context of your question, from teacher to student. Only a person who has shakti can transmit it. Yet proclaiming oneself to be a guru with the ability to transmit shakti is a barrier to the transmission of that spiritual energy. No teacher owns shakti; only the almighty Divine Being possesses it—and when the teacher stands between the Divine Being and the student, that energy cannot flow.

It is good to have faith in a teacher, but that faith must not blind you. Keep your eyes open and watch those who claim to have received shaktipata. How joyful are they? Are they easily disturbed? How much transformation do you see in their lives? They receive "shaktipata" and for a couple of days they are blissful, singing the glory of the guru who gave it to them. Fine. But as soon as they find themselves engulfed in day-to-day reality they still become angry and impatient. It means that the effect of this so-called shaktipata did not last and was of little value.

Shaktipata that shows its effect on the physical level is also meaningless. If shaking is a symptom of kundalini awakening, then how do you distinguish somebody suffering from Parkinson's disease from someone whose kundalini is aroused? If you squint hard or put pressure on your eyelids, you see lights. Deprive yourself of food, sleep, and water and you will begin to see colors and perhaps hear voices. These are not signs of spiritual awakening or the rising of kundalini. Spiritual awakening in the true sense brings about a long-lasting transformation. Shaktipata is the transmission of divine energy that engenders such an awakening.

Q **Suppose I receive shaktipata from someone who is truly a conduit for shakti: since the grace of the Divine would now be flowing in me, isn't it true that I would not have to do any further practice?**

Absolutely not. Regardless of how genuine your teacher or how powerful the transmission of spiritual energy, you must not abandon your practice. In a sense, receiving shaktipata is easy—it is being bestowed on everyone all the time. We just don't know how to recognize it or assimilate it. Practice opens our mind and heart, and without such preparation this ever-flowing grace washes over us in vain.

Even when we have prepared ourselves to receive that grace and thus are able to experience it, an even more intense level of practice is necessary if we are to retain that energy. Divine grace flows over us without any effort on our part; receiving and assimilating it requires self-effort. Only an ignorant person sitting in the place of a teacher would advise students to have faith in the teacher and discount the practices and the importance of self-effort.

Q Can shaktipata be transmitted through non-human agents?

Spiritual energy is quite subtle; it is potent because it is not dependent on any material means. Shakti often expresses itself through non-human conduits. For example, a mountain peak can be a transmitter of knowledge, wisdom, peace, tranquility—a channel through which the divine grace flows to you. When that happens the mountain itself is honored as a guru. This is why people consider specific locations to be the abode of God—Mount Kailas in Tibet, Nanda Devi and Kedarnath in northern India, Mount Arunachala in south India, and Mount Sinai in the Middle East, as examples. These places are sacred because they are charged with divine energy and spontaneously emit transformative power.

Q If shaktipata depends on the unconditional grace of the Divine and can be transmitted through non-human agents, why is it important to practice under the supervision of a teacher?

A living teacher is invaluable. If you are not guarded and guided by a teacher, the mind can easily trick you. It may convince you to design and undertake a practice that simply pleases the mind. Furthermore, non-physical teachers don't give you clear answers to your questions, and if you are making a mistake in your practice they don't correct it. But a teacher who has been trained in an authentic tradition has direct experience of the problems students ordinarily encounter. An experienced teacher can detect a student's problems long before they surface and guide the student to correct them before they become intractable. In the case of shaktipata a teacher can tell you when your imagination is running away with you. These are a few of the reasons why you need a teacher, preferably one trained in an authentic tradition.

Such teachers are themselves under the supervision of their own master. According to the tradition, the Divine Force is ultimately the master of all masters. Authentic teachers never work independently of it—they always act under its will or guidance. When they feel a surge of love and compassion in their heart, the desire arises to share whatever they themselves have received, and guided by that surge of compassion, spiritual energy is transmitted spontaneously. That is shaktipata.

In most cases spiritual energy is transmitted in small amounts—enough to bring about the transformation needed for that particular student's spiritual development. The teacher is a conduit, transmitting a spark that lights the lamp of the seeker. You then begin to live in the light of the lamp; and when you assimilate that level of light, another, more intense flood of energy comes forth. The light within becomes brighter and burns impurities at an even subtler level, further illuminating the interior of your being.

That is how the kundalini shakti in you is awakened, step by step, with ever-increasing intensity and brightness. And that is what shaktipata is all about. Self-effort is never left behind; but even though you keep working hard, you give credit to the almighty Divine Being, the one who is the source and center of divine energy. This is the One who is lighting your lamp.

the Science of life

REJUVENATION TECHNIQUES

Q Why are ayurveda and yoga said to be sister sciences?

Philosophically, both yoga and ayurveda spring from the common ground of Sankhya philosophy. The goal of both is to eradicate pain and misery. Although scriptures such as the *Charaka Samhita* claim that ayurveda can help us attain freedom from all levels of pain and misery—physical, mental, and spiritual—its focus is mainly on preventing and treating physical illness. Yoga texts such as the *Hatha Yoga Pradipika* and the *Yoga Sutra* focus on disciplines related to the mind and senses.

Today many people are drawn to yoga in order to reduce stress, lose weight, and keep fit, rather than for its spiritual benefits. On the other hand, many who do come to yoga for spiritual reasons are often struggling with stress, physical problems, and the effects of aging, so despite their intense desire they are not able to practice many of the yogic disciplines. This is where ayurveda can support the practice of yoga.

According to the *Yoga Sutra* (1.1, Vyasa's commentary) there are five states of mind: disturbed, distracted, stupefied, one-pointed, and well-controlled. The body and mind are intertwined, and ordinarily those in the first three states of mind are not in good physical condition. Yoga, as the great masters in the past intended it to be practiced, can be undertaken only after both body and mind are healthy and balanced. Ayurvedic rejuvenation techniques can nourish and revitalize the body so that we can develop a productive yoga practice.

What is ayurvedic rejuvenation?

The general goal of ayurvedic rejuvenation is to make the body healthier, stronger, less toxic, more flexible, and more energetic. It also aims to clear the mind and free it from sloth and inertia. The ultimate goal is to make it possible to undertake rejuvenation techniques that can reverse the aging process and unfold the extraordinary abilities of the body and mind so that eventually we can reach the highest state of *samadhi* (spiritual absorption) in our meditation. In today's quick-fix culture, however, most rejuvenation programs are simply stress-management programs for revitalizing and energizing the body for short periods of time.

Ayurvedic rejuvenation programs are more comprehensive and vary in length and intensity. An authentic rejuvenation program involves both cleansing and nourishing. According to ayurveda, *ama* (any undigested and unassimilated food in the body, as well as undigested thoughts in the mind) floats into the system as waste matter, blocking our *shrotas* (arteries, veins, capillaries, nerves, etc.) and our *nadis* (energy channels). The forces of nourishment can rejuvenate the body (and even reverse the aging process), but only if they are not counteracted by waste matter contaminating the system.

There are hundreds of recipes for herbal preparations in ayurveda, and an expert *vaidya* (ayurvedic physician) knows how to custom design each one to suit individual needs. But the rejuvenating herbs of classic ayurveda, especially the *bhasmas* (medicines prepared from metals and minerals), are too powerful to be assimilated by those whose systems are weak or blocked by toxins.

Ayurvedic rejuvenation programs aim to serve three groups: those recovering from illness; those who are already in fairly good health but who want to revitalize their body and mind; and those who because of their interest in spiritual attainment want to increase their longevity and unfold an extraordinary level of physical and mental ability.

In most cases, people in the first group are the ones who seek a rejuvenation program. In treating them, a team of ayurvedic doctors and trained yoga therapists follows a standard procedure. Together, they evaluate the preexisting condition of the participant to determine their present energy level, stamina, digestive power, breathing habits, and stress level. They also assess the participant's mental and emotional condition, with special attention to emotional scars caused by trauma such as grief and fear.

Based on this information they design a treatment plan, including elements from both disciplines—a specific diet, an exercise regimen, breathing exercises, counseling, and biofeedback, as well as a systematic plan for relaxation, physical therapy, and ayurvedic massage. The most important component of this treatment plan is the application of ayurvedic herbs, tonics, and medicines known as *vaji karana* and *rasayana.* At this initial level of rejuvenation, when the participant is recovering from an illness, gentle herbs and tonics are prescribed and administered carefully so the participant can assimilate them.

Q What is the difference between ayurvedic and yogic rejuvenation techniques? Which is better?

Detoxification—cleansing—is the main goal of both, but their orientation is different. The ayurvedic *pancha karma* is part of a medical system; the yogic *shat kriyas* are part of a spiritual system. Pancha karma grants mainly a physical level of cleansing; the shat kriyas lead us to mental and spiritual purification. Because some of the pancha karma procedures are invasive, they must be done under the supervision of a properly trained physician, especially during *virechana* (purgation therapy) and *rakta moksha* (bloodletting). The yogic shat kriyas can be practiced without the help of a physician. They are undertaken in several steps and are therefore milder at first, but they can become intense as a practitioner becomes more expert.

A combination of both pancha karma and the shat kriyas can be more productive than either alone, but it is crucial that a proper assessment be made of how best to combine the two therapies. An expert yogi and an ayurvedic doctor make an excellent team. Together they can make an initial evaluation of personality type, energy level, and previous medical history, and design an appropriate detoxification program. This may involve either pancha karma or shat kriyas or a combination of both.

The pancha karma practices of *vamana* (vomiting therapy) and *virechana* are almost the same as the upper wash and the complete wash, respectively, of the yogic shat kriyas. The only difference is that in pancha karma herbs and oils are used to induce vomiting and peristalsis, while in the yoga system normal saline water and willpower are used (along with some yogic techniques) to accomplish the same result. For optimal results, the *snehana* (oleation therapy) and *svedana* (sudation therapy) aspects of pancha karma can be combined with the yogic shat kriyas, as well as with other yoga practices.

The remaining four shat kriyas—*neti* (the nasal wash), *dhauti* (a technique for cleaning the stomach), *nauli* (a technique for activating the solar plexus), and *trataka* (gazing)—can help us remove toxins and waste matter not eliminated by the practice of pancha karma. Furthermore, neti, nauli, and trataka not only detoxify, they also energize the system. In the advanced stages, nauli and trataka can awaken startling dormant forces, resulting in an extraordinary level of health as well as expanded consciousness.

The next stage in a rejuvenation program is that of nourishing, and there are many ayurvedic guidelines for this. Then, after the body has detoxified and come back to normal, the regimen requires help from experts in both disciplines. Some of the techniques come from yoga and some from ayurveda, and the prescription for proper diet, exercise, herbal tonics, breathing practices, and relaxation techniques, as well as a healthy routine—all integral to a rejuvenation program—will vary from person to person.

What is more, it is important to introduce only such herbs or ayurvedic preparations *(rasayana)* as can be easily assimilated, for ayurvedic herbs and the rasayanas prepared from them are not like the herbal teas used to balance the body's three *doshas,* or humors *(vata, pitta,* and *kapha).* They are medicines. For example, ashwagandha and vacha are traditionally used as tonics for the body and brain, respectively. They are quite effective when the person taking them is in fairly good health, physically and mentally, but they can be overwhelmingly powerful for those with a weak body and mind. The combination of ashwagandha and black musli is even more powerful than ashwagandha alone. If the patient is weak, another herb, punarnava, may be the best one to begin with. Later, other more powerful and effective herbs can be introduced as that person gains strength. There is no counterpart to ayurvedic medicines in yoga. This is one of the reasons a complete rejuvenation program should combine elements of both disciplines and be supervised by both an expert yogi and an ayurvedic doctor.

Q **Can an ayurvedic rejuvenation program help if the illness is alcoholism? If so, can you give some specifics?**

Yes, ayurveda can be useful in rejuvenating someone who is recovering from alcoholism. Because a rejuvenation program must be custom designed, however, the only way to offer specifics is to present a case study. Here, we'll discuss a participant that we'll call Sean. He is a 45-year-old businessman, married, with two children. In evaluating Sean's condition, the team of ayurvedic doctors and yoga therapists discovers that he is pittic by nature—ambitious, intense, restless, and often impatient. He has a quick mind and a good sense of humor.

All of Sean's health problems are related to alcohol consumption—three months ago he was diagnosed with an ulcer, and more recently he was hospitalized with a mild case of pancreatitis. He has been a weekend binger for years, but recently there have been intervals in which he has drunk heavily for three or four days straight. He has had several DUI offenses in the past year and has participated in inpatient and outpatient rehabilitation programs without success. Recently, however, he has joined an AA program and stopped drinking. His only medication is an antacid.

Sean is fond of red meat, especially spiced varieties like sausage and beef jerky. He is also a fan of chips and salsa. His favorite alcohol is beer, although he is not averse to whiskey, gin, or vodka. He also loves pretzels and pickles. He used to smoke, but stopped after he got married. He drinks three to five cups of coffee a day, down from eight to ten cups.

Sean was an athlete in high school and college. He is still reasonably strong, as he works out at a gym and jogs in spurts. He keeps a disciplined schedule for a while, then goes through periods when he does no exercise at all, even though he recognizes that exercising helps him handle stress. He is a chest breather; he holds his breath and sighs often.

Based on these observations, the first step in Sean's rejuvenation program will be to detoxify his body. As he is strong, a course of pancha karma will be used to cleanse his system initially. After this has been completed, he will need to continue detoxifying himself with the help of the yogic shat kriyas, especially the nasal wash, the upper wash, and the complete wash. In addition to a course of ayurvedic herbs, the following regimen of exercise, breathing, relaxation, and diet will be prescribed:

Sean will do a course of hatha yoga practice for one hour a day, with an emphasis on breath awareness in postures. His typical routine will consist of the sun salutation, the standing balance poses, the bow, the boat, twisting poses, the forward bend, and the plow. Breathing exercises will include five to ten minutes of sandbag breathing, diaphragmatic breathing in the crocodile pose, alternate nostril breathing, and *shitali* pranayama. The asana and breathing exercises will be followed by a 31-points or 61-points deep relaxation.

As part of his detoxification program Sean will need to sweat at least once a day, and so he will either do some aerobic exercise or take a sauna or hot bath. To help him reestablish a healthy breathing pattern, he will have morning and evening biofeedback sessions. Every fifth day he will be reevaluated, and his program will be changed and modified as necessary.

Sean will drink wheat grass, carrot, and green amaranth juice—either singly or in combination—as well as fennel tea, as these beverages are excellent for overcoming addiction and detoxifying the body.

A properly trained ayurvedic cook will provide delicious dishes consisting of the following ingredients: vegetables; rice; wheat; tapioca; buckwheat; mung beans; germinated gram; cereals consisting of rolled oats, barley, amaranth, and cracked wheat; buttermilk; fruit—and other ingredients which do not increase acidity.

This diet will exclude sour substances, such as tamarind and vinegar (although lemon in moderation is all right); tomatoes, turnips, and other vegetables that are sour, pungent, or astringent in taste; deep-fried foods; eggs; oil; coffee, tea, and other substances containing caffeine; and hot spices. Sugar will be replaced by maple syrup, honey, or jaggery.

The main ingredient in Sean's herbal medicine will be four out of the five master herbs: punarnava, ashwagandha, brahmi, and shankha pushpi. The doctors will monitor Sean constantly to determine the proportion of herbs in each dose.

In addition to this mixture, Sean will be given an ayurvedic tonic that will accelerate the detoxification process and nourish the brain, the nervous system, and the endocrine system. This tonic will be prepared fresh every day, using the following ingredients: almonds, poppy seeds, black pepper, fragrant rose petals, and fennel, as well as pumpkin, cucumber, brahmi, and shanka pushpi seeds. It will be sweetened with the unprocessed crystals of sugarcane syrup.

This is just a brief description of a rejuvenation program for someone with Sean's characteristics who is recovering from alcoholism. The details have to be filled in by the ayurvedic healthcare team on a case-by-case basis.

Q Meditation teachers often say that the first step in practice is to attain steadiness and stability of body, because without that there can be no progress. My own teacher told me to begin by sitting with the support of a wall to keep the spine properly aligned and to focus only on my posture, noticing where it is tight and where there is pain, and then to use asana to free those places. Only then should I go on to the next step: establishing a serene and steady flow of breath. The problem is that after two years of working with asana to get rid of a sharp pain in my shoulder, it remains a source of distraction. What should I do?

This is where ayurveda and other systems of therapy that do not bombard the body with heavy-duty drugs can complement yoga. Hot baths, massage with medicated herbal oil, acupressure, acupuncture, or ayurveda's *marma*-point therapy are often effective in relieving shoulder pain.

But if the pain is chronic, you will have to find its underlying cause. One way of doing this is to study the pain, identify its nature, and classify it under one of three main categories: *vata, pitta,* or *kapha.* Deep throbbing pain at the level of the nervous system, which is accompanied by restlessness, is caused by derangement of vata. A burning pain at the level of the skeletal system is due to derangement of pitta. If the pain is in the muscles beneath the skin and is accompanied by a sense of heaviness and immobility, its source is derangement of kapha.

Usually pain in the shoulders is accompanied by stiffness in the shoulder blades and upper arms and is therefore likely to be a kaphic symptom. (In our modern culture, we are primarily exposed to kaphic/tamasic food, water, air, thoughts, and feelings.) To overcome this pain, I advise you to first minimize kaphic food and increase the intake of sattvic food; then activate the fire element at the navel center, and with the help of pranayama, let the fire circulate throughout the body. Without putting strain on your body, do exercises that loosen your shoulder joints and connective tissues. Shoulder pain may also be due to a weak spine, and if that is the case, practice the postures that strengthen the spine.

These yogic techniques can be complemented by taking the standard ayurvedic herbs known as *dasha mula,* "the ten main herbs," especially if you are a woman. (Traditionally, all women in India take a preparation of these ten herbs after delivery.) According to ayurvedic texts, these herbs are strong yet safe—they are not known to have any side effects. They heal muscle trauma, soothe the nervous system, restore vitality, and tone the overall body. If after applying these measures for several months the pain still persists, you will need to consult an expert who can administer stronger ayurvedic preparations.

HERBS

Q There is growing interest in ayurvedic herbs these days. What is the difference between an ayurvedic herb and herbs in general? Does an herb have to grow in India to be ayurvedic?

It is easy to understand the difference between ayurvedic and other herbs in general when we know what ayurveda really is. The word *ayurveda* means "science of life" or "science of longevity." The techniques of ayurveda integrate body, breath, mind, and consciousness in the treatment of all ailments, from the simplest illness to the most complex disease. But ayurveda is not the science of disease, it is the science of health. Its goal is to make it possible for us to live a healthy life until our last breath. Any herb that helps us become healthy, retain our vitality, and live the full span of life can therefore be called ayurvedic.

Because ayurveda developed in India, ayurvedic experts studied the healing and rejuvenative properties of the plants that grew there and used those plants in their preparations. But don't make the mistake of assuming that only herbs grown in India are ayurvedic. A number of the herbs mentioned in ayurvedic texts also grow outside India. Many plants with properties similar to the ones mentioned in ayurvedic texts grow in Europe and Central America, for example.

Any herb growing anywhere can be adopted into the ayurvedic system of healthcare, provided it has the necessary properties.

Furthermore, herbs that have become popular in, say, India or China have come to be regarded as Indian or Chinese, even though they are widely used elsewhere. Den shen, for example, is known as a Chinese herb, but people in other parts of the world have been using it for thousands of years; in North America it is known as red sage. People have been using the same powerful rejuvenative herb under the name ashwagandha in India and withania in the West. Another "Indian" herb, vacha, has long been used by Europeans under the name calamas and under other names by Native Americans.

Q Is it appropriate to combine herbs not mentioned in ayurvedic texts with other herbs?

Yes, this is perfectly fine. However, to do this effectively the herbalist, pharmacist, or alchemist who combines them must have a comprehensive knowledge of the herbs, their unique properties, and what makes them compatible. Herbalism is a vast subject, one which was practiced in all cultures before the advent of modern medicine. In earlier times, however, herbalists were knowledgeable only about the herbs that grew in their own region. They worked with them and came to know their properties intimately. There was very little interaction with herbalists from different parts of the world, and so their knowledge was limited to local plants.

Today the situation has obviously changed: herbalists are no longer limited to plants that grow locally. Herbal treatments—whether for prevention, healing, or rejuvenation—can be more effective if the best herbs from different regions are combined. And this can be done only if ayurvedic experts further their knowledge by researching and studying the science of herbs developed in various cultures. Without solid, scientific research the current interest in herbalism will fade without making any significant contribution to raising the overall standard of health and well-being.

Q How important is it to use only organically grown herbs? In a time when almost the whole planet is contaminated with chemicals and other toxins, how can we obtain herbs that are pure?

It is very important to use only organically grown herbs in herbal preparations, whether they are meant for healing our body or for uplifting our consciousness. Unfortunately today the entire planet is suffering from contamination from chemicals and other substances and so are the herbs, but there is still some relatively pristine land left. If we refrain from polluting it and use the herbs that grow there, that will be a good start.

But obtaining herbs that are pure requires more than organic farming methods. Just as a human being consists of body, mind, and soul, herbs also are composed of these three components. To ensure their physical health we must grow them organically so that the plant is free from toxins and grows in accordance with nature. To ensure their mental health we must maintain a harmonious and cheerful environment where the herbs are growing. This means that the place and its immediate surroundings must be free from the negative energies of fear, anger, and violence. The ancient Vedic herbalists supplied food for the soul of the herbs by repeating mantras and making fire offerings. According to them only healthy and happy herbs can engender health and happiness in humans and other living beings. Only when herbs are awakened in the first place can they awaken those who use them; only when they are enlightened can they enlighten those who use them.

The Vedic method for growing herbs, therefore, is much more sophisticated and complete than what we call organic farming. There is a complete set of mantras for planting, weeding, watering, harvesting, and processing herbs for ayurvedic preparations. There are specific rituals, along with specific fire offerings, for nourishing the herbs at a spiritual level and uplifting their consciousness. If herbs are cultivated in this manner they will have a miraculous effect on our body, mind, and soul.

Q Can you explain the role of herbs in spiritual practices? How can they enhance our spiritual growth?

In ancient times the Vedic people experienced nature as the Divine Mother because they recognized that everything evolved from her. They called her Prakriti. Everything that existed in her and evolved from her was saturated with consciousness. According to ayurveda, especially the tantric version, herbs are the embodiment of the living goddess. If applied properly they release divine energies—to heal not only the physical aspect of our being, but the mental and spiritual aspects as well. People in ancient cultures lived close to nature and had great sensitivity toward the consciousness localized in these herbs. They knew intuitively in which plants the divine energies are concentrated and they knew how to invoke these energies and bask in their light. Holy basil *(Ocimum sanctum)*, neem *(Melia azadirachta)*, pipal *(Piper longum)*, bael *(Aegle marmelos)*, mandar *(Erythrina indica)*, and haridra *(Curcuma longa)*, for example, were worshipped by the Vedic people as living gods and goddesses.

Just as some species of animals are more evolved than others, and some humans possess a higher degree of intelligence than others, there is a greater degree of consciousness, intelligence, and healing power inherent in certain plants. In ayurveda such plants are called herbs. This definition may or may not accord with the botanical definition, but this is how the ancient scriptures, such as the *Atharva Veda* and tantric texts, differentiate herbs from other plants. There are a host of mantras that describe not only the medicinal properties of these herbs but the spiritual powers they embody as well. For a practitioner of yoga these herbs can bring about a remarkable transformation.

Q Can you give an example of using herbs as part of spiritual practice?

This concept is briefly introduced in the first *sutra* of chapter four in Patanjali's *Yoga Sutra.* It is greatly elaborated in the tantric scriptures, as herbs play a significant role in the advanced practices of tantra and kundalini yoga. Working with the forces of the *muladhara chakra,* for example, mandara (*Calotropis gigantea,* a variety of the milkweed plant) is used. In this practice a square yantra or an elephant-like figure is prepared from the root of this plant for purposes of concentration and visualization; the mala used will consist of either turmeric root or the root of the mandara plant.

This is an advanced practice, and it is supposed to be done in a garden of mandara plants. According to legend, Krishna brought this plant from heaven (which may mean that Krishna was the first to discover the spiritual uses of this plant). Therefore the practitioner always invokes the spiritual guidance of Krishna while undertaking this practice.

In another practice, this one to develop retentive power *(medha),* a heavy dose of vacha *(araceae)* is taken under the strict supervision of an expert, who has previously successfully completed the practice. Using vacha involves a long preparation, consisting of *mantra sadhana* and the ability to regulate sleep and withstand the cold.

Another example of using herbs for spiritual purposes is a special practice known as *aparajita sadhana,* which is done while sitting under a canopy formed by the aparajita plant *(Clitoria ternatea).* The scriptures prescribe this practice to conquer the tendency toward an inferiority complex or feelings of worthlessness, abandonment, hatred, or jealousy.

I have heard that if herbs are prepared in a tantric fashion and taken in a tantric manner, they will have an immediate, miraculous effect. If this is true, what makes a procedure "tantric"?

When someone makes claims about the power of tantra or talks about tantric magic, watch out. Most of what people hear comes from a rudimentary and fragmented understanding of the subject, coupled with an overactive imagination.

Tantra is the most profound and scientific aspect of spirituality. It is like an ocean. Just as it is impossible to explore the entire ocean and everything that exists in it, so is it impossible to know all the mysteries of tantra. Just as we try to make the best use of the ocean's resources without having complete knowledge of the ocean, so do we attempt to make use of tantric wisdom without knowing everything about tantra.

Tantric masters have explored the possibility of potentizing herbs and herbal preparations for quick and lasting results, and they have compiled authentic tantric herbal formulas—but their significance is obscure. The formulas can be understood only if we comprehend the interconnection among different branches of knowledge, including ayurveda, alchemy, astronomy, astrology, gemology, numerology, and *svarodaya* (the science of breath), as well as the sciences of mantra, yantra, and personified forms of deities and how they correspond to the subtle forces of the human personality. Tantric philosophy and metaphysics provide the interconnection among these different branches of knowledge. A perfect blend of all these sciences and practices is called "tantra."

How can an herb be potentized in a tantric fashion?

There are certain mantras, yantras, and rituals which can be used to awaken and intensify the medicinal properties of an herb. There are also certain times when the energy of an herb awakens by itself. For example, the herb called vacha is frequently used in ayurvedic medicines to promote health, but the texts do not mention its spiritual uses. As was mentioned above, a single dose of this herb unfolds an extraordinary level of retentive power *(medha)* if it is taken at the proper time and if you are following specific spiritual observances under the guidance of a competent teacher. This herb is hot in effect and is therefore used in conjunction with cooling herbs. (A particular variety of herb from this family has been found to be carcinogenic; therefore vacha should be taken only under the supervision of an expert.) Because of its heating properties, vacha can be unmanageable, overwhelming, for those who are weak, pittic, or spacey. In ayurvedic preparations this herb is used in small proportions, along with herbs that have cooling and nourishing properties.

I will give you a brief explanation of the tantric way of using vacha. According to Indian astrology, when Jupiter and the eighth constellation (Pushya) are aligned, the conjunction is known as *pushya amrita yoga*. At least seventy-two hours before this alignment occurs, an expert tantric who has completed an entire course of the *gayatri purash charana* practice goes to the place where the herb is growing and invokes and awakens the subtle force of the herb with appropriate mantras and rituals. The adept then waters the plant while fully absorbed in the *bija* mantra known as *sarasvata bija* and attends the plant for three days, energizing its retentive power *(medha shakti)* through certain specified practices. Then when Jupiter and Pushya come into alignment the adept harvests the plant, root and all, without cutting or harming it in any way. The plant is then kept on the tantric's meditation altar until the time for taking it arrives. The adept who harvested this herb can take it for their own benefit or can administer it to someone else. It is taken on the seventh day of the waxing moon in the month of Magha *(achala saptami)*, a date that usually falls in the last portion of January or the first portion of February. This herb is taken only once in a lifetime.

The person taking the herb bathes a couple of hours before the astrological occurrence, meditates on the sarasvata bija mantra, prepares a paste by crushing and grinding the root, and when the paste is ready, liquefies it with milk. (For the sake of brevity I will omit the elaborate procedure for preparing the paste.) The candidate then walks into a river until the water is up to the upper chest or neck, and faces downstream. They then drink the preparation and remain in the water for at least an hour, doing *japa* the entire time. If the candidate feels nauseated, they must stay in the water until the nausea passes. If the nausea induces vomiting, the vomitus must not come in direct contact with the skin (which is why the candidate is facing downstream). When the liquid has passed from the stomach to the intestines, it is safe to come out of the water.

If the preparation is digested, the effect will last a lifetime. If it is expelled, it means the candidate was not prepared. Before taking the preparation again, the body will need to be strengthened and detoxified and the fire within will need to be awakened by yoga practices, including *pranayama* and the *gayatri purash charana.*

I have met a few aspirants who have undergone this tantric treatment, and these encounters have convinced me that this *kriya,* known as *sarasvata oshadhi prayoga,* can have a miraculous effect on one's retentive power and creativity.

There are other ways of using herbs in a tantric manner, such as tying the herbs to the arms or using them as incense, but the most effective method is to offer the herbs into the fire, provided the entire ritual (which involves worship of yantras and mantra recitation) is done with precision.

Q Can gems be used along with herbs as a part of spiritual practice? Some teachers prescribe both herbs and gems, claiming they will accelerate spiritual practice or remove obstacles, while others condemn such practices. What do you think?

The science of herbs and gems and their relationship to spirituality is subtle, profound, and often mysterious. The scriptures mention herbs and gems along with mantras, *tapas* (austerity), and *samadhi* as means for yogic accomplishment. But there is not a single scripture that gives complete information on the subject.

The ancient scriptures that mention the spiritual significance of herbs and gems also state that these powerful substances, which embody divine forces, withdrew their luster and power in the Kali Yuga [the Age of Darkness]. In fact, most of the herbs and gems mentioned in these scriptures no longer exist. Just as many of our own inherent spiritual forces have become dormant, the supernatural abilities of those herbs and gems still in existence have also fallen asleep. So if we are to use them for spiritual awakening, we need someone who is already awakened, and who knows the system of awakening the dormant forces in these substances.

But even if the dormant forces have been activated, we still need to know the right method of using herbs and gems for spiritual purposes. Just as a hearing aid will not work if it is inserted in the nose, herbs and gems must be used in the correct manner. This is a complex science and requires more knowledge than is generally understood (the method that I described of how to use the herb vacha in a tantric fashion is just one example). Yet there are many so-called teachers who claim to be masters of this science and say that the herbs and gems they give will have a miraculous effect, provided you have faith.

These days many people have become fanatic about wearing gems and taking "spiritual herbs" every day. (Similarly, there are many who carry yantras and mandalas in the form of rings or lockets, and who meditate inside pyramid-shaped structures.) These practices create momentary enthusiasm and excitement, but I have noticed no significant effect that demonstrates purification of heart, one-pointedness of mind, and expansion of consciousness—which are the hallmarks of true spiritual awakening.

working with body and breath

HATHA YOGA

Q I have taken yoga classes with many teachers. They all teach basically the same exercises and say they are teaching hatha yoga or asana. Most of them give the impression that in addition to being good for the body, asanas are also a means for inner unfoldment; some even claim that asanas can help you awaken your kundalini. I don't see any relationship between these postures and spirituality. What am I missing? How can asana help us grow spiritually?

There is a vast difference between the way asanas were thought of and taught originally and how they are taught now. In ancient times, meditation was the goal; asanas were a means of enhancing the capacity of the body and mind so that a person could sit in meditation for long periods with as few distractions as possible. Only when the body is healthy and the mind one-pointed and inward does a person have a chance to discover the inner dimensions of life. This self-discovery is the essence of spiritual practice.

In the process of self-discovery an aspirant begins to see the connecting link between body and breath, breath and mind, mind and soul. But today people often go to "yoga" classes to enhance their physical fitness, and in most classes asanas are taught as a means of addressing the concerns of the body, with little or no attention given to cultivating this inner connection between body, breath, mind, and soul. Yoga is the path of union, and yoga practices help us come to the realization that there is a connection among the different aspects of ourselves. The physical level of asana practice is not yoga and does little to help us grow spiritually.

For example, the practice of *pranayama* (control of the breath) is said to be one of the surest ways to attain mastery over the modifications of the mind, making the mind one-pointed and inward. Separating the asanas from breathing practice is a modern invention. Nowhere in the scriptures are asanas taught without pranayama. In spite of this, many modern teachers do not include the discipline of pranayama when they teach asana—and yet they call what they teach hatha yoga. While this kind of asana practice may promote health, it will fail to increase clarity of mind and cannot therefore engender spiritual awakening.

In other words, the classes you describe are not hatha yoga classes. According to the scriptures, hatha yoga is a complete path leading to physical health, mental clarity, and spiritual illumination. Hatha yoga practices combine asanas (physical postures), pranayama (breathing exercises), concentration, and meditation. The word *hatha* is itself an indication of the goals and objectives of this practice: *ha* means "sun," and *tha* means "moon"; thus hatha yoga is the practice that enables a practitioner to balance solar and lunar energies. Hatha yoga practices create a state of harmony in body and mind by balancing the solar and lunar, masculine and feminine, active and passive aspects of ourselves. Unless we combine the disciplines associated with breathing and meditation with the physical postures, we cannot expect to achieve this harmonious state. And without this inner harmony, we waste a great deal of our time and energy fighting the distractions and disturbances arising from both the inner and outer worlds.

Q **I have always thought asana was a synonym for yoga and that meditation was a separate discipline. But you are saying that asana is only one component of hatha yoga and that unless asana practice is accompanied by pranayama and meditation it is not hatha yoga. Why is there no connection between asana and meditation in the modern world?**

I come from a background in which yoga pervaded every part of our lives. We didn't think of it as a distinct path or discipline—it was a way of life. I grew up practicing yoga, but it was only when I came to the United States at the age of twenty-six that I realized what I was doing. When people first asked what kind of yoga I practiced, I didn't know what they meant. To me, yoga was yoga. I wasn't familiar with the technique of isolating one component from a comprehensive body of knowledge and focusing exclusively on that. Another thing that took me by surprise was the focus on the physical postures—I had always practiced the postures in conjunction with pranayama and meditation.

Spending an hour or more systematically stretching the body is both calming and energizing. The results are immediate and unmistakable. The result of working with the breath and the flow of energy throughout the body, which is one of the benefits of pranayama, takes longer to manifest; although these benefits are powerful, they are more subtle. Subtler still are the fruits of meditation. When yoga was introduced in the West, the postures were easy to popularize—people readily understand the concept of working with the body. But they are not as receptive to the concept of working with the breath and mind. Therefore asana practice has been easy to market, while the subtler practices of pranayama and meditation are not nearly as marketable. Thus the practice of asana has been divorced from the practice of meditation and cultivated for its own sake, and "asana" has become synonymous with "yoga" in the minds of most people. They have no idea that meditation is the essential technique of yoga.

Thinking that there is any difference between yoga and meditation is a form of ignorance. In the scriptures you will not ever find them described as separate practices. In fact, the *Yoga Sutra,* the most authoritative text of yoga, defines "yoga" as mastery over the modifications of the mind; the techniques that enable an aspirant to achieve that mastery are the techniques of yoga. And according to all the commentators, both the perfectly balanced state of mind and the path leading to that state are yoga.

Q So you are saying that yoga is actually a systematic path leading to enlightenment and self-realization, and that the goal of this path is to attain perfect control over the modifications of the mind. Yet most yoga centers and teachers offer instruction only in yoga postures and breathing exercises, with an occasional nod to psychology. Most do not teach meditation, and the few that do confine themselves to basic techniques. Why?

Yes, the goal of yoga is gaining control over the modifications of the mind and, finally, attaining the direct experience of one's inner self. More than two thousand years ago, when the sage Patanjali codified the system of yoga, he did not put much emphasis on physical exercises and included only advanced pranayama in his system. In those days, either hatha yoga and pranayama practices were so common that they didn't need to be mentioned, or people lived such balanced, harmonious lives and were in such good health that they did not need to make the physical postures and the breathing exercises an integral part of their spiritual practice.

Today, however, we seem to be stuck at the level of body consciousness. More than half of our time and energy is spent in dealing with mental issues, and what remains goes to addressing physical complaints and survival issues. This leaves little time for purely spiritual pursuits and for answering the essential questions: What is our origin? What is the purpose of life? Is there any higher reality than the one we perceive? What is the relationship between our individual consciousness and Absolute Consciousness?

A second reason yoga teaching lacks depth is that many of today's yoga centers are run by teachers whose knowledge of yoga is confined to physical postures and simple breathing practices, so this is what they teach. This is also the area of yoga that interests the greatest number of students. After practicing hatha yoga for several years and studying yoga texts, some students begin to yearn for deeper dimensions of yogic wisdom. They naturally develop a commitment to the spiritual dimension of yoga. But even these inspired students face the same problems as everyone else: their physical energy is depleted and their minds are scattered. Consequently, they cannot afford to exclude asana and breathing exercises from their spiritual discipline.

There are some teachers who know the inner essence of yoga and who have inherited the wisdom of the ancient yoga scriptures. But in a materialistic society such as ours it is very difficult for them to teach. It takes money to advertise that the teachings are available, and even when they manage to do this, such classes are poorly attended. However, any student who is prepared and who is earnestly searching will find qualified teachers and the authentic teachings, which lead to the supreme goal of yoga: self-realization.

Q **In practice, what makes hatha yoga spiritual?**

Including the *yamas* and *niyamas* in your daily life is the first step in transforming hatha yoga into a spiritual path. The yamas are the practice of non-violence, truthfulness, non-indulgence, non-stealing, and non-possessiveness. These five principles help you restrain yourself from living in an unhealthy way. The niyamas are a set of five observances—purity, contentment, self-discipline, self-study, and surrender to the Divine—that help you make a commitment to living a healthy life. By practicing these ten principles along with asana and pranayama, you begin to transform yourself from inside out and outside in.

Meditation on sacred sounds and sacred symbols is the next step in transforming hatha yoga into a spiritual path. This helps you connect yourself with the Divine. It is only when a practice is undertaken with a spiritual end in view that it becomes spiritual. Meditating on a spiritual object is a spiritual practice; meditation that aims only at cultivating a one-pointed mind or psychic powers is not. To achieve a spiritual goal one has to use spiritual means.

The asana component of hatha yoga can introduce you to your body. Pranayama can help you gain access to your energy sheath. The technique of concentration can help you cultivate a one-pointed mind. But none of these disciplines necessarily initiates a process of spiritual awakening.

Not all forms of meditation are spiritual. You can meditate on water and thereby cultivate a calm and one-pointed mind. You can meditate on fire and cultivate a vibrant mind and improve your energy level. You can meditate on certain mantras that can help you gain extraordinary powers, such as clairvoyance or the ability to heal others. But even though you have gained these extraordinary abilities through your yoga practice, you may still be far away from your inner self.

Turning the mind inward is not easy. The charms and temptations of the world are powerful and the mind has formed a habit of running from one object to another. Even when it has cultivated one-pointedness, it does not see a reason to go inward and seek the Divine within. You have to convince the mind that worldly experiences and the objects of the world are short-lived, while the Lord of Life residing within is eternal. The relationship with that Divine Being is eternal, and the joy that we receive from embracing the Divine within supersedes all sensory pleasures. Only this understanding can inspire us to turn our mind inward. Meditation with that motive not only helps us cultivate a one-pointed mind, it also helps us turn our mind inward. That is how the inward journey begins—a journey that is rewarding at every step.

Q Can you elaborate on the role of hatha yoga in increasing energy and boosting stamina?

The dynamics of human energy and stamina are subtle and involve more than muscle strength. I remember reading about a study that compared the stamina of varsity football players with the stamina of a group of two-year-olds. The football players were each assigned a two-year-old and told to imitate the child's every move for a day. After spending eight hours doing everything the children did—running, falling, getting up, rolling, clambering over furniture—the football players were exhausted, while the children had energy to spare. According to the yogis, this is because the energy channels *(nadis)* of the child are unobstructed, while the men's were clogged.

The great master Guru Gorakh Nath said, "The body is like a mansion. It is built on the foundation of Providence. This structure is held in place and sustained by the pillars and beams of the pranic force." The pranic force is the vital energy within us. Food is only one source of energy. Another, more significant, source is our own *nadi* system, the energy channels through which the pranic force travels, sustaining both body and mind. The more awakened the pranic field, the more energetic we feel.

The physical elements constituting the body are arranged around the pranic force. The navel center is the main hub of the network of energy channels through which this force flows. Just as the Sun is the center of our solar system, the *manipura* chakra (the navel area) is the center of vital energy in the body. That is why to stay healthy and energetic we must keep our navel center active.

By practicing hatha yoga we gain access to the pranic field, which in yoga is known as the *pranamaya kosha* ("the body made of prana"). With the help of pranayama in the form of the classical yoga breathing exercises we can awaken the pranic force, purify the energy channels, and allow vital energy to travel freely through these channels.

The journey from matter to energy—from body to the pranic force—is possible only when we practice postures and pranayama together. In fact, asana without pranayama is not yoga and is of little value. According to the acclaimed text the *Hatha Yoga Pradipika,* asanas help us prepare to do pranayama, but it is the energy released by the practice of pranayama that awakens the dormant forces within. Only when the pranic force awakens do we overcome sloth, inertia, and laziness. When the pranic force travels through the energy channels unobstructed, we are filled with vital energy. We are also able to truly rest and therefore require less sleep.

Q There are three aspects to physical fitness: aerobic fitness, strength, and flexibility. Can hatha yoga deliver on all three?

Yes. To my knowledge there is no system of exercise that is as complete as hatha yoga. When classical asanas are done at a moderate pace, in coordination with the breath, the main benefit is flexibility, but there are also secondary strengthening and aerobic effects. Flexibility is the hallmark of all hatha yoga practices—the asanas are focused primarily on developing and preserving suppleness in the spinal column and the joints.

There are certain postures and practices, however, that are intended primarily to strengthen the body. This involves more than building muscles in arms, shoulders, and thighs, although the postures also have this effect. According to yoga, strength comes from the navel center. The energy generated from this center not only provides strength but also increases both energy and stamina. The practices of *agni sara, bhastrika, kapalabhati, mula-bandha,* and *nauli* energize the body. According to my own experience, the practices of *agni sara* and *yoga mudra,* along with a special sequence of leg lifts, are among the best hatha yoga practices for energizing the body.

If you are interested in increasing the aerobic effect of the postures, this can be done by linking a few of the asanas and practicing them a number of times at a fast pace. The sun salutation done repeatedly and quickly will elevate your heart rate. In my own practice I often rapidly alternate legs in the lunge (the monkey pose from the sun salutation). In other words, I start with the right foot forward, then bring it straight behind as the left foot comes forward between the hands, continuing to alternate leg positions for a minute or two. My other favorite, which has the added advantage of activating the navel center, involves moving rapidly from a supine posture to the hip-balance pose *(utthita hasta pada asana).* From a supine position, I use the strength of the abdominal muscles to quickly and simultaneously lift the legs and torso into a hip balance, hold for an instant, return to a supine position, and repeat as many times as possible.

The purpose of the intermediate level is not only to maintain the progress you have already achieved, but also to unfold the human potential which usually remains dormant within us. The intermediate level includes classical yoga exercises, yogic cleansing techniques, and pranayama—*nadi shodhanam, kapalabhati, bhastrika, ujjayi, bhramari,* and *agni sara.* Practicing these postures and breathing techniques regularly will strengthen not only the muscles but also the internal organs. These practices will also enable you to clean your system at a deep level by activating such organs and glands as the heart, liver, lungs, pancreas, ovaries, and testes.

Classical yoga postures and pranayama techniques are designed to provide an equal workout to the left and right sides of the body and brain, and because of this, they have an amazing effect on the sympathetic and parasympathetic nervous systems. Both active and passive, solar and lunar, and male and female energies are forced to flow in a balanced manner, cleansing and nourishing the nervous system. This cleansing and nourishing is an important preparation for undertaking the advanced practices of yoga, which unleash the powerful dormant energies of the body and mind. A weak and impure nervous system may be jarred, even shattered, when this dormant force awakens. Therefore I would advise against jumping into advanced yoga disciplines if you are not comfortable and regular with the practices of the intermediate level. You need a solid base from which to jump.

If you are honest with yourself you will automatically know whether or not you are ready for advanced practices. Signs and symptoms of perfection at the intermediate level include having a strong digestive fire, with balanced *vata, pitta,* and *kapha;* feeling light and energetic at the physical level; feeling cheerful, inspired, enthusiastic, and motivated at the emotional level; and feeling a strong hunger to gain more knowledge and experience at the intellectual level. When these signs are clearly evident you are ready to move on to the advanced level.

The advanced stage of yoga is custom designed to fit your individual needs and goals. At this stage you need to have already perfected one sitting posture, and to have formed the habit of always doing pranayama with the *bandhas* and *mudras.* Advanced techniques of concentration, visualization, breath retention, and mantra japa can be learned only from a competent teacher. Such a teacher will never

Q I have often read that advanced yoga practices should not be undertaken until the nervous system has been strengthened. What are such advanced yoga practices, and how can I prepare myself for them?

Generally speaking, yoga practices can be divided into three main categories: initial, intermediate, and advanced. The initial stage of yoga practice may consist of basic hatha yoga postures and simple breathing exercises. The purpose of yoga at this stage is to maintain or regain a normal level of health. In today's fast-paced, stressful society most of us suffer from substandard health: a stiff body, low energy level, weak organs, and a mind filled with fear, worry, and anxiety are common to most of us. As long as we are struggling with these problems we should undertake only a simple yoga routine, focusing especially on those practices which specifically help us to overcome them. Sleeping and waking up on time, eating the right kind of food in the right proportion, and doing gentle exercises—such as some stretching, forward bending and backward bending, and postures to loosen the hips, open the chest, and make the spine strong and flexible—are part of the initial phase of yoga practice.

In addition, we may also employ simple breathing exercises whic enable us to regulate the motion of the diaphragm, eliminate che breathing, remove jerks and noise in the breath, and strengthen tho organs that are involved in the process of breathing—abdominal mu cles, diaphragm, and lungs.

As you continue to practice you'll gain more awareness and c trol of your body and breath. You'll know you're ready for the stage when diaphragmatic breathing, instead of chest breathing become your normal habit; when your body has become fle enough so that you can sit comfortably with your head, neck trunk straight; when you've increased your stamina to the poir you can walk fast or exercise for an hour without getting tired you've formed the habit of eating, sleeping, and waking up o and when your bowel movements are regular. When you are accomplish this, and when it has become part of your normal you can gradually move to the next level of yoga.

teach advanced techniques of yoga unless the student is fully prepared—physically healthy, emotionally mature, and intellectually sharp. Without these prerequisites, and without proper guidance, a student who attempts to do advanced practices may have a more negative than positive experience, for the student's nervous system is not yet fully prepared. There is no such risk in the initial and intermediate stages. That is why it is important to perfect them slowly and systematically before moving on to advanced practices.

Q **What is the best way to strengthen the nervous system in order to undertake advanced practices of yoga?**

It is very simple. Practice one step at a time. Perfect each level before moving on to the next. Laying the groundwork is essential; the rest falls into place naturally. After the basic practices of the initial phase are routine for you, strive to master the practices of the intermediate level. Stay at the intermediate level for a long time. The practices of this level—the classical yoga asanas, pranayama, and cleansing techniques—are the way to strengthen your nervous system.

You will find that at some point in your practice you will feel the need to place more emphasis on pranayama, especially the pranayama techniques that energize your navel center. This is a clear indication that your nervous system is now clean enough; it is ready to absorb and assimilate the additional pranic force that is generated from the navel center. An unhealthy and impure nervous system and *nadis*—energy channels—become irritated and sluggish when the vital energy tries to travel through them. It is like providing food which is heavy in nutrients to someone whose digestive system is weak.

Asanas such as the complete spinal twist, the peacock, and the headstand; pranayamas such as *bhastrika*, *kapalabhati*, and *surya bhedi;* and other practices such as *mula-bandha, uddiyana-bandha, trataka,* and *nauli kriya* are some of the techniques at the intermediate level of yoga which strengthen and energize the nervous system. Continue to do these practices regularly and patiently, and in time you will reap the benefits and be able to do advanced practices.

ASANA AND PRANAYAMA

Q If a mind turned inward is the vehicle for completing the spiritual journey, why is it necessary to spend so much time working with my body and breath?

Turning the mind inward is the most important step—but the body, breath, mind, and soul are intertwined. That is why your spiritual practice will be more fruitful if it includes techniques for working with your body, breath, mind, and soul simultaneously. A productive practice is one that is designed to enable you to penetrate the deeper layers of your being while reducing the obstacles you encounter on the outer layers—the body, breath, and mind.

A tired body, an erratic breathing pattern, and a scattered mind are not fit tools for the spiritual journey. That is why yogis invented physical postures *(asanas)* to energize the tired body, a system of relaxation to restore the vitality of the nervous system, and breathing exercises to regulate the breath and to revitalize the body and mind. By incorporating yogic exercises, breathing practices, and relaxation techniques into your daily routine along with your meditation practice, you can reach the summit faster and more easily. Working with the body and breath while training the mind is the best way to prepare a solid foundation for an ever-advancing spiritual practice.

Q The books I've read on yoga and holistic health indicate that breathing plays an important role in our physical and mental well-being. Can you explain why this is so and give me a sequence that can help prepare me for yogic breathing practices?

The scriptures say that "breath is life and life is breath." Through the breath you receive vitality from the atmosphere. Further, the breath is the link between the individual and the Cosmic Being, as well as between the body and the mind. Yogic breathing practices are called *pranayama*, which literally means "expanding the vital force," or "gaining control over the activities of the vital force within."

In a healthy breathing pattern the breath flow is deep, smooth, and silent. There is no pause between inhalation and exhalation, which are of approximately equal duration. Even though the breath is deep, there is little movement of the upper chest. This is an indication of diaphragmatic breathing, which is basic to yogic breathing practices. Diaphragmatic breathing enables you to balance and control your emotions. It also reduces fatigue and stress and helps you feel your best.

The first step in training yourself to breathe diaphragmatically is to strengthen the diaphragm by working with a sandbag. For this practice you'll need a five-pound sandbag packed tight enough to retain its shape but not so tight that it is rock-hard. You may use another kind of weight, but make sure it is relatively soft and that you are comfortable when it is placed on your abdomen.

Begin by lying on your back and relaxing your body systematically from head to toe. Calm your breath. Now gently place the sandbag on your abdomen. If you have heart problems, lung problems, or blood pressure abnormalities, place the sandbag on the muscles below the navel; make sure the sandbag is supported by the abdomen, not by the pelvic girdle.

Close your eyes and breathe. You must make an effort to inhale, but the exhalation should be effortless. Notice how the sandbag rises as you inhale and drops as you exhale. After three to five minutes, remove the sandbag and relax on your back for a few more minutes.

In addition to strengthening your diaphragm, this practice will help to regulate the motion of your lungs in concert with the movement of the diaphragm.

After several weeks you may want to increase the weight of the sandbag. If you do this gradually, staying within your comfort range, you may ultimately increase the weight to ten or fifteen pounds.

Q Can you elaborate on the benefits of diaphragmatic breathing and explain in more detail how to develop the habit of breathing this way?

The diaphragm is the muscle that divides the torso into two separate chambers: the thorax and the abdomen. It forms the floor of the thorax, and rests against the base of the lungs. The lungs are like sponges. As they contract and expand, the used-up gases are expelled and oxygen is absorbed. During exhalation the dome-shaped diaphragm muscle relaxes and presses up against the lungs. Inhalation follows as the diaphragm contracts away from the lungs, allowing them to expand.

This is the way our bodies were designed to breathe—all of us breathed diaphragmatically as babies. In a healthy person, the movement of the diaphragm is responsible for seventy-five percent of the exchange of gases in the lungs. In many people, however, the diaphragm is tense and blocks natural breathing. This causes fatigue, tension, and more serious problems. One of the first aims of yoga is to reestablish good breathing habits. Restoring the habit of diaphragmatic breathing accomplishes this.

You can learn what a correct diaphragmatic breath feels like by lying in the crocodile posture. To assume the crocodile, lie on your abdomen with your legs a comfortable distance apart. The toes can be pointed in or out, whichever is more comfortable. Fold the arms in front of the body, resting each hand on the opposite arm above the elbow. Position the arms so that the base of the rib cage touches the floor.

Place the forehead on the forearms. As you breathe, the diaphragm moves vertically, pressing against the lungs from below.

When you inhale, the abdomen expands, pressing against the floor, and the back rises gently. As you exhale, the abdomen contracts and the back falls gently. Both of these effects are produced by the movement of the diaphragm.

You can establish the habit of diaphragmatic breathing in daily life by practicing the crocodile pose three times a day for five to ten minutes. When you are finished, roll onto your back and observe your abdomen as it expands and contracts with the breath. Next, sit in a chair and again watch your breathing, keeping your abdomen relaxed. The last step is to stand as you continue to breathe diaphragmatically. Practice regularly until diaphragmatic breathing becomes a habit.

Q **I have been feeling very nervous and agitated lately. Is there a breathing practice that can help me?**

Alternate nostril breathing, also known as *nadi shodhanam,* or channel purification, is a means of purifying the subtle energy channels in the body and bringing the activities of the nervous system to a state of balance. This practice is done as follows:

1. Sit with your legs crossed in the easy pose or on a chair with your feet flat on the floor. Make sure your head, neck, and trunk are aligned.
2. Bring your right hand to the nose, folding the index finger and the middle finger so that the right thumb can be used to close the right nostril and the ring finger can be used to close the left nostril.
3. Close the left nostril and exhale completely through the right nostril.
4. At the end of the exhalation close the right nostril and inhale through the left nostril slowly and completely. The inhalation and exhalation should be of equal duration.
5. Repeat this cycle two more times.
6. At the end of the third inhalation through the left nostril, change the pattern by keeping the right nostril closed with the thumb and exhaling completely through the left nostril.

7. Then close the left nostril and inhale through the right nostril.
8. Repeat this pattern two more times. This completes one round.

This cycle can be repeated. Make your exhalations and inhalations even, beginning with a duration that is well within your comfortable capacity. Many people begin with a six-second breath—exhaling for three seconds and inhaling for three. As you continue to practice, you will gradually lengthen your breath.

Q The air where I live is polluted. Is there a breathing exercise that will help keep my lungs clean?

The 2:1 breathing practice is an absolute necessity for people living in cities where the air is polluted. This practice cleans the lungs and purifies the blood. In addition, the practice is relaxing and has the effect of increasing your vital energy.

You may practice 2:1 breathing either in the corpse pose or in a sitting posture. Begin by establishing a pattern of even breathing. You can count to make sure that your inhalations and exhalations are of equal length. This may take several practice sessions.

Once you have established a comfortable pattern of even breathing, begin to exhale longer than you inhale. For example, count to ten while inhaling and to twelve while exhaling. After a period of days or weeks, try lengthening your exhalation by a few more counts until you are inhaling for ten counts and exhaling for twenty. This may take two or three months of daily practice. As with all yoga practices, be sure to stay within your comfortable capacity.

When you have been breathing at a rate of ten-count inhalations and twenty-count exhalations for several weeks, begin expanding the length of the inhalation while continuing to make the exhalation twice as long. For instance, if you inhale for twelve counts, exhale for twenty-four counts. Take your time and expand your capacity until you are inhaling for fifteen counts and exhaling for thirty. If you spend five minutes at least once a day breathing in this manner, you will be ridding your lungs of toxins from the polluted air around you. You will also find the practice very relaxing.

What creates blockages in the energy body?

Bad food, an unhealthy lifestyle, sense abuse, and, most of all, suppressed desires, feelings, and lower urges. The seeds of mental and pranic disharmony are sown when we keep ignoring the voice of the heart—our conscience. This is the enlightened part of us that spontaneously tells us what is right and what is not. Because of fear, attachment, social pressure, or simply out of negligence, we keep making the same mistakes despite the repeated warnings of our inner voice. The result is guilt and self-condemnation, which weaken us, drain our vital energy, and create mental, pranic, and physical obstacles.

To some degree, it is possible to unblock energy in the body by working with asana, pranayama, and *mudras*. However, those suffering from deep mental distress must not push themselves to practice advanced yogic techniques, especially pranayama with breath retention, for doing so could strengthen and magnify such mental states, creating even bigger blockages in the pranic sheath.

If I feel a blockage in the flow of energy during the practice of asana or pranayama, how can I work through it?

Be gentle with yourself; don't push yourself to the point where you risk shattering your body and nervous system. First, work with the musculoskeletal and nervous systems. Cleansing techniques, such as the nasal wash, upper wash, complete wash, and *agni sara* will help you cleanse and energize your system. If you have taken drugs in the past, then gentle pranayama, such as alternate nostril breathing, and occasional juice fasts will also be helpful.

In the beginning, stay within your capacity. Then gradually expand it, a step at a time, and see how your body reacts. Nothing you do should make your body uncomfortable. A slow and steady regular practice will unblock and release your healing energy, enabling you to heal subtle physical or emotional injuries at the same time. As the *Yoga Sutra* says: "One can grasp the true intent of yoga through the practice of yoga. Yoga is the way to gain knowledge of yoga. One who is not negligent in yoga practice remains established in yoga and enjoys the highest fruit of yoga forever."

Q How will I know if I am practicing correctly?

As a result of practicing asana you begin to understand your own body language. The body develops its own sensitivity and knows whether the food you eat is good for you or not. Your internal clock regulates your schedule precisely, and your body lets you know if you're exercising too much, if you're sleeping too much, and so forth.

Something deep within will not allow you to indulge in unnecessary gossip or other useless sense activities. The body will find great delight in maintaining a peaceful relationship with worldly objects. A true practitioner of hatha yoga is not disgusted by worldly objects, yet feels uncomfortable with noise, in a crowd, or with the excessive company of friends and relatives. At the mental level, such a practitioner develops a great deal of tolerance to the pendulum swings of life's "pairs of opposites"—such as pleasure and pain, honor and insult, and so forth.

Progress in pranayama can be observed in several stages. In the first stage, the nervous system is being cleansed and strengthened, so your body may occasionally jerk and tremble as the *prana shakti* unblocks the *marma sthanas* (vital points). After that, you may perspire a lot. In the third phase, the body feels light. In the fourth, the body begins to slim down, and you become radiant and energetic. The surest sign of success in pranayama is that a practitioner's thinking is clear and, deep within, the veil of ignorance is destroyed by the radiance of the inner light. At this point, if a student has the guidance of a master, then advanced hatha yoga practices can be used to awaken kundalini. Such an awakening will bring delight without any of the side effects (shakiness, visual and auditory hallucinations, etc.) of which modern students frequently complain.

Q How do you practice asana and pranayama together? Is it a matter of breathing a certain way in the postures, or are the pranayamas done separately?

Ideally in the practice of every asana your movement is coordinated with your breath. All movements in asana practice involve either stretching or contracting. The general rule is that you inhale when stretching and exhale when contracting. Both your movements and your inhalation and exhalation must be smooth and fully coordinated. Then, when holding a posture, breathe gently, smoothly, and diaphragmatically.

Breath awareness and mindfulness are the key to enhancing the quality of your hatha yoga practice. For example, in the seated forward bend *(pashchimottanasana)* inhale while reaching upward with your arms and exhale while slowly bending forward, moving your hands toward your toes and your head toward your knees, timing your movements so that you complete your exhalation when you are fully into the posture. While holding the pose, relax your lower back and abdominal region and inhale and exhale from the diaphragm. When you are ready to release the posture, inhale gently and completely while lifting your torso and raising your arms.

In addition to coordinating your movements with your breath, there is also a regimen of pranayama practices that is an integral part of a fruitful hatha yoga routine. In my personal practice I have divided the entire series of postures into four categories.

First I do the standing poses and then the sitting poses. While doing the sitting poses, I practice some of the vigorous pranayamas, such as *bhastrika, kapalabhati,* and *surya bhedi* pranayama.

Before moving on to the next group of postures I practice some of the *mudras,* which by their own nature combine postures with pranayama, especially retention. One of my favorite practices is *yoga mudra.* This is an advanced yoga technique, as it combines the practices of *padmasana,* the forward bend, three locks (the root, navel, and throat locks), breath retention, repetition of mantra, and visualization. This practice should be learned from a qualified teacher, and the full-fledged *yoga mudra* should be practiced only by those who are proficient in the postures and are free from all medical complaints.

After completing a sequence of sitting poses and pranayamas, I move on to the supine postures (the plow, bridge, shoulderstand, etc.), and then to the asanas done in a prone position, specifically the locust, boat, bow, and peacock. I end my asana practice with the headstand and a relaxation in the corpse pose.

After the relaxation I practice the pranayamas that purify the energy channels and energize my body and mind while leading my mind toward meditation. Such pranayamas are *nadi shodhanam* and internal and external *kumbhaka* (breath retention). I recommend that you practice these only under the guidance of a competent teacher.

Q **Is it possible to use pranayama and asana to forcibly awaken kundalini shakti? If so, what are the effects?**

The aim of the classical yoga postures is to unfold the inner forces that lie dormant within. This process is accomplished first by bringing the solar *(ha)* and lunar *(tha)* energy currents to a state of harmony, and then by igniting the inner fire known as kundalini shakti. However, many of the exercises taught in yoga classes today are not standard, classical yoga asanas, but preparatory practices. We cannot expect to awaken kundalini shakti by doing such warm-up exercises.

Asanas that directly aim at awakening kundalini include *siddhasana, matsyendrasana, pashchimottanasana,* and *yoga mudra.* These postures require a great deal of preparation, and this preparation must be completed before committing yourself to the intense practice of asana. A flexible body and a balanced nervous system are indispensable.

If you aspire to true attainment in hatha yoga you must pay attention to regulating the four primitive urges: food, sex, sleep, and the desire for self-preservation. These urges eventually come under your control when you incorporate the following principles in your day-to-day life: eating moderately, in balanced proportions; living in solitude without suffering from loneliness; observing silence for certain periods of time every day; remaining free of expectations; controlling the senses; and having as few possessions as possible. As you work with them, you will come to understand how these six observances help regulate the primitive urges and how they help deepen the practice of hatha yoga.

According to Patanjali, the codifier of yoga science and philosophy, you should commit yourself to the practice of pranayama only after mastering one of the sitting postures. If asana (posture) is not correct (i.e., comfortable and steady), you should work only with simple breathing exercises while continuing to refine your posture. Powerful pranayamas, which in most cases involve breath retention, should be practiced only after asana is perfected—and even then, only under the guidance of a competent master.

In addition to mastering asana, there are other prerequisites for practicing advanced pranayamas: first, eliminate jerks and noise in the breath and reduce the pause between inhalation and exhalation. Only when diaphragmatic breathing has become natural and effortless, and the spinal column has become flexible and strong, can an aspirant begin to practice pranayama to awaken kundalini shakti.

turning inward

THE PRACTICE OF MEDITATION

Q What is meditation? Why is it important?

If you want to learn about meditation, you first need to know something about concentration. According to yoga, concentration means focusing the mind on one object. An undisciplined mind—the kind most of us have—tends to shift continually from one object to another. Steadying the mind by focusing it on one object helps you to gradually overcome this ever-wandering habit of the mind. With persistent practice, the mind is able to focus on one object for longer and longer intervals. When the mind remains concentrated on one object for a period of twelve breaths, this is called meditation. Thus meditation can be defined as the uninterrupted flow of concentration.

The human mind has an infinite capacity to think systematically, to grasp things that seem to be beyond ordinary perception, and to gain knowledge instantly. It has the power to command not only the body and senses, but also the events that take place in the external world. Poor concentration—which stems from the mind's own habits of unrestrained anxiety, craving, and attachment to its previous experiences—robs the mind of its infinite power. Without the ability to concentrate, the mind becomes weak and loses self-confidence and willpower. Meditation seems to be the only way to train the mind thoroughly and to bring it back to its natural state.

Meditation practice enables a human being to attain control gradually over the mental modifications (or thought constructs) that continually disturb the mind-field. Meditation is a systematic discipline for working with all faculties of the mind and organizing them in a manner that allows the mediator to become more efficient and creative, as well as more calm and peaceful.

Because the mind is connected to the body and the external world, any valid method of meditation also includes other disciplines, which may seem unrelated at first glance. These include a healthy diet, exercise, and a disciplined approach to interactions with others. That is why practicing the following principles in a balanced way is said to be part of a meditation practice:

Yama: the five restraints—non-harming, non-lying, non-stealing, moderating sensual gratification, and non-possessiveness.

Niyama: the five observances—purity, contentment, practices that bring about perfection of the body and the senses (acts that increase spiritual fervor), self-study, and surrender to the Ultimate Reality.

Asana: physical exercises or postures.

Pranayama: breathing exercises.

Pratyahara: withdrawing the senses and the mind from unwholesome objects.

Dharana: concentration.

Dhyana: meditation.

Samadhi: spiritual absorption, the culmination of meditation.

Q What is the difference between concentration and contemplation? How does contemplation lead to spiritual awareness?

As I've just defined, meditation is the uninterrupted focus on one object for a prolonged period of time. All meditation begins with a simple process of concentration: focusing the mind on a given object. In time, as this focus becomes steady and the mind is no longer distracted by other thoughts, concentration becomes meditation.

A one-pointed mind is cultivated through constant practice. Good software programmers, for example, have one-pointed minds because they are constantly practicing concentration—solving a problem by working out a series of minute details. That kind of one-pointedness or mindfulness makes a good software programmer, but it does not necessarily give a person the ability to withstand the storms of disturbing thoughts and emotions that have their origins in the external world or in the depths of one's own mind. Spiritual literature contains numerous accounts of meditators who gained an awesome ability to concentrate either by practicing *trataka* (fixed gazing) or by focusing their mind on a compelling object. This gave them extraordinary powers of concentration, but they remained prey to ignorance and the pains and miseries that ignorance breeds: egoism, attachment, aversion, and fear. Meditation—prolonged, sustained concentration—helps one cultivate a one-pointed, steady mind, but it is ultimately the contemplative aspect of spiritual discipline that enables the practitioner to channel the mental energy cultivated by meditation in a spiritually fulfilling and enlightening direction.

In other words, the one-pointedness of mind that comes from the ability to concentrate must be used to sharpen the intellect, but that sharpened intellect, in turn, must be used to understand the higher purpose and meaning of life. Meditation becomes a spiritual practice only when the aspirant contemplates the following questions one-pointedly and sincerely: Who am I? Where have I come from? What is the purpose of being here on Earth? Where will I go after I leave this platform? Whose footsteps am I walking in? What kind of footprints am I leaving behind? How much have I contributed to God's creation? Am I wiser than I was when I was younger? Is there anything I must do so I will not regret leaving it undone with the last breath of my life? Have I done anything more than eating, sleeping, going to the bathroom, and growing older? Through my asana, yoga, pranayama, and meditation practice, in the study of spiritual principles and the lives of the masters, how much inner contentment have I gathered?

Transformation requires contemplation, and contemplation is not the same as sitting for meditation. Contemplation is a tool for self-reflection and self-study, but it must not be tainted with worry and anxiety. If it is, it is no longer contemplation but degenerates into mere worry. Cultivating true contemplation, however, will infuse your meditation practice with spiritual fervor. Only then can you expect true and everlasting transformation from meditation.

Q Can you give me specific instructions on how to do a meditation practice?

There are many methods of meditation. In all of them, the most important thing is to be systematic. Even the best method of meditation, if not done systematically, is of little use. The following nine points are indispensable in a systematic practice:

1. Before practicing, freshen up and prepare yourself psychologically. Wash your hands and face and put on loose, comfortable clothes. The room where you meditate should be clean and the temperature moderate.
2. Do a relaxation practice and several rounds of alternate nostril breathing to overcome fatigue before sitting for meditation.
3. Make a mental resolution that for the next twenty to thirty minutes you will entertain neither your memories of the past nor your anxieties about the future.
4. Either sit on the floor in a comfortable cross-legged posture or sit in a chair with your feet flat on the floor. Make sure that your head, neck, and trunk are aligned. Relax your shoulders, and let your hands rest on your knees or thighs.

5. Close your eyes and withdraw your mind from all directions. Mentally draw a circle of light around yourself, separating yourself from all external affairs. Fill your mind and heart with the feeling of divine presence. Remind yourself that the Divine Light pervading the universe is present within you and that it is a privilege to attend it. After establishing the presence of the Divine, bring your attention to your breath.
6. Breathe gently and naturally, without jerks, pauses, or noise. Make sure your breath is flowing smoothly, evenly, and soundlessly. As soon as you have completed your inhalation, begin exhaling; begin inhaling as soon as you have completed your exhalation. Thus you inhale and exhale as if the breath were an unbroken circle. To make sure that you are breathing diaphragmatically, be aware of the gentle outward and then inward motion of your abdomen as you inhale and then exhale. Your chest should move only slightly or not at all.
7. Focus on your breath and watch how it flows from your nostrils to your heart center as you inhale, and from the heart center to the nostrils as you exhale. Notice the breath as it passes the point where your nostrils meet your upper lip.
8. Now deepen your concentration on your breath. Allow your mind to follow the flow of your breath. With each inhalation try to feel that your mind is traveling between your nostrils and your heart, and with each exhalation, back from the heart to the nostrils. Thus your breath and mind are flowing together as one inseparable stream of awareness. Go still deeper into your breath and you will hear in your mind a sound that naturally emerges from the breath. That sound is "so hum."

   Focus mentally on the sound "so hum." While you inhale, listen to the sound "sooooo," and while you exhale, listen to the sound "hummmm." Let your mind, breath, and the sound "so hum" flow together. Stay with this practice for as long as you find it enjoyable.
9. The next step, for those who have received a personal mantra through formal initiation, is to focus on that mantra. If you

have received mantra initiation, follow the meditation instructions given to you at that time, even if they conflict with these general guidelines.

Why is it so important to sit with your head, neck, and trunk straight when you practice meditation?

There are three main reasons.

1. This is the healthiest and most comfortable way of sitting. In this pose, the spine is stretched up, the chest is expanded, and the head is held in place effortlessly. Due to the straight spine and expanded chest, the lungs, the heart, and the diaphragm work efficiently and in a relaxed manner.

   The weight of the whole body is centered on the base of the spine and distributed through the buttocks. This creates pressure on the bottom of the spine, and the pressure, in turn, creates heat. As the heat increases, the pranic force at the base of the spine expands and rises. Because the spine is straight, the pranic energy flows freely upward along the spinal column toward the head, burning up sloth and inertia while providing nourishment to the organs located between the base of the spine and the top of the head. As a result, anyone sitting in this pose will be relatively free from sloth, heaviness, and inertia, yet will remain relaxed.
2. At the base of the spine, between the first and second chakras, an energy channel called the *kurma nadi* originates. It runs all the way to the hollow of the throat and regulates the stability of the body and mind.

   According to yogic mythology, there is an enormous and powerful *kurma* (tortoise) on whose back sits *shesha naga* (the cosmic snake). This snake has a thousand heads and it holds the Earth on one of them. When it shifts the Earth from one head to another, earthquakes occur. The most powerful earthquakes come when the tortoise—who holds the snake who is holding the Earth—moves slightly.

The root of the kurma nadi is the tortoise. The stability of the spine (the shesha naga) and all that is centered around it depends on the strength of the kurma nadi. By keeping the head, neck, and trunk straight and by sitting in a meditative pose, one attains firmness in the energy that is controlled by the kurma nadi.

3. Sitting in the same pose every day is a way of training our body and mind to be aware of the Truth on which we meditate. The pose and the practice that goes with it are instrumental in the formation of a fruitful meditative habit. The following story illustrates this point:

   Once upon a time there was a student. He was sincere, hardworking, and quite intelligent. But his teacher was somewhat bewildered because this young man seemed completely incapable of giving the correct answers in the classroom. The teacher spent extra time with him, reviewing each lesson again and again and asking, "Do you follow?" The student would always say, "Yes sir." But the next day, his mind again seemed blank. Finally one day the teacher lost his temper and kicked the student so hard that the poor fellow fell down. (Thank God this didn't happen in the West—a lawsuit would have been filed.)

   As the student rolled on the ground, his memory returned and he recited the entire lesson flawlessly. The teacher immediately understood the problem and admonished him: "Son, study your lessons sitting with your head, neck, and trunk straight, not reclining on your bed."

   Time, space, and causation are basic conditionings of the mind. How we sit and where we sit creates a deep groove in the mind. It is important, therefore, to sit for meditation every day and to sit in the same meditative pose each time. The best pose is the one in which the head, neck, and trunk remain in a straight line.

Q I have a severe curvature of the spine that cannot be straightened by surgery or any other treatment. Therefore I can't sit with my head, neck, and trunk in a straight line. Perhaps this condition explains my year-long struggle with meditation. Despite reading, studying, and taking courses on meditation, it continues to be a daily trial. How can I intensify my meditative experience?

Please do not struggle with your sitting posture. Try to find a pose that is comfortable for you during meditation, even though you cannot keep your spine straight. You have just one curvature in your body, whereas there have been great meditators and yogis who have had more than one and still attained the highest illumination. One great yogi, Ashtavakra, had eight curvatures in his body (at least a couple of which were undoubtedly in the spinal column).

A correct posture allows us to use the body as an efficient tool for working with the mind. But if there is a basic problem with the tool itself, then it is best to bypass it. In your case, go directly either to the *anahata* chakra (the heart center) or to the *ajña* chakra (the center between the eyebrows), and maintain your meditative awareness there. If you push your body too much, you will simply meditate on the pain rather than on your mantra or any other meditative object you may have chosen.

Even meditators who have perfectly healthy spinal columns eventually cut down on their sitting meditation practice because as physical strength declines, the spine loses its strength. Sooner or later, everybody is defeated by old age. At that time, skilled meditators maintain a natural meditative state called *sahaja samadhi,* which entails constant awareness of the inner reality. For this awareness, a meditative posture is not absolutely necessary. A loving attitude toward yourself and others, a devotional attitude toward the Divine, and contentment in regard to your physical condition are the grounds for maintaining sahaja samadhi. Why not maintain that state from the very beginning?

Q Does what I eat affect my meditation practice?

Yes, food has a great effect on the quality of our meditation. Only food that is *sattvic* is conducive to meditative awareness. Sattvic food is fresh, light, and nutritious. It is cooked and seasoned so that it still retains its vitality. Heavily processed food is not sattvic. One of the indications of whether food retains its vitality is if it keeps its original fragrance, flavor, color, and texture after it has been prepared. It should not lose its identity during the cooking process. However, even fresh food that is light, properly cooked, and nutritious remains sattvic only if it is eaten in the right proportion, at the right time, and with the right attitude of mind.

Just as we carry the subtle impressions *(samskaras)* of our deeds, food also carries samskaras. Food assimilates samskaras from a variety of sources: fertilizers, water, soil, and air. The most powerful samskaras are created by how food is harvested and how it is handled from the time it leaves the field or orchard until the time it reaches your table. When food is mass-produced and we get it from supermarkets, we have very little control over these conditions. It is difficult to get reliable information about how the food has been grown, harvested, and handled. Thus it is almost impossible to determine whether the food is sattvic. The best solution is to eat organic fruits, vegetables, and grains, and to try to get your dietary needs met as close to the source as you can. Two ways of doing this are buying from local farmers and growing some of your own food. With packaged food, my experience is that the shorter the list of ingredients and additives, the better the quality.

If we want to live happy, healthy, and spiritually productive lives, we must overcome our taste for modern luxuries and learn to live on a diet of rice and other whole grains, legumes, vegetables, dairy products, and fruit. Reducing our intake of soft drinks, fake fruit juice, and popular snacks that are loaded with sugar and salt will automatically increase our intake of sattvic food.

Eating sattvic food makes the body light and bowel movements regular, and improves the function of our liver and kidneys. When the body is comfortable, the mind feels good. A cheerful mind is needed for meditation.

Q Is it possible to have a good meditation practice and still eat meat?

Meat is not something terrible. A vegetarian diet is not the sole—or even the most important—criterion for being a yogi. However, the type of meat that is available in markets is not pure meat—it contains chemicals that have come either from the animals themselves or from the butchering, processing, and preserving process. When we eat this meat, we are also taking these chemicals into our bodies.

Because animals have a more evolved consciousness than plants, meat products carry more powerful samskaras, and eating them invites these animal tendencies into our internal systems. Plants are also alive, but because their self-identity is less evolved, their samskaras are less powerful. Therefore, with a vegetarian diet we get vitality from the food we eat, but are less affected by the samskaras of what we eat. If you read about the origin of the meat that is available today—how the animals are raised and fed, and how the meat comes to the market—you will not eat meat, even if you have no interest in meditation.

But to answer your question directly: Depending on how sincerely you practice and how you arrange other factors that are an integral part of meditation, you can have a good meditation even if you eat meat. However, just as the food we eat is the most important factor in our health, it is also crucial to spiritual development. A balanced vegetarian diet, one that provides enough protein and vitamin B_{12}, is more conducive to meditation than a non-vegetarian diet. Compared to most components of a vegetarian diet, meat is not sattvic.

Q Famous texts, such as the *Hatha Yoga Pradipika,* advise practitioners to include an ample amount of clarified butter, other milk products, fruit, and sweets in their diet. But today we read everywhere that to stay healthy, a person should avoid fat and sugar.

We have abused ourselves so much by indulging in excessive eating and other unhealthy habits that we no longer have the capacity to eat good, sweet, rich, delicious food. By the time many people become health-conscious, they have already consumed enough sugar, fat, and salt to last several lifetimes! That is why in modern times, students who start their yoga practice late in life must confine themselves to lowfat milk, skim milk, or perhaps even whey. To make up for the damage they have caused to their kidneys, liver, heart, and circulatory and nervous systems, they must stick to a pure, sattvic diet—one that contains the least possible amount of fat, salt, and sugar.

Some people have been fortunate enough to have missed all these luxuries or, driven by Providence or by their innate inspiration, began leading a healthy, yogic lifestyle at an early age. The ancient dietary prescriptions still apply to such people. It all depends on your physical condition. For someone with a normal, healthy body and mind, yogis prescribe three different sets of dietary rules at three different stages of practice. Swami Rama has distilled the essence of the dietary instructions found in the ancient yoga manuals and presented them in Volume 1 of his book *Path of Fire and Light* as follows:

Diet During Beginning Levels of Practice. Normally, this is a balanced vegetarian diet, based on grains with legumes, fresh-cooked green vegetables, fresh milk products, and fresh, raw fruit. Clarified butter *(ghee)* is used sparingly as a cooking medium. A variety of seasonings and spices may be used, but harsher spices, such as chili peppers, raw onions, or garlic, are avoided.

Diet During Intermediate Levels of Practice. At this level, diet will be based on specific grains, usually wheat and barley, which are often fried in ghee with mild spices, such as ginger, and which may be cooked with sugar. Legumes are used less frequently and may be restricted to fresh (not dried) beans such as chana (which is similar to garbanzos). Fruit and milk play an increasing role.

Diet During Advanced Intensive Practice. When advanced practices are being done, most solid foods are dropped, though fresh fruit may still be taken in moderation. Milk, especially milk rich in butterfat, becomes the focal point of the diet, and is taken, as always, after boiling. It may be combined with water, spices, or sugar.

When should I meditate, and for how long?

The best time to meditate is in the early morning. Wake up before sunrise. Before beginning your meditation, empty your bladder and bowels and brush your teeth. Take a bath or shower, if you wish, and spend a few minutes stretching or doing some gentle asana.

In the beginning, meditate only as long as you enjoy it. Don't push yourself beyond your capacity or make meditation a chore. Simply form a habit of meditating regularly—ten or fifteen minutes a day is a good start.

Later, try to meditate in the evening as well as in the morning. It's best to meditate at a set time, but if that is not possible, make a habit of meditating just before you go to bed. Again, ten or fifteen minutes is enough in the beginning. Once you are accustomed to meditating for a short period, gently begin to expand your capacity by gradually lengthening the time that you spend in meditation.

Is it true that it's best not to meditate when you're not feeling well?

If the nature of your physical complaint makes meditation impossible, then certainly you should not attempt it. If meditation seems like work and requires a great deal of physical effort, then do not make yourself worse by meditating. But if you have been practicing for a long time, if meditation has become effortless and a source of joy, then certainly you should meditate, because it will make you feel better.

If you have experienced the subtle distinction between body and mind, you will have noticed that the mind is the primary tool in meditation; the body is secondary. For a meditator there can be no better therapy for any illness than meditation itself. Ideally you should learn to meditate even in the grimmest situations so that during your last breaths, when conditions are really grim, you will be able to stay in a meditative state and make your exit peacefully and gracefully.

Q **Doesn't an object of meditation, such as a mantra or yantra, automatically pull the mind in a spiritual direction?**

In theory, yes. But in practice, it depends on a number of factors. Who gave you that mantra? Was the person who initiated you connected to the Source? Is the mantra you were given an awakened mantra, or is it simply a word or phrase taken from a book? The fruit of your meditation also depends on how lovingly, faithfully, and one-pointedly you meditate on your mantra. Are you really practicing with full determination, or are you just experimenting with a technique that you've heard leads to enlightenment? All these factors make a big difference in mantra practice.

An even more significant factor is how you manage your daily life outside your meditation sessions. Even if you behave like a sage during the thirty minutes you meditate every day, if during the remaining twenty-three and a half hours you are not mindful of your thoughts, speech, and actions, it's like pouring a cup of milk in a barrel of muddy water and expecting to get a barrel of milk.

Greed, selfishness, and an overbearing ego are deeply rooted in our unconscious mind. Constant meditation, which is supported by self-observation and self-analysis, can help us identify these subhuman characteristics in ourselves. Once we recognize them and come to know their patterns and in which areas of life they spring up most frequently, we can begin to work with these characteristics. This requires contemplation, which is why the prominent yoga texts, such as *the Yoga Sutra* and the *Bhagavad Gita,* constantly advise us to make *svadhyaya* (self-study) an integral part of our practice.

Why is it said that the object of meditation is more important than the technique employed?

All kinds of meditation techniques have been invented and trademarked by various people. I have seen those calling themselves meditation teachers who prescribe meditation on an actor or actress or on a beautiful piece of artwork. Some tell their students to meditate on roses or some other enticing aspect of the natural world. I have even heard of teachers saying that the object of meditation has to be attractive, colorful, and engaging.

According to the sages, however, you become what you think, and that is why the object of meditation is more important than the technique of concentration on that object. If you meditate on roses, an actress, or some fancy diagram generated by a computer, how can you expect your mind to be infused with spiritual consciousness? How is that possible? You must first decide what kind of transformation you are looking for, and then search for an object which can induce that kind of transformation through its own inherent virtue. If the inward journey to the source of consciousness is the goal, then a divine object which is intrinsically connected with that source will lead your mind to that source.

Where should I focus my attention during meditation?

If you have a weak constitution, suffer from digestive problems, fatigue easily, or have a weak immune system, then the *manipura* chakra (the navel center) is the best focal point. The *anahata* chakra (the heart center) is good for those students with a predominantly emotional orientation who want to transform and channel their emotions for communion with the Divine. Concentration at the *vishuddha* chakra (the throat center) can be beneficial for those inclined toward the creative arts. For those with a primarily intellectual orientation, focusing on the *ajña* chakra (the center between the eyebrows) is best.

But of all places, the best focal point is the *sahasrara* chakra (the crown center). However, leading the mind systematically to the crown center and maintaining your attention there is an exact method that requires precise instruction from a competent teacher. Don't focus at the crown center unless you have received clear instruction to do so, or you feel a natural and spontaneous pull toward that chakra.

Remember that these are just general guidelines and they apply only under the following conditions: when you are trying to learn to meditate on your own; when you are experimenting with various methods of meditation; or when you have chosen a particular sound, a mantra, or a visual object for your meditation because you are attracted to it. Various systems of meditation provide specific guidelines. For example, in certain Buddhist and Zen schools of meditation, the breath is used as a focal point. In mantra meditation, the nature and unique characteristics of the specific mantra into which you are initiated usually determine the center on which to focus.

In traditions that use mantra meditation, the most appropriate center for focusing your attention is the one to which you are directed by the grace of the master or the grace of the mantra. If you have been initiated into a mantra and the person who initiated you belongs to an authentic tradition and has been blessed with the living wisdom of that tradition, then the mantra itself becomes your guide. In other words, the mantra itself will lead you to the most appropriate center. Simply listen to your mantra and you will notice that when your mind is absorbed in the mantra, your awareness becomes condensed and concentrated at one of the centers. Let your mind go there, as this is a sure sign that this center is the center for your concentration.

Mantra is a self-conscious, self-illumined force. The eternal flow of love and divine compassion in the form of sound knows which center is best for you and why. If you have not received clear instruction from your teacher about where to focus, simply allow your mind to be led by the power of your mantra.

Q Can I choose my own focus of meditation based on the observation of my personality traits, or must I seek instruction?

If you are meditating on the breath or on a general object, such as the sound "so hum," or if you have learned meditation entirely in a classroom setting or from books, then follow the general guidelines provided above. However, if you have received personal instruction, and especially if you have been formally initiated into a method of meditation, then discuss this question with the teacher who initiated you. Personal guidance is always more precise and can remove your doubts.

Q Sometimes my center of attention shifts by itself and I seem to be more comfortable focusing on a chakra other than the one I was told to focus on. Why?

This experience is either a sign that your meditation is improving or evidence that your mind is playing tricks with you. If your attention shifts from one center to another within a single meditation session, as well as to other external objects, then your mind may have a roving tendency. If this is the case, make an effort to put an end to this shiftiness! On the other hand, if you are naturally pulled to a different center of focus, you may need to meditate at that chakra. In that case, begin with the assigned chakra, and as your meditation deepens, allow your mind to spontaneously move to where the attention has shifted. Don't interfere with the process.

Q I have seen the chakras depicted in a number of books. Sometimes they are elaborate, sometimes quite simple. The colors also differ. How can I tell which of these depictions is accurate? Are the chakras two-dimensional as pictured in books, or are they three-dimensional? Are they real?

The question of whether the chakras are real, what color they are, and whether they are two- or three-dimensional can be answered only if we know what the chakras are made of. They are not part of the physical body. According to the scriptures, the physical body is superimposed on a subtle body, and the chakras are located in this subtle body. They are energy centers, the connecting hub at which the major energy channels of the subtle body come together. The word *chakra* means "wheel"; each chakra is a wheel of the life-force. The energy concentrated at these chakras nourishes both the physical body and the mind.

In our physical world there is nothing that describes the characteristics and functions of the chakras, and yet yogis have to resort to some sort of depiction that can be understood. Accordingly, in the scriptures each chakra is depicted as a concentrated field of energy which manifests in the form of sound and light. Sound in all cultures is considered sacred, and from this concept comes the idea of the sacred word, or mantra. Light too is associated with the sacred. Whenever we think of light we associate it with color—the spectrum of light that illuminates the physical realm can be divided into seven bands of color. Experientially yogis may have known the chakras in an entirely different way, but to communicate this experience they had to lend it shape and color, and so the chakras came to be depicted in their present form. In reality, however, there is nothing like a fixed shape or color.

According to the scriptures, the chakras are radiant fields of energy. Moreover, this radiant energy is intelligent. The power of will, the power of knowledge, and the power of action are intrinsic to these energy fields—they are self-guided and self-illuminating. It is from these fields of energy that the forces of healing and nourishment flow to both body and mind, which is why the scriptures describe the energy at these centers as deities or goddesses. Thus the clear-cut answer to your question is that none of these depictions are perfectly accurate. The chakras are neither two-dimensional nor three-dimensional, because dimension corresponds to the physical world and our sense perception. In one sense they are real, for they are based on the direct experiences of the sages who perceived them through the eyes of intuition. In another sense they are not real but simply symbolic representations of a pure energy field.

Q I have sometimes had psychic experiences in meditation. What is the meaning of these experiences?

Psychic experiences are a signal that you are moving in the right direction. They come and go. Such experiences can inspire you and reassure you that you are making progress. Like any experience, they last for a specific period of time—two minutes, five minutes—and vanish. But before they vanish, they leave a strong and delightful impression on your mind. It is important to assimilate these experiences and use them to strengthen your faith. This will help keep you moving along the path.

However, many people cannot distinguish between truly spiritual experiences and hallucinations. No matter how unusual or supernormal an experience is, if it does not add to the purity of your heart or the one-pointedness of your mind, then it should be ignored. A spiritual experience is always illuminating and uplifting. If you do not find these characteristics in your so-called psychic experiences, then simply disregard them. And even if your experiences do have these characteristics, do not become complacent. Keep practicing and keep yourself open to the next and higher level of experience. This is an ongoing journey. You are infinite, your journey is infinite, and the experiences you gain along the path are also infinite. Don't get stuck with the experiences you have had; there are many more to come.

THE SACRED SOUND

Q What is a mantra and why is it considered to be divine?

The mantra is a word, a syllable, or a series of sounds revealed to the sages in deep states of meditation. These sounds were neither uttered nor heard. Rather, they emerged from the center of silence, from the center of consciousness, and the sages "saw" them through the eyes of intuition. That is why the sages to whom these mantras were revealed are called *rishis* (seers).

According to the scriptures, these mantras do not belong to a language that humans speak with their tongues. Mantras come from the realm of universal language. (In biblical terms, this is the language that the children of God spoke before the Tower of Babel was built. Afterwards a confusion of tongues arose.) However, when the seers communicated this revealed knowledge to their students, they had to speak in a language that the students could understand and replicate. So at this point, mundane language became the vehicle for the revealed mantras. Languages such as Sanskrit, Prakrit, or Tibetan were used to create an external approximation of what the rishis heard internally.

There is an important subtle distinction here: intellectually we may call the external manifestation of the mantra an approximation. However, according to the tradition of *mantra shastra,* the mantra you receive from your teacher during initiation is the actual sound that was revealed to the first seer.

The power of a mantra lies in its ability to lead a meditator to the same state of consciousness as that attained by the seer of the mantra. In that state, the meditator will be blessed with the same revelation. But according to the scriptures the true form of a mantra is not contained in what we see when it is written or what we hear when it is articulated. Rather, the essence of a mantra is *nada*—the pure, unstruck, eternal sound. This state of unstruck, eternal sound is what the apostle John was referring to in the Bible when he stated, "In the beginning was the Word, and the Word was with God, and the Word was God." *Nada* contains everything—not just words and meanings, but the entire universe in its unmanifest form.

The principle of the mantra or the Word is the only common link among all of humankind's many spiritual traditions. Some traditions use it as a tool for focusing the mind; others use it as a means of channeling love and devotion toward God. When such sounds are used silently for focusing the mind and turning it inward, it is called meditation; when these sounds are spoken aloud, it is called prayer.

Q Do I need a mantra to practice meditation?

Although it is not absolutely necessary to meditate on a mantra, meditators from all traditions have found the mantra to be the most effective object of concentration. From a spiritual perspective, the object of meditation is more important than the process of concentration itself. If gaining concentration is your only goal in meditation, you can achieve that by focusing your mind on any object that attracts you. But if the inward journey to the source of consciousness is the goal, then having a divine object which is intrinsically connected with the source will lead your mind to that source.

Spiritual lore contains countless tales of meditators who gained enormous powers of concentration, either by practicing *trataka* (fixed gazing) or by focusing their mind on an attractive object. Such meditators attained great powers of concentration, but they were not transformed. They remained prey to ignorance and all the pains and miseries that originate from it—egoism, attachment, aversion, and fear.

If you meditate on a mantra, you may not notice an instantaneous improvement in your concentration (although your concentration is bound to improve to some degree). But self-transformation and the unfoldment of higher virtues, such as love, compassion, and tolerance, are inevitable.

How can I learn a mantra?

A mantra is given rather than learned. It is passed directly from teacher to student in a process called mantra initiation. Only someone who has practiced mantra meditation, studied the science of mantra, and—most important of all—been directed by their own teacher to initiate students can give mantra initiation.

I would caution against rushing into mantra initiation. There are many reasons for this, but the major one is that if you have any lingering idea that yoga is a religious practice, you may create an internal conflict with your religious background and views by receiving mantra initiation. Practice instead with the sound "so hum." Meanwhile, keep expanding your understanding of what a mantra is and why it will help you. When you find yourself comfortable with a teacher and a particular yogic tradition, ask for initiation.

To use the sound "so hum" to deepen your meditation practice, bring your awareness to your breath. Observe it as it flows from your nostrils to your heart center with the inhalation. Mentally listen to the sound "so" as you inhale. With the exhalation, observe your breath as it flows from your heart center back to your nostrils and listen to the sound "hum." When you find your thoughts straying, gently but firmly return your attention to your breath and the sound.

Why not choose a mantra for myself instead of seeking a formal initiation?

There are thousands of books on any subject you can think of; yet people still undergo formal education. Similarly, it is necessary to undergo proper training and discipline in the practice of yoga. Proper training begins with formal initiation.

It is impossible for a novice to figure out which mantra is best. That is one reason for not choosing your own mantra. Another is that the teacher directly sows the seed of spiritual wisdom in the heart of the student through the process of initiation. With the passage of time, as the student practices, the seed sprouts, grows, and yields its fruit. If someone works very hard, it is possible to gain some intellectual knowledge of mantra science, but when a mantra is received through proper initiation, it illuminates the whole being, not only the intellect.

In most traditions, mantra initiation is a process, not a one-time event. The scriptures call this initiation *krama diksha.* Often a teacher will give a *bija* mantra, a seed syllable, as the first step. Then as the student practices, the teacher will impart additional *bija* mantras or a specific mantra central to that particular tradition.

Initiation also is a way to establish the intimate relationship between student and teacher, which is necessary in the ongoing process of spiritual unfoldment. Mantra initiation is a big commitment on the part of both teacher and student. Therefore I suggest that before undertaking this commitment you first overcome your own skepticism and doubt. Watch your natural inclinations and study the intensity of your desire to know your true self. That will help you know when the right time has come for receiving a mantra. If you're honest with yourself about what you're looking for in life, the voice of your heart will tell you whether you've found the right tradition and the right teacher.

Q I know several mantras in addition to my personal mantra. Does it matter which one I use?

The word *mantra* means "that which protects," and one mantra is enough. Sometimes a teacher will tell you to do a practice with a mantra other than your personal mantra. Such practices usually involve doing a certain number of repetitions of that mantra or working with it for a specific period of time. When you've completed the practice, you return to your personal mantra. The following story is instructive:

Once two students were doing mantra practices. They decided to test their mantras and find out if the power of these mantras really did protect them. They climbed a tall tree and crawled out on a branch. The first student jumped. He was using only his personal mantra, and landed unharmed. But as the second student was about to jump, he stopped and thought, "Should I use the first mantra that was given to me? But the second mantra was given later, so it must be more advanced. And then there's a third mantra that I learned from a tape, and I read in a book somewhere that it burns all karmas, so it must be very special." So he repeated the last two mantras, but still kept the first in mind. His mind couldn't decide which one to hold on to, so when he jumped, he broke both legs and his collarbone.

One mantra, one guru, one wife, one husband—this is the surest way to lead a happy life.

Q **I've heard that for a mantra to show its effect, it has to be said in the correct way. At my age I'm never going to be able to learn to pronounce a Sanskrit mantra perfectly, so where does that leave me?**

When you are initiated by a person who is authorized by the tradition, there is no way that you can mispronounce your mantra. At the time of initiation the mantra is placed in the deepest recesses of your heart. Your vocal organs may have a hard time voicing it, your tongue may have a hard time pronouncing it, but the mantra is repeating itself somewhere deep in your heart. Let it happen.

A mantra is the divine sound, which is being vibrated in every single cell of your body. The eternal sound of the mantra is inseparable from your life-force—it is ringing in the interior of your mind and heart whether you are aware of it or not.

Once the teacher connects you to the divine source within you, the mantra cannot be incorrect. This is true even if you received the mantra from someone who did not know how to pronounce it properly. If your heart and mind are in the right place, if you are sincere and honest but somehow ended up with a teacher who did not know how to pronounce the mantra properly, the true teacher, who dwells in your own heart, corrects it. When we do something with a good heart, God takes care of us and guides us. How can the heart be incorrect?

So once you have received a mantra, try your best to pronounce it as well as you can, then leave the rest to the One who dwells in your heart, the One who witnesses every single thought, word, and action and guides you in the right direction.

Should I coordinate mantras other than "so hum" with the breath?

If you are an ex-smoker or have in some other way formed the habit of shallow breathing or chest breathing, it is better to coordinate the mantra and breath, thus regulating the motion of the lungs. This will help you establish a natural pattern of deep, diaphragmatic breathing. You'll notice a cleansing effect, as well as increased physical and emotional stability. While coordinating the mantra with the breath, however, make sure that the sound of the mantra is not creating a jerkiness in the flow of your breath.

For mantras other than "so hum," you have to be very careful about breath/mantra coordination. Although some mantras must be coordinated with the breath in order to take the mind inward, most mantras will create some jerkiness in the breath if you try to coordinate the two. Many mantras are too long, or their vibratory pattern does not match the pattern of the breath. Therefore it's best to seek advice from the person who initiated you, or from someone else truly knowledgeable in the science of mantra.

What's the difference between meditation and japa?

The process of meditation and japa are similar but not the same. During meditation you are not aware of the number of mantra repetitions nor the pace at which you are repeating the mantra. In fact, if you are meditating, you don't repeat your mantra; you simply listen to it. Deep within, you are still. The sound of your mantra is already there and you simply listen to it quietly. You listen so attentively and peacefully that you are not aware of any thought other than the continuous flow of your mantra. That's the ideal, or let's say, that's what should be happening during mantra meditation.

But an untrained, undisciplined mind has a hard time remaining still and attending only to the mantra. The mind begins making excuses: "Oh boy, I forgot to write that letter!" "I should look at today's stock market report," and so forth. It finds a reason to do other than what it has been told to do, and to be somewhere other than where it is supposed to be. In the beginning stages of self-discipline and self-transformation it's best not to fight with the mind. Rather, skillfully give it more than one object to contemplate.

Japa, remembering the mantra with mala beads, is a way to constructively provide your mind with more than one object. During japa you use the same pose that you would use for meditation. Sit in a chair or cross-legged on the floor, with the head, neck, and trunk straight. Place your hands on your knees, and hold your mala with your fingers. Hold the mala so that your fingers, palms, hands, arms, and shoulders are free of tension while you are moving the beads. Usually you move the beads only with the thumb, middle finger, and ring finger, because this seems to be the most relaxing method.

Remember your mantra as silently as possible while you move the beads. The pace at which you remember the mantra and move the beads should be fully coordinated. After a few days or weeks of japa your fingers become adjusted to the beads and move them effortlessly. Remember, you don't move a bead unless you repeat the mantra, and you do not repeat the mantra without moving a bead. If the mind starts wandering, the mala is sure to stop or at least slow down. This immediately reminds you that your mind is wandering. On the other hand, the moment you become lazy or drowsy, your fingers become less active, while the call of your mantra turns your attention to the beads.

Mala and mind form a partnership; they help and motivate each other. The result is that you remember your mantra with fewer distractions and disturbances. (Moving the beads does create some degree of distraction; however, that is still better than having the mind wander from one object to another ceaselessly.)

While doing japa you might start touching a deep state of meditation, so that moving the beads seems to be a lot of work. If your posture is correct and the mala and fingers are really familiar with each other and do not require even the slightest attention from your mind, then japa with the mala continues, although you are neither aware of the beads nor of the process of moving them. However, it is rare to experience such a meditative state of mind while doing japa. Usually before the mind slips into deep meditation it goes through a state of natural disinterestedness in moving the beads. In that case, let your mala drop and allow your mind to dive into the depths of that meditative joy and stillness. This state may not last long, and your mind may soon start traveling to other thoughts. The moment you realize that is happening, gently pick up your mala and resume your japa.

This journey—from japa to meditation and back to japa—is the best way to train and discipline the mind for the inward journey without fighting with your habit patterns. In your own personal practice, observe yourself and see whether it is better to concentrate on japa or meditation.

Q **Should I always practice with mala beads? Should I practice japa for a while before committing myself to a longer period of meditation?**

Immediately after you have been initiated into a mantra, it's good to practice with a mala, especially if the mantra is relatively long or consists of sounds that are unfamiliar. It takes a while for the mantra to create a strong groove in your mind; before that happens, you have to make a conscious effort to repeat it and meditate on it.

To step into the practice of meditation systematically, it's best to design a gradually increasing course of japa (a specific number of repetitions of your mantra within a certain number of weeks or months). For example, the first week after initiation commit yourself to doing one round of japa with your mala every day. This is 108 repetitions, and it may take only five minutes to complete. Then, if you have time and enjoy your practice, continue listening to your mantra without using the beads.

The next week you can do two rounds, the third week three rounds, and so forth. Expand your practice until you reach either the limits of your capacity or the limits of the time you have available.

Maintain your practice at that level for three months. Then one day try to meditate on your mantra for the entire period without using your beads. Watch how your mind behaves. If you notice that you want to open your eyes or look at your watch to see the time, you need to keep doing japa.

Practicing japa prepares a solid ground for meditation. The more you practice japa, the more solid the ground.

Q Is there a particular way to hold a mala? Does it make any difference if I hold it in my left hand or my right hand?

Make a circle by lightly touching the tip of the thumb to the tip of the ring finger. Hold the mala with the thumb and the third finger, while gently supporting it with the ring finger. You may use any of these three fingers to turn the beads. However, turning the beads with the thumb seems to be the easiest. For some reason, the scriptures advise us not to use the index finger for doing japa.

If you are doing japa for a short period of time, hold the mala in front of the region of the heart. In a prolonged practice, however, this method becomes tiresome and can create tension in your shoulders. When that happens, part of your mind automatically goes to the shoulder and upper arm so you are no longer focusing one-pointedly on the mantra. Furthermore, if your mala is made of heavy beads, the weight will be a distraction. Therefore keep your hands on your knees or somewhere on your thighs and do your japa comfortably.

This principle of being comfortable and minimizing distractions also applies to the question of whether to hold the mala in the left hand or the right. If you are left-handed, it is usually easier to hold the mala and move the beads with your left hand; otherwise, use your right hand.

Q When I'm in a meditative state I feel like I'm not repeating the mantra clearly. Some syllables seem to be missing. Is it important to remember every syllable of the mantra distinctly, with the same clarity as it is pronounced verbally?

In a deep state of concentration only the feeling of the presence of the mantra remains; the individual syllables may be blurred. Your logical mind, which perceives things in a linear order, merges into pure, non-objective awareness and comprehends things spontaneously in totality, rather than in segments. That's why, in this state of awareness, mantra remains, but the mind, absorbed as it is in non-objective awareness, doesn't register every single syllable or phoneme.

If this happens, it's wonderful—but make sure this experience comes from deep meditation and is not simply the result of spaciness. There's a subtle line between merging into non-dualistic, non-objective awareness and sinking into oblivion. The sense of delight—the feeling that the burden of your mind is being lifted—is a sign of deep meditation. During deep meditation your whole body is charged with the divine energy of your mantra. Afterwards, you feel like a child of bliss—a princess or prince of freedom. In contrast, if you were just spacing out, your head will feel completely empty. You do not gain knowledge from a spacey state and you don't return a wiser person, as you do from a deep state of meditation.

Until you have reached a deep state of meditation make a conscious effort to remember every single syllable of your mantra distinctly. Gradually articulation of the mantra becomes secondary, and *bhava* (pure feeling) takes over. Just let it happen.

Q I have heard you and other teachers speak of the joy that comes in meditation once the mind begins to be absorbed in the mantra. I have been meditating for five years and my mind shows no signs of being led by the mantra. I doubt that I have been able to remember my mantra for more than ten or fifteen seconds at a time without other thoughts intruding. For me, meditation is not a joy, but a losing battle. Willing myself to concentrate on the mantra when I sit for meditation every morning doesn't work. Are there techniques I can practice to improve my concentration and strengthen my resolve to remember my mantra?

You are not the only person facing this problem—this is an experience a great number of seekers have in common. There is no need of abandoning your mantra meditation and trying other techniques, because this virus of frustration will infect those techniques too. It is better to try to understand the basic cause of this problem and resolve it.

You have not yet been convinced of the importance of going inward because you do not understand the value of the everlasting wealth within. Nor have you grasped the role of mantra in leading you inward and unveiling that wealth. Because of the shallowness of your knowledge regarding your mantra, you have not yet fallen in love with it. In the back of your mind you still feel that the mantra is merely a device for focusing your mind. You are not fully convinced that the mantra is actually the Lord of Life, the Word that existed in the beginning of creation, was with God, and is God.

There may be several reasons why you do not feel that the mantra is a living reality in the form of sound. These days there are many people running around giving mantras, and there are numerous books cataloguing mantras. You can easily get a mantra from a book, from a tape, or from mantra initiators for somewhere between ten dollars and a thousand dollars. So what's the big deal?

In the commercial atmosphere that has developed in the yoga community, it is quite natural to treat a mantra superficially. When we do that, meditation on a mantra does not transform our attitude, but forces us to remain active in the process of remembering the mantra on a technical level. This prevents us from cultivating *bhava* (feeling).

A meditation without bhava is too weak to face the challenges posed by our conscious and unconscious minds. When you understand that the Divine Being has entered the inner chamber of your heart in the form of the mantra and that you are fortunate to be there to attend that Divine Being, who has blessed the cave of your heart so graciously and lovingly, you will not entertain other thoughts, feelings, and memories during your meditation.

Let me give you an example. Suppose you are an unsuccessful, but ambitious, politician. You have only the faintest influence over the people of your county, yet you dream of becoming the president of the United States. You attend city council meetings and belong to the Rotary Club, but you have no access to higher political circles.

However, after years of hard work, skillful strategic planning, and a little luck you have managed to get the president of the United States to accept an invitation to make an appearance in your town. He has also accepted the invitation to stop by your home afterward for a cup of tea. This is a real coup, as it is understood that he is a very busy man and that the only reason he would give you fifteen minutes of his time is that you are a valuable person.

After the public appearance, he arrives at your home. You realize that you are incredibly fortunate. While you are talking to him about the possibility of his support of your candidacy for the congressional seat in your district, you notice the mailman driving up. Will you leave the president to get your mail because it might contain some catalogues? Is junk mail more important than the president?

Similarly, if you really come to understand that all the thoughts, memories, anxieties, and emotions that pop up during your meditation have the same value as the junk mail that fills your mailbox every day, you will never, ever allow your mind to be distracted. You will feel fortunate to attend your mantra. Therefore continue studying, keep gaining knowledge about the purpose of life, and continue to expand your understanding regarding the mantra and the state of tranquility that it induces.

What do you mean when you say, "Remember your mantra along with its meaning"?

This means do your japa with feeling. Don't let your mantra become a mechanical repetition in your head. Dry repetition without feeling leads to boredom, because the mind perceives it as monotonous. If your mantra has a literal meaning, then contemplate on that meaning as part of your meditation. Ponder the meaning, relate yourself to it, and assimilate it in your heart and mind. When it matures, this contemplative exercise is transformed into pure awareness.

For some people, trying to remember a literal meaning of the mantra will disturb the process of meditation. Because the mantra is an unfamiliar sound and seems to be a word, you naturally translate its meaning into your own language. Thus there is a tendency to replace the mantra with one or more words in your native language, and then attempt to grasp its meaning from the translation. Avoid this tendency. Simply maintain the feeling.

Is a mantra effective even if it is repeated without feeling? How do you get the feeling if you don't know what the feeling is?

Feeling and the purification of the heart go together. You need both. They appear together, like a sprout and the shadow of a sprout. The mantra is the seed that sprouts. The feeling is the shadow that follows the sprout of purification. Keep doing your mantra meditation sincerely and regularly. It will sprout naturally one day; both the purification and the feeling will grow together.

You are already inspired and have a somewhat purified heart; that's why you started practicing mantra meditation. But keep making efforts to purify yourself further by cultivating sattvic qualities in your thoughts, speech, and actions. Try to slow down and eliminate useless talk. Do your best not to hurt yourself and others. Even in your jokes, try to eliminate foul language. Watch your diet. This is the way to purification.

A purified mind and heart are like a blossoming flower. Feeling is the nectar. They go together. When the flower blossoms, it sends an invitation to all the nectar lovers. Thus mantra meditation, accompanied with feeling and purification, sends an invitation to the Lord of Life, the Supreme Being. The moment of union that comes when the mantra fully blooms is called *samadhi,* the state of ecstasy.

Q **I have heard meditation students who are more experienced than I am talking about doing a practice called *purash charana.* What is it?**

Purash means "first" and *charana* means "step." Thus purash charana is the first step toward the experience of the Divine. When you undertake a purash charana you make a commitment to recite a mantra a specific number of times within a specific period of time. The number of repetitions depends on the mantra. A purash charana of the *gayatri* or *maha mrityunjaya* mantra, for example, is usually 125,000 repetitions. A mala has 108 beads, so if you do 10 rounds a day it will take you 125 days to complete the practice. If you do 5 rounds a day, you will complete the practice in 250 days. (Even though the mala has 108 beads, you take only 100 repetitions into account because traditionally 8 repetitions out of the 108 are dedicated to honor the force that enables us to complete a round.)

Once you have developed a regular meditation practice you impose the discipline of a purash charana on yourself as a means of strengthening your self-discipline and subduing the mind's deceptive tendencies. When you make a commitment to repeat your mantra a certain number of times each day, you are much less likely to let the mind play tricks on you by coaxing you to cut your practice short today and do a longer practice tomorrow. Without a purash charana the mind might say, "Well, I did enough today" or "I have lots of work today; I'll catch up tomorrow." With a purash charana, you don't allow your mind to deceive you: you attend your purash charana, and your purash charana attends you. As a result, one day you and your mantra become good friends.

When you commit yourself to a purash charana, you are undertaking a higher practice. The higher the practice, the more intense the need for self-observation. So when you undertake a purash charana, it is important to prepare yourself to confront bigger temptations and to strengthen your resolve not to be swayed or distracted from your purpose.

What do you mean by temptations? Why would they become stronger when a person undertakes a purash charana?

The logic is simple: the higher the peaks, the deeper the valleys. Once you have become established in your daily meditation, there is no challenge—it becomes a routine part of your life. The issues you confront are usually related to your daily life and you manage them as a matter of course. But once you undertake a purash charana (for example, repeating the *gayatri* mantra 125,000 times within 125 days) you will find yourself facing bigger challenges. The part of you that rebels against self-discipline will show up. You will be caught in the war between your power of determination and your lack of self-confidence, between your power of resolution and your tendency to procrastinate.

The urge to go against our determination is a hidden tendency that looks for an excuse to manifest. Anything that serves as an excuse is a form of temptation. In the normal course of practice we have no chance to observe this tendency in ourselves because unless we present ourselves with a challenge it remains dormant. By undertaking a purash charana we impose a stricter than normal discipline on ourselves, thereby challenging our ingrained habits. To prevail we need God's grace, the blessings of the saints, firm conviction, and strong willpower.

Q Can anyone undertake the practice of a purash charana? And if so, how do I know what level of japa I should undertake?

It is best to undertake such a practice only after you have established a regular schedule and formed the habit of eating, sleeping, and meditating according to an established routine. Regularity is the most important factor in such a practice. To understand why, let us take a fruit tree as an example. After the seed has been planted, it first sprouts and then eventually grows into a tree. Before it can produce fruit a specific amount of time must pass, and further, the tree must be exposed to a certain amount of light and heat and consume a certain amount of nutrients and water. If it does not get these elements in appropriate amounts and at the appropriate time, the tree's growth will be stunted; it may even die before reaching maturity. Light cannot be substituted for water; heat cannot be substituted for nutrients. If it is deprived of the proper amount of light for months and is suddenly bombarded by intense light for days at a time, what will happen to that poor tree?

When we undertake a purash charana we are planting a spiritual tree that must be nurtured and encouraged through steady, regular practice. Once you are sure that your schedule is well-established and that you will neither starve nor overfeed your spiritual plant, go ahead and undertake a purash charana. As to how large a purash charana you should undertake, that depends on how long your mantra is, what your capacities are, and how much time you have at your disposal. The subtle but crucial details of how to sow the seed and tend the plant once it begins to grow must come from an expert gardener—a spiritual teacher.

Q I have heard that there are certain mantras which can help us destroy (or at least attenuate) negative tendencies while bringing forth positive tendencies to counteract the negative ones. What are these mantras?

According to the sages there are two ways of overcoming obstacles to our spiritual unfoldment: overcoming our weaknesses and thereby becoming strong, or strengthening that part of us which is already strong and thereby overcoming our weaknesses. The first method is predominantly cleansing and the other predominantly nourishing. In the Vedic tradition the two best-known and most widely practiced mantras are the *gayatri* mantra and the *maha mrityunjaya* mantra. The gayatri mantra focuses on cleansing and is one of the most potent mantras for overcoming weakness, while the maha mrityunjaya mantra focuses on healing and is one of the most powerful strengthening mantras. Although they approach the goal differently, both are given for the purpose of eliminating obstacles. Ultimately they have the same result.

The gayatri mantra works with karmic impurities, the subtle impressions of our mind that are the source of negative thinking patterns. This mantra calms mental noise, washes off karmic impurities, purifies the ego, sharpens the intellect, and illuminates our inner being. It connects us with the inner teacher so that we become more receptive to inner guidance and illumination. This mantra is particularly suitable for those who are struggling with confusion, doubt, skepticism, lack of self-trust, and lack of direction.

The maha mrityunjaya mantra is a healing and nourishing mantra. By awakening the inner healing force, it strengthens our power of will, knowledge, and action. It helps us to receive and assimilate the nourishment from food and herbs as well as from the spiritual disciplines we have undertaken. This mantra is often given to those who are struggling with low energy, a sense of hopelessness, grief, or illness, as well as from lack of enthusiasm, courage, and determination. It is particularly suitable for those in the healing professions, as it helps prevent burnout by continually replacing the healing energy that a healer transfers to the patient.

The scriptures call the gayatri mantra "the mother of the Vedas" and the maha mrityunjaya mantra "the heart of the Vedas." Many practitioners combine the two mantras to experience optimal progress. Scriptures such as *Gayatri Panchanga* and *Netra Tantra* describe the general and specific techniques of meditating on these mantras for unique spiritual results.

FREEDOM FROM MISERY

Q I have been trying to understand how misery arises. What is the cause of the unhappiness we see all around us?

The scriptures tell us that the mind is the source of both misery and happiness. Even though no one wants to be miserable, we seem unable to rid ourselves of unhappiness. We run in all directions trying to discover the source of our suffering and remove it, but we fail because we are not able to accept the truth: the source of our displeasure is within us. We prefer to attribute the cause of our problems to an external source.

The mind is adept at perceiving what lies in the external world, but it does not know how to turn itself inward and see what is inside. Even if we suspect that the source of our unhappiness is within and that we need to work with our own mind and heart, we still try to find an external cause. It is easy to find validation for doing so—the whole world operates this way—but deep down we know that our misery is self-created. Persisting in our attempts to locate our unhappiness elsewhere only makes matters worse.

The atman, our inner self, is ever awake. It is always with us—telling us what is true and what is untrue, what is right and what is not right. But fear, lack of discipline, absence of self-confidence, and the habit of leaning on others causes us to ignore it. Every time our inner self counsels us to avoid a harmful action and we take that action anyway, we feel guilty. We tell ourselves we will not make the same mistake again—but driven by our inner weaknesses, by our habit patterns, or by social pressure, we repeat it. Again our inner voice says, "Hey, don't be foolish. Why are you inviting misery for yourself?" We hear it—and yet we make the same mistake again. This time we feel even guiltier. We keep piling guilt upon guilt, going against the inner voice, and repeating our mistakes over and over. This leads to self-condemnation, and eventually the mind becomes so cluttered and so noisy that it drowns out the voice of the soul.

Living with guilt and self-condemnation is intensely uncomfortable. So what do we do? If we have not learned to turn the mind inward, we turn it outward and look for an excuse to blame someone else. Blaming people and external circumstances provides momentary relief, which is why we cultivate the habit of finding all kinds of problems in the external world. We think: "He's a bad person ... She's unfair ... Had those hateful people not done what they did, my life would be delightful ... Other people are nasty ... The world is ugly and cruel ..." Once this habit is well-established we begin to build a wall and isolate ourselves from others. But that fails to bring either peace or happiness. We begin to lose self-respect and finally isolate ourselves from ourselves. Now our misery is complete.

Q **How can I learn to put an end to this self-created misery?**

All problems, pains, and other miseries originate in the mind. The only way to overcome misery is to make the mind composed and peaceful. The scriptures tell us to protect our mind. And further, they say that once the mind is protected we will find safety and protection everywhere.

A mind governed by fear becomes defensive. As part of its self-defense it reacts violently, hurting itself and others in the process. The rules imposed by our society and the laws imposed by our government may offer short-term ways to reduce the causes of misery in the external world, but ultimately we, as individuals, have to take responsibility for eradicating the agony rooted in the depths of our own mind. That is why the scriptures talk about the process of self-transformation, and tell us that it is only through self-transformation that we can expect reformation and improvement in our external environment.

The process of overcoming misery begins with reflection on the purpose and meaning of life. Understanding this purpose intellectually creates an interest in finding it, and through further self-reflection, contemplation, and self-inquiry we nurture this interest. Eventually it matures into a burning desire to find the meaning and purpose of life here and now instead of postponing our happiness for tomorrow. Even the simple realization "I am on the path of self-discovery and freedom" becomes a source of joy, enthusiasm, and self-motivation, and we find delight in working toward that goal.

In other words, the first step to overcoming misery is to realize that there is a higher purpose and meaning in life. Everything—all experiences and objects—is simply a means to achieving this goal. As long as we know this, we will not become attached to the means but will learn how to skillfully use them to achieve the end.

The second step is to understand that happiness is the foundation for all success, both worldly and spiritual, and that happiness is a virtue of your own mind; it is your own creation. If you expect some achievement to make you happy, you will always be disappointed. Happiness comes from a decision. You can be happy only when you decide to be happy. If your happiness is conditional, it vanishes when that condition is removed. For example, if you are relying on your spouse to make you happy, sooner or later you will be miserable. If you expect happiness from your children, your wealth, your friends, or your property, you are going to be disappointed sooner or later because everything changes. Just as you are interested in your happiness, others are interested in their happiness. Just as you think others are the objects of your happiness, they think you are the object of their happiness. As long as you fulfill their desires they respect you, but when you do not they consider you useless.

Don't let this knowledge disappoint you. This is the nature of the world. But when you learn to live in the world joyfully and perform your duties skillfully and lovingly with full realization that you own nothing, you don't create an ocean of misery for yourself to drown in. Decide to be happy no matter what comes. When someone you love leaves you or you lose a material object you value, stick to that decision. Then you will have inner peace.

With a peaceful mind continue walking on the path. Make the best use of the resources around you, without fear or attachment. Discard useless memories and anxieties that haunt your mind and do no good. Remind yourself every day that you are on a mission to know who you are, why you came to this world, and what you are supposed to learn. How far have you succeeded in knowing that which is to be known? If you had to drop your body at this very moment, would you have any regrets? This simple contemplation will help you stay on the path and attain freedom from all misery.

Q **I have read that this whole world is maya—illusion— and we must get rid of it if we ever hope to be eternally happy. Can you explain maya? As part of this world, aren't we also part of maya?**

Frankly, this maya business is as confusing as confusion itself. The doctrine of maya in its fully developed form comes from one of the most influential teachers in Indian history, Shankaracharya, who maintained that Brahman, Absolute Truth, is the only existent reality. Brahman alone exists. To explain the existence of this world, Shankaracharya puts forth the concept of maya, and states clearly that it does not exist. Yet he also claims that it is through the twofold function of maya—called *avarana shakti* (the power to veil) and *vikshepa shakti* (the power to project)—that this world comes into existence. In other words, this mysterious maya, which does not exist, somehow exerts her veiling power, thereby hiding Brahman, the

Absolute Reality; by exerting her power of projection, maya paints the illusion of the world on the canvas of non-existence. Thus, the world appears. But how can ordinary people, like us, manage to grasp that a non-existent maya can put a thick veil on Brahman? What could be more confusing?

In the past twelve hundred years a host of philosophers have grappled with this question. Some have offered arguments in favor of the doctrine of maya, and some have attempted to refute it. In doing so they have produced hundreds of texts, yet the concept of maya remains as impenetrable as ever.

To my knowledge, there are only two groups of philosophers, both tantric in nature, who have not gotten entangled in the confusing net of maya. They are the tantric masters belonging to the traditions of Kashmir Shaivism and Sri Vidya. These masters have skillfully eluded this net simply by regarding maya as Maya Shakti. They maintain that maya is not illusion; nor is maya non-existent. Rather, it is Shakti, the creative energy of Brahman. (In these two schools Brahman is also known by many other names: Shiva, Bhairava, Yamala, etc.) This Shakti, or creative energy, is intrinsic to Brahman, and therefore it is not different from Brahman. In this sense Brahman can be compared to a powerhouse of infinite capacity, and Shakti to the power contained in this powerhouse and flowing from it. An infinite number of universes spontaneously flow forth from this powerhouse, and according to these tantrics it is totally irrelevant whether the world is created by Brahman or by Shakti, or whether the world evolves from Brahman or from Shakti—Maya Shakti and Brahman are one and the same.

Now let us look at ourselves and the world, first in the light of the doctrine of maya and then in the light of Maya Shakti. It is discouraging to believe that we have come from maya (illusion), and that life and the world in which we live is the product of illusion. This is the most pessimistic of all possible worldviews. If everything is maya—our body, mind, senses, temples, churches, teachers, scriptures—then where can we turn? What tools and means are left to transcend this maya? This doctrine of maya becomes a source of endless questions and does not offer a single answer.

By choosing to regard maya as Maya Shakti, however, all such questions vanish. Brahman is divine; so is its intrinsic creative energy, Maya Shakti. Just as a mother plays hide and seek with her child, Maya Shakti plays hide and seek with us. By using her veiling power *(avarana shakti)* she hides herself, and by using her power of projection *(vikshepa shakti)* she creates an illusionary appearance of the world in which we try to find her. To those who understand and embrace this philosophy, this world is a divine playground. They know that throughout this game of hide and seek, the Divine Mother and her "soul" (Brahman) is hidden here, somewhere. They experience joy while seeking, and immerse themselves in joy when the seeking is over.

When I was a young man struggling with the concept of maya, I complained a lot. To me, the world was a miserable place. But ever since I realized that Maya Shakti is my mother, full of love and compassion, I have had no complaint about the world within me or outside me. What a relief!

Q If the Divine Mother herself manifests in the form of the universe, how do you account for the existence of evil?

In *shakti sadhana,* in which the Divine Mother is considered to be the source of all that exists, there is no evil. This beautiful world evolves from her, as do we, her children. The whole universe is the manifestation of the Divine Mother, who is the embodiment of beauty and bliss. Therefore, according to this school of tantra, the world is saturated with beauty and joy.

To explain the relationship between the Divine Mother and the world, practitioners of shakti sadhana use the analogy of the ocean and its waves. The Divine Mother is the ocean of beauty and bliss; the world and everything that exists in it are the waves. In essence, there is no difference between the ocean and the waves that arise from it and subside in it. The Divine Mother is also known as Sri, the Auspicious One. The world that manifests from her and exists in her can only be auspicious. Therefore to these tantrics the very idea of evil is totally groundless.

Q In the course of my life I have encountered people whose minds were filled with evil. The *idea* of evil may be groundless, as you say, yet evil obviously exists.

The fact that someone's mind is filled with evil does not mean that evil really exists. The tantrics hold that belief in evil is a form of ignorance—a false belief. The power of false belief is well-documented in the realm of psychology—it is one of the major causes of insanity. According to tantrics, believing in evil and struggling to attain freedom from it is spiritual insanity.

Still, as you point out, this form of insanity is not uncommon, and for that reason tantric masters have come up with a variety of spiritual formulas to cure it. Some felt it was better not to further confuse the victims by telling them that evil does not exist, and they developed the system of exorcism—which implies that evil exists and there is a way to remove it. In other words, they used one false belief to get rid of another.

Other tantrics chose the path of transformation. Like the exorcists, they did not attempt to contradict the belief in the existence of evil; they maintained that evil can be transformed into good. Evil is evil only if it harms you. If you are wise and skillful, and if you are equipped with insight and inner strength, you can transform your self-created evil into a benevolent friend. This second approach is the better of the two. In this process, you are simply working with your own creative energy, and thus the energy which, due to your ignorance and negligence, had been manifesting as evil is now manifesting as divine. This is what the practitioners of Sri Vidya in the tantric tradition try to accomplish. According to this scheme, the forces of anger, hatred, jealousy, lust, and so on are worshipped as manifestations of the Divine. To such tantrics, these forces are not evil, nor are they obstacles, and therefore one does not have to get rid of them.

There are still other tantric masters who dismiss the idea of evil altogether. They maintain that whatever you think is evil does not exist to begin with. In their teachings, they use the example of someone who is terrified of snakes. While he is walking in the darkness, this snake-phobic person suddenly panics when he sees what he thinks is a snake. He freezes in terror; he has no courage to continue walking. Along comes the tantric therapist, who immediately shows that his fear is baseless. The master lights a torch, picks up the object which the poor fellow thought was a snake, and shows him that it is only a rope. Such masters lead their students to the understanding that evil is only as real as the snake in the rope.

Q **In my reading I have come across phrases such as "piercing the veil of maya" and "the chakras have seals over them." To me, this implies that we are not supposed to remove the veil or unseal the chakras. Otherwise, why would God have veiled maya and sealed the chakras?**

God is perfect. She is the master of all the forces. There are no veils hiding God's beauty, which is why it is said that in him, beauty is unsurpassed. If God were human, all of her chakras would be completely opened because all the powers in the universe are at her command. This beautiful and perfect God created us in his own image. Creation of the perfect can never be imperfect. How can one who does not have any veils veil her own children? How can God seal our chakras and keep his own chakras open?

This compassionate and omniscient God did not create misery for us, yet we are miserable. Neither did God create our veils, yet we are veiled; nor seal chakras, yet our chakras are sealed. All traditions in the world recognize this and attempt to eliminate misery, tear the veil of ignorance, and unfold the dormant energy which lies within us. The problem is that our actions, motivated as they often are by greed, ego, attachment, desire, anger, hatred, jealousy, and so on, taint our mind and heart, which in turn attracts miserable conditions. It is our job to purify our mind and heart by removing the taints of greed, ego, attachment, and so on. It is also our job to tear the veil of ignorance.

God did not create the veil. Yet, because we do not know how it was created and who or what created it, religionists describe this veiling as "original sin" for the sake of convenience. Yogis do not use this term. Rather, they call it indescribable, beginningless *avidya* (ignorance). According to them it is fruitless to discuss how, when, where, and why ignorance came into being. These are imponderables and it is too late to brood on them. Yogis recognize the pressing need to discover how to end this ignorance. They are firm in the conviction that God is delighted to see her children—you and me—working to eliminate ignorance. This endeavor to root out ignorance is *bhakti* (love for, and devotion to, God). Working toward the elimination of ignorance and cultivating divine qualities is the truest form of worshipping God.

Joy is our nature. We are blessed with an intrinsic abundance of joy. We enter this world endowed with bliss and with the freedom to enjoy it simultaneously at all seven levels of our existence, known as the seven chakras. Fear, insecurity, and defense mechanisms engendered by our primitive instincts seal our lowest chakra, located at the base of the spine. A host of cravings, with the sexual urge heading the list, blocks the second chakra. The third chakra, at the navel center, is blocked by power issues, such as ambition and the desire to dominate others. Hatred, duality, and selfishness seal the fourth chakra, the heart center. Self-condemnation, lack of confidence, apathy, and a negative attitude toward oneself and the external world cause blockage in the fifth, or throat, chakra. The sixth chakra, at the center between the eyebrows, is partially dammed by our uncontrolled thoughts, emotions, and feelings. Ignorance, which is too subtle to be described in words, blocks the pathway that leads to the seventh chakra, at the crown of the head.

The different paths of yoga each offer a unique approach to attenuating and eventually eliminating the impurities that block these chakras so that we can enjoy the infinite potentials intrinsic to us. Of these paths, kundalini yoga incorporates the most direct techniques for unblocking the chakras. According to kundalini yogis, the way to serve God is to purify and unlock the gifts of the Divine, which are deposited at these different chakras. In so doing, we allow the bodies we inhabit to be transformed into shrines.

KARMA: THE MAKER OF DESTINY

Q The word *karma* is used loosely these days. What is its actual meaning?

Karma is the law of cause and effect, action and reaction: as you sow, so shall you reap.

Q How does karma come into being?

Subtle impressions of all our actions—mental, verbal, and physical—are stored in the mind in the form of memories. When we keep performing the same actions, we reinforce these memories. At some point they become so strong that they turn into habits and start dictating our behavior.

As long as we remember the cause of these habits and the consequences of giving in to them, we can change them. If our power of will and determination is strong and we have a fervent desire to overcome our habits, we can gradually erase the habit patterns until they again become simple memories.

But through constant reinforcement some habits become so strong that they create deep grooves, not only in the conscious mind but also in the nervous and glandular systems, our musculature, and the senses, and reach all the way into the unconscious mind. These strong impressions of actions, having the unconscious mind as their domain, influence the entire personality. When powerful impressions are created by taking potent substances, such as psychoactive drugs, we use the term "addiction." We call other strong impressions, which we have forgotten about with the passage of time but which have become part of the personality, "unconscious material."

In yogic literature, the name for this unconscious material is *samskara.* Samskaras are subtle impressions of our previous actions that normally are not known by our conscious mind, but which influence our present activities. Depending on the nature and characteristics of a particular samskara or group of samskaras, we find ourselves inclined toward a particular lifestyle, environment, academic discipline, type of entertainment, and so forth. For example, two children in a family have the same upbringing and exposure to the world, but one child seems to be more interested in art and music and the other is more interested in science. Although we cannot find a direct cause for these differences, yoga philosophy says that they are due to the children's samskaras.

Samskaras seem to be more powerful than the forces of our conscious mind and intellect. From deep within, the samskaras influence our mind and intellect. As a result, we often know what is right and yet do not find ourselves fully motivated to do it, just as we know what is wrong and yet, under the influence of an unknown and irresistible force, we do it anyway. Such situations reveal the conflict between our conscious understanding and our samskaras. We find ourselves being impelled by our samskaras in spite of our conscious awareness that we are failing to do something that ought to be done or doing something that ought not to be done.

The progression from action to memory, from memory to habit, from habit to compulsion, and from compulsion to samskara finally results in the formation of karma. At this stage, the samskaras (which have now become karma) are so subtle and so deeply imbedded in the recesses of the unconscious that they are completely outside of our awareness. Because we do not even know they are there, we have no means of bringing them into our conscious awareness. They have survived so long and have been so well-nourished that they are the most powerful aspects of our personality. In fact, they are the makers of our interior being. Karmas keep influencing and manipulating our body, senses, mind, ego, and intellect as long as we are alive, even though we are blind to that influence.

When the bond between the body and the mind is severed by death, they become the sole motivating factors. The journey of life after death is carried on by our karmas.

On a practical level, how do our karmas affect our lives?

Our karmas influence not only our behavior but also our surroundings and the circumstances of our relationships. Karmas are the makers of our destiny. This is why the scriptures say, "It is karma that brings us into the world." It is karma that makes us feel that someone is our soul mate. Karmic factors stir the subtle realm of providence, resulting in such events as winning a lottery or becoming the victim of a natural disaster. The most satisfactory answer to the question of why one person seems to be prosperous, healthy, and lucky while another suffers from poverty, disease, and misfortune can be found in the law of karma.

According to this law, everyone is responsible for their own actions. No one can reap the fruits of another's actions nor escape the fruits of their own actions. When we do not know the exact cause of a particular event, we call it an accident—but nothing happens accidentally. We sowed the seed of that so-called accident in the form of our previous actions, whether in this life or in a previous one.

There is no reason to blame anyone for our current problems and circumstances. Whether we know it or not, we are bound by the ropes of our own karma. It is through our karmas that we reward or punish ourselves, bind or release ourselves. Our karmas are also our innate guides; they guide us in the form of our inner inclinations, tastes, and interests.

It sounds like you are saying that people get what they deserve. In other words, victims of war and poverty have brought their misfortunes on themselves. I find this concept troubling.

According to the law of karma, our present lives are a continuation of the eternal stream of life from the point where they stopped last time. Any significant action that we are inclined to perform is an action that gathered momentum in a previous lifetime but couldn't be completed because the vehicle disintegrated before the destination was reached. Similarly, events that have a significant effect—pleasant or unpleasant—on our life are not accidental either. The seed of karma was planted long ago, but before it could grow and yield its fruit, we migrated from one body to the next. Eventually our personal karma blossoms and bears fruit. When it does, we are drawn or driven by nature to reap those fruits.

It is the law of karma that triggers our unconscious desires, attachments, and sentiments, and influences our freedom of choice at a subtle level. Under the influence of this law we are born into a particular family, raised in a particular religion, and go through myriad physical, psychological, and spiritual experiences. These events do not occur in isolation. The karmic fruits we are reaping in our present life are linked with the lives of many others. As we attempt to accomplish our major goals, we undertake many auxiliary actions, which, in most cases, involve other people. When these actions bear fruit, the lives of others are also influenced. Although the person who is the principal agent of the action reaps the greater part of the fruit, others will suffer or prosper along with that person.

The key is putting this knowledge in the right perspective. Great teachers of the law of karma yoga do not tell us to disregard others' suffering by attributing it to their karma. It is a grave mistake to discount those who appear less fortunate by thinking, "Oh well, it's their karma and who am I to interfere with the law of providence?" The law of karma should be applied to oneself and to oneself alone. Even then it must be done with a transformative attitude. This concept must not be used to judge others. If you judge others, the law of karma dictates that you will be judged.

If you are not so affected by adverse karmas as many others seem to be, then make the best use of your good karmas, which have started yielding their fruits. Sow the seeds of other good karmas for the future. One of the best ways to do that is to serve those who seem to be less fortunate than you are. Remember, do not judge anyone, for doing so is a very powerful action which will come back to haunt you.

Are we totally at the mercy of our karmas?

The answer is both yes and no. By virtue of being born as humans, we possess a more evolved body, brain, senses, and mind than do other creatures. Our innate abilities and intelligence enable us to build comfortable shelters, move from one place to another, and explore ways of improving the quality of our lives. Plants and animals don't have that privilege. But how we use this privilege is totally up to us. Making the best use of the unique gifts that distinguish us from the other forms of life here on Earth can free us from being the victim of our karmas, at least to some degree.

However, we must not forget that our knowledge, capacities, and resources are limited. Even the most knowledgeable, powerful, and resourceful person has limitations. No one has complete freedom to choose, change, and transform the circumstances that are the result of their own karmas.

We have very little freedom when it comes to working with our karmas. The greatest limitation is that our knowledge of the unconscious mind is insufficient and we do not have the means of attaining perfect control over it. We also lack knowledge about how to withdraw our senses and mind from the external world and turn them inward to penetrate the subtle mystery of *karma-shaya,* the realm of the mind-field where all karmas are deposited. Even our inclination to gain knowledge about our own mind, withdraw the senses and mind from the external world, and turn them inward is influenced by our karmas. This is the classic chicken-and-egg dilemma.

Can we know what our karmas are?

No. Definitely not—unless we are omniscient. Even if by some miracle we know our karmas related to a dozen lifetimes, that knowledge is just a drop in the bucket.

It is impossible to know what all our karmas are, nor is it necessary. All we need to know is how to get around them. Yoga masters and texts advise against brooding on the past. Live in the present. Learn to perform actions that nullify the effects of bad karmas and activate the good karmas so that they ripen faster, making the present productive.

This is the purpose of spiritual practices—the fire of knowledge that is produced by spiritual practices burns your karmas. The love and devotion that naturally unfolds as an aspirant persists in practicing a spiritual discipline protects that aspirant from the fangs of negative karmas. The spiritual practices that belong to the path of karma yoga help replace negative karmas with positive ones. Spiritual practices affect our karmic field, making our present brighter, freer, and more productive. Once this process begins, we will naturally overcome our bad karmas, whether we know what they are or not.

Undertaking spiritual practice is like turning on a flashlight to remove the darkness rather than counting how many objects lie concealed in the gloom and brooding about how long they have been lying there. Achieving freedom from the bondage of karma does not require knowing what our karmas are, how many there are, and where they are stored. What it does require is coming to know who is truly responsible for performing actions, storing them in the form of karmas, and ultimately reaping the fruits.

In other words, the only thing that matters is that you are here as a result of your karmas; it is through the karmas you are creating here and now that you can rid yourself of your past. The degree and intensity of your determination is what decides how much of your karma can be worked out, how fast, when, and how. Yoga is learning the art of performing positive actions lovingly and wholeheartedly. As the *Yoga Sutra* states, "*Yogah karmasu kaushalam*—Performing one's actions skillfully is called yoga."

Ultimately, according to yoga, the only way we can acquire freedom from karma once and for all is to acquire knowledge of the real doer of all actions and to realize that we bind ourselves by mistakenly considering ourselves to be the doer.

Q How is it possible to know which actions I must perform and which I can bypass?

Acquiring knowledge is not a one-time event, but a matter of gradual unfoldment. The first step is to understand your position in relation to your immediate environment—that is, your family, your children, your professional life, or the people you interact with most often. You need a clear understanding of the difference between your real duties and useless involvement. By "useless involvement" I mean meddling in the lives of others and—out of ignorance, attachment, and desire—regarding such meddling as your duty. Neither such actions nor the pleasant or unpleasant experiences you share with people in the course of such actions are necessarily due to your previous karmas.

If you cannot tell the difference between actions you must carry out because of the accumulated power of your karma and those that are unnecessary, you are performing your actions blindly. The fruit of such blind actions will blind you further. Eventually, you will reap the fruit of this blind karma.

Gaining a clear understanding of this process and acquiring the ability to distinguish between your duty and unnecessary actions require effort. For that, you need to sit at the feet of accomplished teachers, such as the seers of the Upanishads. But don't be discouraged. Such seers are right in the cave of your own heart, although you must have the desire and the courage to stand at the entrance to the cave and persist until you gain entrance. One of the best methods of accomplishing this is contemplation, which is a whole other subject.

The next step in gaining knowledge is to learn how to liberate yourself from the karmas that you cannot ignore. These karmas have started bearing fruit, and dealing with them is your duty. If you ignore them, they chase you. If you face them, they may frighten you or wear you down. At this stage, knowledge involves understanding that this world consists of both good and bad, pleasant and unpleasant, and that experiencing these pairs of opposites is part of life.

Once you are embroiled in a situation it is useless to brood about whether the experiences you are going through are due to your karma or whether you have involved yourself in something that could have been avoided if you had possessed sufficient knowledge. The only way to liberate yourself is to focus your energies on the higher goals of life. This will help free you from complaints about the past and worries about the future, which drain your energy to no purpose. Gaining knowledge means convincing yourself that life is not confined to the trivial issues and circumstances that confront you daily. With the help of this knowledge you can preserve the greater amount of your time and energy for moving forward, rather than wasting it in judging yourself and others on the basis of limited facts gleaned with your senses and processed through the lower mind.

I want to stress again that this knowledge is not something that you acquire in one day, nor is it true that once you have it, you don't have to work for it anymore. Constant study, contemplation, and interaction with those who live by this knowledge are required. This will allow you to refine continually and reinforce what you already know and to expand your knowledge further. This is the process of gaining spiritual maturity.

The knowledge we have been discussing is explained in spiritual texts that belong to the Sankhya and classical Yoga systems of philosophy. As this knowledge matures, it is left behind. Finally, the aspirant glimpses an even higher truth, technically known as Brahman. At the dawn of this knowledge the aspirant experiences the universal nature of the individual self, which is identical to the Universal Self. In the light of this knowledge even life's greatest calamities become irrelevant. This light is so bright that it burns all karmas in an instant. For one fortunate enough to attain this knowledge, the current karmic circumstances are like the ash of a rope that has been burned but still retains its shape. That karmic ash may look like a rope, but it no longer has the power to bind.

TRANSCENDING DEATH

Q Is there a concept in yoga that parallels the Western concept of the psyche?

Yes. The concept of the psyche is very close to the concept of the *bhokta*. This is the individual soul, which identifies itself with the mind, senses, and body and is thus affected by the experiences that the body and mind undergo. According to yoga, or more specifically to Vedanta, the word *atman* refers to the soul in its pristine state. Pure existence, consciousness, and bliss are intrinsic to the atman. It is perfect and eternal. However, due to its false identification with the body, senses, and mind, this eternal perfection is veiled; it assumes an individual identity and thus feels as though it is separate from the Universal Self. Such individuated consciousness is called *jiva*. When it loses sight of its own perfection, the jiva begins to believe that the experiences occurring in the body, senses, and mind are occurring in it. When that happens, it becomes involved in pleasant and unpleasant experiences and is known as the bhokta, the enjoyer. The bhokta is the lower self as opposed to the higher self, the atman, which knows itself as uninvolved, pure, and perfect. In Western terms, the psyche is parallel to the lower self, whereas the soul is parallel to the higher self.

Q Is it the psyche or the soul that is caught in the cycle of birth and death?

The psyche. As the scriptures clearly state, "The mind is the cause of both bondage and liberation." The fragment of consciousness that is trapped in the body, senses, and mind—the psyche—is like the fragment of the atmosphere trapped in a tiny bottle. Until this fragment of individuated consciousness re-experiences its unity with the all-pervading, omniscient consciousness, it undergoes the pain of isolation and loneliness, which it is constantly striving to overcome so that it can again experience the boundless joy it once knew.

Although it is constantly searching for the source of this joy, it is searching in the wrong place. Using the body, senses, and mind, this wisp of consciousness tries to find completion in the external world. It undergoes the constant flux of union and separation in relationships with people or objects, and in doing so accumulates attachments and aversions. Thus it journeys through life, pushed and pulled by attachment and aversion, allowing itself to remain involved in worldly relationships, looking for its completion there.

At the time of death, when the body and senses are no longer available as vehicles for continuing its search and the mind alone is its locus, the poor jiva does not know how to manage its miserable loneliness. Helplessly, it chooses to go back to the same world of pleasure and pain, loss and gain, union and separation. According to yoga, spiritual training is simply a means of reminding the jiva of its oneness with infinite consciousness so that it can stop this endless journey through the cycle of births and deaths.

Pure consciousness is eternal, all-pervasive, and omniscient. It is never in bondage and is never caught in the cycle of birth and death. It is unitary consciousness. In this state of consciousness, the sense of individuality does not exist. It is the consciousness of the psyche that mistakenly identifies itself with the body and thus becomes the victim of birth and death. When it enters a body, it feels it is born. When the body is destroyed, it feels that it dies. At the moment of enlightenment, it recognizes its folly and is liberated.

Why does the individual self identify with the mind and ego and become separated from Universal Consciousness in the first place? Does it separate itself first and then become identified with the mind and ego? Or is its identification with the mind and ego the cause of this separation?

The answer the scriptures give is itself the source of numberless questions: the Supreme Self or the Universal Being throws the blanket of illusion over itself and simultaneously veils its true nature, projecting a multitude of images. Each of these images now contains only a fragment of the Universal Self. Because a veil covers the self-shining glory of the Universal Truth, these images now appear to be born in time and space. They also seem to die.

Why the Universal Being throws this blanket of illusion over itself and projects a multitude of images is another question. The scriptures tell us that this is an eternal process. Evolution and involution, manifestation and dissolution are intrinsic attributes of the transcendental Truth.

The law of karma dictates that individual souls who already happen to be separated from Universal Consciousness must go through the cycle of birth and death. In the long journey of life, individual souls—jivas—have accumulated a vast range of karmic impressions. They cannot go back to their pristine state of unity with Universal Consciousness unless their karmic impurities have been removed, their minds have become transparent, and their egos have been dissolved. This process of washing away the karmas cannot begin if the individual soul remains suspended in death. Primordial nature—*prakriti*—pulls together all the conditions necessary for an individual soul to be reborn. Nature is stirred by the force of compassion to bring the souls to birth. Birth is the only way to attain freedom not only from death but from the entire cycle of birth and death.

This purpose can be accomplished only by making the best use of all the resources that come with being born as a human. If we somehow fail to use these resources correctly, or if we abuse them, we remain caught in the wheel of karma and perpetuate the cycle of birth and death. Therefore scriptures such as the *Isha Upanishad* tell us,

"Krato smra, kritam smra...—Know what you are doing now and know what you did in the past. By knowing that, decide the right course of action for the future and attain freedom in this lifetime."

Q What does yoga have to say about the astral body?

The concept of the astral body is more elaborate in the yoga tradition than it is in the West. In their efforts to study the totality of the human being, the yogis developed the concept of the five sheaths *(koshas)* to describe the composition of our being, layer by layer, from the grossest to the subtlest. These five layers are known as the *annamaya kosha* (the physical sheath), the *pranamaya kosha* (the energy sheath), the *manomaya kosha* (the mental sheath), the *vijñanamaya kosha* (the sheath of intellect), and the *anandamaya kosha* (the sheath of bliss). Except for the first sheath, that of the physical body, the sheaths are part of the astral body.

The yogic tradition further divides the astral body into the subtle body and the causal body. The mental and intellectual sheaths are part of the subtle body, which consists of the essence of the five gross substances—earth, water, fire, air, and ether. The subtle essences corresponding to these five gross substances are the principles of smell, taste, sight, touch, and hearing. In addition to these five principles, the subtle body also includes the forces of the five active senses, the five cognitive senses, the mind, the ego, and the intellect. Thus the subtle body is composed of these eighteen principles.

The pranic sheath is the connecting link between the subtle body and the physical body. It is through the pranic sheath that the physical body receives guidance and motivation from the subtle body. At the time of death the pranic thread is broken and the physical and subtle bodies are separated. Then the subtle body can no longer use the physical body as a vehicle and must resort to the causal body to complete its unfinished business.

The causal body is made of *vasanas,* the subtle impressions of previous deeds. They are stored in the unconscious mind, known as *chitta.* The realm of chitta, in a sense, is heaven and hell. At the time of death, when the body and brain fall away, the conscious mind with all its feelings and preferences merges into the causal body, the domain of the vasanas. In the model of the five sheaths, the astral body corresponds to the anandamaya kosha, the sheath of bliss. This is the first and foremost veil. It causes the soul to lose its awareness of its vastness and creates the illusion that its existence and bliss are confined to the domain of the vasanas. The vasanas become its total wealth.

This is the origin of the psyche, the place where its sense of disconnectedness from the universal pool of consciousness begins. Depending on which kind of vasanas are stored in this domain, the psyche trapped in the subtle body experiences heavenly pleasures, hellish misery, or a combination of both. Fed up with the miserable memories stored in the chitta and driven by a longing for sensory pleasures, the psyche again searches for a suitable physical body. And so the cycle continues.

Q **Yoga tells us that the world is illusory and atman alone is real. What does this mean?**

The world is unreal in the sense that everything in it is constantly changing. Objects of the world are transitory: they are all subject to destruction, death, and decay. It is one thing to say this, however, and quite another to really grasp it. Lack of knowledge about the real nature of objects is the source of disappointment. Usually we forget that the objects we ourselves possess are subject to destruction and decay. For example, your own body is an object and is subject to nature. When you are young, you don't really believe you will become old, although you see those around you age. When your own old age approaches, you are surprised and disappointed. You try to escape this disappointment by using herbs, medicines, and cosmetics, or by keeping yourself busy. But nothing really helps. That which you think you are is constantly slipping through your fingers.

In your relationships with others, the situation is even worse. The person who seems to love you today doesn't care for you tomorrow. Your children say they love you, but eventually they marry and devote themselves to their spouses and children. You are left alone with your own I-am-ness—which is undependable because it is constantly in flux. It is in this sense that the scriptures say the world is illusory. This fact should not dishearten you or make you sad. Simply accept the nature of the world as it is.

While you are trying to assimilate the knowledge that worldly objects are illusory, contemplate on the Truth that is immortal and not subject to destruction, death, and decay. The Truth remains unchanged and witnesses the changing states of all worldly objects, including your body and mind. Once you know this eternal Truth, life's successes and failures, losses and gains will no longer be disappointing. Instead of viewing this stream of change as destructive, you will see that it is the source of continual renewal. You will appreciate the process of change, for you will understand that without it the world would become stale and stagnant—a boring place to live!

Q How does an individual soul, which has just sparked from Universal Consciousness, incur karma? If it doesn't have karma to begin with, how can it be involved in paying off karmic debts?

According to the scriptures, each *jiva,* each individual human being, has some karma, which is why it sparks from Universal Consciousness in the first place. The manifestation of the universe is not a one-time phenomenon. There is nothing like creation and annihilation. Instead, consciousness is constantly expanding and contracting. Through mortal eyes, this is seen as creation and annihilation, birth and death.

Life is an ever-flowing stream of consciousness. When and how it started, no one can say. This current creation had its beginning somewhere in the dissolution of the previous cycle of creation. During the time of dissolution, individual souls—which are numberless—fall into cosmic slumber. When, under the will of the Divine, nature comes out of this slumber, these individual souls also wake up. We call this the beginning of creation. Just as a night's sleep does not dissolve yesterday's unfinished projects, the long sleep between cycles of creation does not clear up our previous karmic debts. When we wake up, our karmas wake up along with us and we start the cycle all over again. Those who break this cycle are fortunate.

People who are unfamiliar with the boundless domain of knowledge and consciousness may still argue that there has to be some beginning. But trying to find a beginning of the beginningless is a fool's errand. That is why in regard to these questions a great master like Buddha remained silent, and why the sages of the Upanishads simply smiled and said, "This is a wonder."

If atman is not subject to birth and death or to bondage and freedom, then why do we need to do spiritual practice? Who does the practice and who receives its fruit?

Atman is pure and enlightened, subject neither to birth nor death, and therefore does not require freedom from bondage. It is never bound by any law. It is the mind that ignorantly believes itself to be in bondage and strives for liberation. Spiritual practices are meant to liberate the mind, not atman. Mind, with its employees—the senses and the body—does the practice and, if it's lucky, gets the reward. Atman, the pure self, stands still from eternity to eternity and witnesses the play staged by the master magician called mind. Once the mind creates the concept of bondage and is convinced that it is bound, it cannot rest until it is convinced that it is totally free. Unfortunately, its conviction of bondage is so strong that it must go through an arduous process of freeing itself from its own restraints. That is called intense *sadhana.*

Q But why practice? Why not just study, contemplate, and gain the conviction that you are the pure self and become one with the One?

Through study and contemplation on the truth described in the Upanishads you transcend false identification with the non-self, which is destroyed by knowledge of the true self. You experience yourself as a pure, unalloyed, totally independent wave of consciousness. This can be achieved by virtue of your contemplative knowledge. But in what sense are you a perfectly free being? The unlimited grandeur, knowledge, and bliss within can be brought forward only by awakening and unfolding the infinite power of atman. You awaken it through *sadhana*.

It is as if you are a billionaire who has completely forgotten about the money you have in the bank and have come to think of yourself as poor. You cannot claim your wealth if you don't know it exists. If you remember you are a billionaire, you no longer think of yourself as poor. But you still need to know which bank your wealth is stored in, how to withdraw it, and how to find your way to the bank. For that purpose, you need convincing knowledge that cannot be contradicted by arguments. You gain that knowledge through spiritual practice.

The experiences the sages have recorded in the scriptures, confirming the existence of atman and its infinite power—*atma shakti*—is like a passbook. Your unshakable conviction, fully supported by reason and logic, is like recognizing your name on the passbook, opening it, and reading the balance. On the ground of this knowledge, desire grows to find the source of your wealth. Learning the proper system of sadhana is like acquainting yourself with the route to the bank. Seeking direct guidance from a teacher is like overcoming doubts about which way to turn at the crossroads. Reaching the source and gaining access to that which was already yours is called spiritual accomplishment—the realization of who you are and how great and infinite you are.

Once you have a direct experience of Truth, are you really free from the bondage of birth and death? Do you become immortal, as the scriptures say?

A knower of the eternal self, atman, becomes immortal. This does not mean that you will never die. Rather, you transcend your attachment to worldly objects, including your own body, and maintain the joy of simply being. Death is a habit of the body, which is composed of different elements and so must decompose one day.

While we are alive we are motivated by our desire to undertake certain actions. In most cases these actions are goal-oriented. Attachment to the fruit of an action leads to disappointment and misery. If we fail to achieve the fruits of our actions, we are depressed. If we succeed, we become attached. This attachment is a source of fear, because sooner or later we lose what we have gained: either we must leave those objects we worked so hard for, or they are destroyed. But desire itself is never destroyed. Insatiable desire forces us to perform actions, which create misery. To overcome these self-created miseries we perform more actions, thinking this will liberate us. Many desires for performing actions and receiving the fruits of our actions are not fulfilled in this lifetime. Those unfulfilled desires create the psychological conditions for continuing the cycle of birth and death.

To free yourself from this cycle you must cultivate an attitude of non-attachment toward worldly objects. This is possible only when you know that there is a higher truth. Then you will no longer be tempted by the charms of the world. After knowing the higher truth *(para vidya),* lower truth *(apara vidya)* loses its binding power. In the light of higher truth, lower truth is seen as provisional. An enlightened person knows that the external world is like the water in a mirage. It is a waste of time to run after such water; it cannot quench your thirst. Ignore such appearances and seek the oasis of peace and happiness: Brahman, the highest truth.

After knowing Brahman, do you really experience oneness with Universal Consciousness?

Yes. The knower of Brahman becomes Brahman *(brahmavit brahmaiva bhavati).* If you know only the lower reality, that is the reality you believe in. For you, it is the only reality. Your concepts of pleasure and pain, loss and gain, and bondage and freedom are confined to the objects in your field of knowing. In this tiny, illusory world you fashion your self image: you find yourself poorer than someone else, richer than someone else, and so forth. Because of your limited vision you become the victim of numberless, self-created complexes.

If you identify yourself as a merchant, you derive delight from becoming richer than other merchants, and you conceptualize heaven as a place where you will be able to enjoy those riches you were not able to attain on Earth. For those who live in the desert, heaven is filled with oases, and hell has no water. Such concepts of heaven and hell and bondage and freedom parallel our self-image, which itself is a reflection of the circumstances of our little world. In this world, we either love our self-image or hate it. In either case we are afraid of losing it, because we believe it is ourselves. People with superiority or inferiority complexes appreciate or depreciate themselves, but in the final analysis do not want to lose what they are.

Nevertheless, as circumstances change, our self-image changes and falls apart in spite of all our efforts to sustain it. Because we can't stop this process of change, we are insecure and fearful. This process becomes a continuous death, which we experience before the actual death of the body. Thus, the knower of the lower reality remains in the lower reality.

You are whatever you know yourself to be—this is a simple law. Thus, the knower of Brahman becomes Brahman. The moment you know you are inseparable from Universal Consciousness, you become Universal Consciousness. Your faith in that Consciousness will grow, and your self-image will be transformed. You no longer feel superior or inferior to anyone else. You are free from all complexes, for in you all complexes and diversities find their rightful place. They become an integral part of you. Their diverse and seemingly contradictory appearances beautify your unified awareness. You understand that you are not part of collective consciousness—rather, you *are* collective consciousness.

All changes taking place within the realm of consciousness are natural and have no effect on the eternity of consciousness. In this regard, consciousness may be compared with a forest. In a forest there are plants, shrubs, vines, animals, insects, rocks, and so forth. If we look at everything that exists in that forest individually, we will not see the forest as such, although we can't deny the existence of the forest. From the standpoint of an individual tree in the forest, the destruction of a particular plant or insect may be significant, but from the perspective of the forest it is all part of the process of growth. Even if the entire forest were to catch fire and burn down, it would still exist, because the potential for regeneration would remain.

When you identify yourself with Universal Consciousness you experience oneness with all and find great delight in witnessing the changes taking place in the external world as well as in yourself. Fear of destruction, death, and decay vanishes. You become fearless, loving all and rejecting none, for you know that everyone and everything in the universe is simply an elaboration of yourself. In this state of realization, love alone is your spontaneous expression because that has become your nature.

Q **I have heard yogis say that death is a habit of the body. Because habits can be broken, this implies that death can be prevented. Can it?**

The subject of preventing death or at least staving it off has fascinated people throughout the ages. Yogis are no exception. In fact, the early literature focuses mainly on the yogis' quest for immortality. The yogis developed two main ways to approach this goal. One involves making the body indestructible; the other is to identify with that aspect of ourselves that remains unaffected by the changes brought about by death.

According to the first approach, death is a habit of the body, and by changing this habit we can transcend the phenomenon of death. The body is made of five gross elements (earth, water, fire, air, and ether), which are constantly undergoing change. If the simple rules of nature are followed, anyone who is born must die—dust must return to dust. However, by practicing some of the higher techniques of yoga, these simple rules can be transcended and a yogi can achieve complete freedom from old age, disease, and death. This is known as *kaya siddhi.*

The tradition of Guru Gorakh Nath emphasizes this approach to immortality. Its followers maintain that we can achieve the purpose of life only while we have a body and that the greatest loss is to die without knowing ourselves at every level. They also maintain that the human body is fully equipped with all the tools and means necessary for self-realization. According to this tradition, therefore, it is of the utmost importance to remain embodied so that we may realize the self in this lifetime, instead of dying and starting all over again in the next life.

To this end, these yogis developed techniques for rejuvenation and longevity, as well as for disintegrating and reintegrating the molecules of their body at will. The first three techniques are known as *rasayana kriya, kaya kalpa,* and *parakaya-pravesha.* The fourth and finest is *asmita siddhi,* through which a yogi creates their own mind, and from that self-created mind *(nirmana chitta)* creates a body *(nirmana kaya).* One who has mastered this technique is able to remain on this plane of existence at will, thus bypassing the process of death and birth. The emphasis on the immortality of the body gave rise to the techniques found in hatha and kundalini yoga, as well as such esoteric techniques as *vajra kaya siddhi, bala atibala,* and *mrita sanjivani vidya,* which are described in tantric and Upanishadic literature.

The second approach to immortality the yogis developed is to disidentify from the body altogether and identify instead with that aspect of ourselves which existed before conception and which will continue to exist after death. This requires learning techniques for penetrating the different layers of our being—the physical body, the pranic body, the mind, the intellect, and the ego—and finally reaching the transcendental realm of consciousness where the soul dwells in perfect glory and bliss.

This approach is upheld by the yogis of the Upanishadic order. They too are convinced that death is a habit of the body, but according to them it is not worthwhile to devote so much energy to changing this habit. Their approach is to use this body and the wealth it contains to uncover the immortal within. This approach gave rise to the techniques of raja yoga, karma yoga, bhakti yoga, and jñana yoga, as well as to different methods of meditation, contemplation, and prayer.

Q If we do not realize our essential nature before we die, do we have to start all over again?

No. The scriptures clearly tell us we do not start all over; we start exactly from where we stopped in our last life. But it is a long time after we are born before we even think of committing ourselves to finding the purpose of life. First we have to learn to walk, talk, read, write, and accomplish all the other tasks of childhood and youth which the world imposes on us. This is necessary because all of the education and training we receive through our brain and assimilate into the conscious part of our mind is wiped out at the time of death. The soul remains unaffected and travels to the next phase of life, along with the impressions stored in the unconscious mind. These unconscious impressions, known as vasanas, are the factors motivating the unliberated soul to blindly search for a new body.

In this context, an unliberated soul is one that has mistakenly identified itself with the non-self—the body, mind, and objects of the world—and as a result has become a victim of its own attachments, desires, and fears. These false identifications are deposited in the depths of the unconscious mind, and when the conscious mind, brain, and nervous system fall apart at death, these tendencies are the only motivating force for the soul. It is driven by these tendencies without knowing why, where, and how it is being driven. In spite of this helplessness, the unconscious mind of such an unliberated soul is governed by an extremely subtle force: *prarabdha karma.* Prarabdha karma functions like a shipping company working under the will of the Divine—it cannot make a mistake. Prarabdha karma places the unliberated soul exactly where it belongs. Thus we are reborn in the time and place where we will find an opportunity to pay off our previous karmic debts and complete the task of self-realization.

The problem is that by the time we come to our senses and commit ourselves to self-realization, a big chunk of our life has been wasted, and we have created innumerable new entanglements in the form of attachment or aversion to the people and objects we have already encountered. We have gotten so sucked into this world that we hardly have the time and energy to think of the higher meaning and purpose of life. If we are lucky enough to succeed in disentangling ourselves from these worldly snares, there is usually very little time left—our energy is depleted, and old age has started knocking on the door in the form of sickness and despondency. It is in this light that the yogis say that if we do not attain self-realization in this lifetime, we must start all over again in the next.

Q Does this mean that the spiritual understanding we have gained in the previous lifetime is totally lost?

No. Just as *vasanas* remain with us in a dormant form, spiritual knowledge also remains in a dormant form. The scriptures offer a beautiful analogy to explain this: just as a frog burrows in the mud and hibernates during a drought, coming out when the rains return, so does the *jiva* (individual soul) come out of its hibernation in the unconscious when it encounters favorable conditions (a suitable body). And just as the frog comes out of hibernation with its instincts intact, we come back with our memories—both spiritual and worldly—intact. However, unlike the strong instincts of a frog, our memories are faint.

Almost without exception, our education aims to brighten our worldly memories and help us become smart and skillful in the pursuit of survival and pleasure. Spiritual training and practice is at the bottom of the list, and what little we receive is shrouded by the political and economic motives underlying most religious doctrines, dogmas, and superstitions. Therefore there is little to brighten the spiritual understanding we gained in a past life, and so in that sense, spiritual understanding does get lost.

Is there a way of reviving our spiritual memories earlier, before we really get entangled in worldly pains and pleasures?

When we are children, the greatest responsibility for reviving and restoring our spiritual memories lies with those who have the greatest influence on us: our parents. If they can create an environment conducive to spiritual growth, it will certainly help us come in touch with our own spiritual wisdom. An environment rich in love, compassion, selflessness, and tolerance can automatically awaken the higher self before worldly pettiness sets in. So when we become parents ourselves, we need to make a concerted effort to create an environment that will brighten and foster our children's spiritual understanding.

Another large measure of responsibility rests with our system of education. Currently this system is completely unbalanced. Spirituality is an alien element in the public schools because there is no understanding of the distinction between spirituality and religion; in private schools, there is an exclusive emphasis on a particular religion for the same reason. In the first case, students are given no spiritual foundation, and in the second, they receive only a religious orientation and little or no spiritual understanding. Therefore by the time they are mature, students either have failed to develop a sense of the higher purpose of life or they believe it lies in blindly following one particular religious belief.

When we become adults, the total responsibility for awakening our spiritual memories lies with us. We now have the freedom to choose an environment that can remind us of our essential self. Creating and inhabiting such an environment is called *satsanga* (keeping the company of wise people). *Svadhyaya* (the study of scriptures, and self-analysis) is another effective way of awakening our spiritual *vasanas*. Last, but not least, committing ourselves to a meditative practice helps us withdraw our mind from the external world, turn it inward, pierce the interior layers of our being, encounter the spiritual wisdom stored there, and enlarge it until we finally experience the presence of the ever-existent Reality within.

Q What happens at the time of death?

We stop breathing, and the game is over. But before breathing ceases, certain signs and symptoms of impending death manifest in the breath. When a person dies suddenly as the result of an accident or an abrupt failure of the vital organs, we don't get a chance to observe subtle changes in the breathing pattern. But when death is the result of a lingering illness or old age, the breath gradually becomes shallow, and the pause between inhalation and exhalation lengthens. Then, as lack of oxygen causes the thinking process to deteriorate, conscious and linear thinking gradually vanishes, and awareness begins to shift between the conscious and unconscious states. The conscious mind, which always works in coordination with the brain, nervous system, and senses, begins to lose its grip, and the unconscious mind takes over. This is a jumbled state—the dying person is neither fully conscious nor completely unconscious.

In this confused state we are no longer capable of employing the senses and brain to gather data from the external world and process it in a systematic and structured manner, nor can we consciously and systematically retrieve data from the unconscious mind. Clarity is gone, and confusion dominates both the conscious and unconscious minds. Clarity is knowledge, and confusion is maya (the veil of ignorance), and as the veil of ignorance thickens in the dying process, mastery over the self disappears and our sense of self-identity becomes muddled. In this disjointed state the unconscious mind takes over and creates an entirely new world of impressions.

If at this juncture we can somehow maintain conscious control over ourselves and exercise the powers of will and determination, we can fill our entire inner realm with the train of thought of our choice. When we realize that death is upon us, that the body, breath, and conscious mind are about to fall apart, we can use this chosen train of thought as a vehicle in which to migrate voluntarily from the conscious to the unconscious mind, allowing us to enter the unconscious not as a slave but as a master.

If the train of thought we use as a vehicle is imbued with divine awareness, it can illuminate the realm of the unconscious, and we will not fall victim to an apparently random stream of unconscious contents. But if we cannot maintain conscious control, we will be totally dependent on the nature of the unconscious contents of our mind. It could be heavenly, hellish, or a mixture of both. That is why the scriptures say, "Your train of thought at the time of death determines where you will go."

Q How can we maintain conscious control over our unconscious during the time of death?

The yogis say that we are the makers of our own destiny. They tell us that if we unfold our potential and make the best use of the possibilities life offers, we are certain to live joyfully and leave the body gracefully.

The body is like a rented apartment, and Nature is the landlord. We dwell in our apartment until our lease is over. During our tenancy we must follow the laws set by Nature—violating them causes debility and disease, and this results in eviction. On the other hand, compliance with Nature's laws—including non-violence, truthfulness, compassion, non-attachment, and non-possessiveness—engenders an environment in which we can live joyfully. But we must always maintain the awareness that nothing in this world, including the body, is ours. While we live in this body we must discover the purpose of life, and when the lease has expired we must graciously hand the keys of breath over to the landlord or we will be evicted.

Attachment to the objects of the world creates a deep sense of fear and insecurity at the time of death because throughout our life we have continuously filled our mind with the idea that the objects of the world and the people we love are integral to our existence, that life without them will be empty. But there comes a time when we must continue our journey without our family, friends, and possessions. At that moment we find ourselves at a loss, and even though we know that parting is inevitable, we still attempt to hold on. We fail and are overwhelmed by insecurity, frustration, fear, and grief, which cloud the mind-field and become the train of thought on which we are swept into the next realm.

The alternative is to approach the next realm in full awareness that this entire world has come from the Divine, exists in the Divine, and ultimately returns to the Divine. We can do this by cultivating the understanding: "In this world I own nothing—all the objects of the world are gifts from the Divine, which I must use to accomplish the higher purpose of life. When the time comes I must leave them behind without clinging to them." If we are established in this awareness, it will grant us a great sense of freedom at the time of death. Then we can leave this body gracefully, and our unconscious mind will be fully illuminated.

So it is possible to maintain conscious control over ourselves at the time of death, but only if we have practiced maintaining awareness of the Divine throughout our life. At the moment of death there is usually so much pulling and pushing going on in different levels of our being that there is no time to think about philosophy. Only if the conviction that nothing in this world is ours is a part of our normal awareness will it be possible for us to effortlessly and peacefully drop all our desires and attachments, hand over the keys of breath to Nature, and walk out of this body before maya throws the blanket of confusion over us. The scriptures constantly remind us that we gain firm ground in awareness through prolonged, uninterrupted meditative practice, and that such practice must be accompanied with love and faith.

Q Is there a way of knowing whether we will be successful in creating the train of thought of our choice while we are dying?

How clear and deep the grooves of a specific train of thought are determines how effortlessly we can hold to that thought during the time of departure. And the depth and clarity of the grooves depend on how profoundly that thought has pervaded every aspect of our life. For example, if the grooves related to mantra awareness are deeper than all other thought constructs, and if love and faith in the mantra has pervaded our awareness more profoundly than anything else, then we can predict with certainty that mantra awareness will be maintained during the time of death.

The Bible says, "You cannot serve two masters." To ensure that your mantra will come forward to illumine your path during the time of death, you must channel all your thoughts and emotions toward it, not only during meditation but also during your daily activities. (You may not need to remember the words of the mantra, but its feeling should be maintained day and night.) To test whether or not every moment of your life is filled with mantra awareness, watch your mind when it is not actively engaged in a task you have set for it, and see if it wanders or broods instead of resting in your mantra.

If mantra awareness has become your strongest habit, then it will come forward automatically during the time of transition. Such a habit is an eternal friend, one that wards off all unconscious habits and the confusion created by them.

A graceful departure is the fruit of long preparation, and in yogic terms, this preparation consists of consciously training the unconscious mind. The techniques of meditation help us to do this, and thus we develop the ability to let go of that which is unwanted and retain the memory of that which is illuminating. When we can do this we can maintain conscious control over our unconscious mind during the time of death. Death is then neither frightening nor confusing.

staying on the Path

MAKING PROGRESS

Q I have been using relaxation techniques with some success to train my mind to turn inward and confine its movement to the space occupied by my body. Yet it still pulls my attention here and there. What should I do now?

The first step of meditation is relaxation. In the scriptures the process of relaxation is called *pratyahara* (the withdrawal of the mind and senses). The next step is to focus the mind on one object for a longer period of time. This is called *dharana* (concentration). The best way to begin practicing concentration is to focus the mind on the breath. Observe it as it flows between the nostrils and the heart center: with your inhalation the mind is traveling to the heart center, and with your exhalation it is traveling from the heart center to the tip of the nostrils. Eliminate the pause between inhalation and exhalation and feel as though your breath is an uninterrupted stream of energy traveling between the nostrils and the heart region. Then focus on the touch of cool air at the bridge between the nostrils when you inhale, and the touch of warm air as you exhale. This will confine your mind to the bridge of the nostrils rather than the space between the nostrils and the heart area, and your concentration will become more condensed, potent, and refined.

Soon, however, you will notice that the mind is refusing to watch the flow of the breath at the bridge between the nostrils. Its tendency is to move outward, and it will try to slip away again. To control this tendency, move to the next level of concentration by providing an object of concentration that is more concrete and profound than simple breath awareness. It is at this stage that the yogis introduce meditation on the sound "so hum." While inhaling, mentally listen to the sound "sooooo," and while exhaling, listen to the sound "hummmm." Synchronize the sound "so hum" with the inhalation and the exhalation and let your mind be so absorbed that the sound, the breath, and the mind become an inseparable stream of awareness. This will bring a higher level of joy and restfulness to the mind, enabling it to drop all other objects effortlessly.

Q How do I know whether I am making progress in meditation? How can I progress faster?

There are two ways of knowing. The first is to observe how much mastery you have gained over your thoughts and emotions both in meditation and in your daily life. Do you become agitated and disturbed as easily as you did before you started your meditation practice? When you are disturbed, how long does it last?

Let's say that before you started meditating, if you had a fight with someone in your office you would still be upset when you got home. That feeling might have lasted the whole evening, making it difficult for you to enjoy your family. Nowadays, however, if you have an unpleasant encounter with a colleague, you wash your hands of it when you walk out of the office and are fully present with your family when you get home. That is progress.

When you sit for meditation, distracting thoughts from the day may flit through your mind. If your automatic response is, "Oh, who cares? This is my meditation time," that is a good sign. But if you find yourself caught up in your thoughts, turning events and conversations over in your mind instead of paying attention to your object of concentration, you are not making much progress. In that case you need to practice non-attachment to further vitalize your meditation. Remind yourself that all these events and objects are part of the material world and are ultimately not valuable. Cultivate the knowledge that life is not confined to the realm of the material. When this knowledge becomes vibrant and alive, you are making progress in meditation.

The second sign of progress is that you miss your meditation practice if you don't do it. Let's say you begin your day without meditating. All day long you hear a whisper from the depths of your heart: "I have not done my meditation." Then when you sit down in the evening to meditate, the intensity of your meditation is markedly increased, and you think, "Thank God, I have time to meditate." This is a good sign. If you miss your meditation but the thought of it lingers in your mind, it means you have fallen in love with meditation and are making good progress.

Q **When I started my meditation practice I found it enjoyable and inspiring, but now that feeling is beginning to fade. I can't seem to concentrate on my breath anymore. Why?**

Usually we begin the practice of meditation to overcome specific concerns—stress, fatigue, deeply rooted sadness or anger, a longing to know ourselves, or a desire to experience God. If we are lucky, we find a balanced path of spirituality that consists of techniques for ensuring health and well-being on all levels of our existence: body, breath, mind, and soul. When we commit ourselves to such a balanced path of spirituality, we experience a totally new level of physical and mental bliss.

Usually, focusing on the breath and the sound "so hum" is the first step in cultivating a meditation practice. This is a wonderful aid to concentration, and for a period of time we are content with our practice. But eventually we are confronted with issues and obstacles that had previously been completely outside of our awareness. This is a condition common to all spiritual disciplines.

In the beginning stages of the journey, whether the path selected is the meditative route of the Vedic sages or the contemplative route of Buddhist or Christian saints, aspirants feel as though everything is "fine and divine." As a result of the initial practice of meditation, concentration, prayer, selfless service, and other components of the spiritual path, the mind becomes inward and the heart is purified.

Such an inwardly turned mind begins to penetrate the deeper levels of our being, where subtle impressions of our past are deposited in the form of unconscious memories. Before we start our inward journey we are so busy with our day-to-day worldly affairs that we have neither the opportunity nor the capacity to see how big the pile of trash in our mind really is or how fierce the tornadoes in our heart really are. With the help of our practice, the body relaxes and the senses become calm and tranquil. As a result the conscious part of our mind gets relief from constantly attending to endless worries and concerns during meditation. That is when we say, "I had a wonderful meditation."

During this phase you are simply meditating on your breath or the sound "so hum." You are in a relatively quiet, tranquil state and the mind is following with the flow of your breath. Suddenly a thought sneaks in: "That guy at the gas station was really huge." You realize that you are entertaining a silly thought, and you bring your mind back to your breath or the sound of "so hum." After practicing regularly and sincerely for six months or more, you have overcome the tendency of the mind to brood on trivial things, which is a great relief.

At this point the next phase of the journey begins. As the conscious mind relaxes, the unconscious mind gradually takes over. You are no longer distracted by the memory of the guy at the gas station, the beautiful dress you saw in the store, or what you need to do at the office. Instead, you may begin to experience emotional turmoil that you don't know how to handle. Negative thoughts and strong emotions begin flooding uncontrolled into your mind, but you do not know the cause of such intense anger, sadness, and depression. Attempts to banish these thoughts and feelings by focusing your mind on the sound "so hum" usually don't succeed.

This is the time when you need personal guidance and a more specific object for focusing the mind than "so hum." At this juncture you may need to receive formal mantra initiation. The energy inherent in a mantra will enable you to concentrate your mind more successfully than you can while focusing on the breath or the sound "so hum."

Q What can I do when I can't get negative thoughts out of my mind?

Let such thoughts come and go through the back door of your mind, but do not involve yourself in entertaining them. Letting your thoughts and emotions go requires no effort: you neither make an effort to let them come nor make an effort to let them go (if you were to make an effort, you would be participating in the process of letting go rather than the process of meditation). Another way of looking at it is that letting go is a by-product of meditation, but meditation is not a by-product of letting go.

By cultivating the habit of letting go, you pass through the phase of being disturbed by memories and anxieties during meditation. Ordinary emotions will not be able to distract you. But some of the more powerful emotions will not leave your mind alone, regardless of how diligently you apply the formula of letting go. It seems that some emotions springing from totally unknown sources hover over the mind, and you can't ignore them.

When you cannot let go of thoughts and emotions, you must learn to witness them. This means acknowledging the thoughts and emotions without adding any interpretations and elaborations. Instead of denying them or remaining indifferent toward them, try to understand what they are, what is causing them, and how meaningful they are in the present moment.

As you cultivate this skill, you will find that no matter how pertinent these thoughts and feelings were in the past, they are now virtually meaningless. Only your attachment gives life to thoughts and emotions connected to the past, thereby allowing them to influence the present. By witnessing these powerful thoughts and emotions in a detached manner, you will nullify the influence they have over your mind. Remember, witnessing does not mean involving yourself in a mental debate, but simply letting the facts present themselves objectively. When done skillfully, the practice of witnessing induces a sense of non-attachment and non-involvement. Once this feeling intermingles with the stream of meditation, then thoughts, emotions, memories, and anxieties lose their power to entangle your mind.

Q I've read that meditation deepens in stages. Can you tell me what they are?

The first three stages are outlined in the answers to the previous two questions. The fourth stage begins when we have mastered the skill of witnessing. At this stage, meditation becomes deeper. We begin to experience an inner joy that cannot be found in any other source. The mind has become more one-pointed and subtle. Now it can see through the dark night of the soul.

Now and then during the meditation, the mind gets a glimpse of an everlasting life. It can clearly feel that the kingdom of the soul is more pervasive and richer than any worldly kingdom. It can clearly see the Divine Light, but can't reach it. A thin but mysterious veil hangs between the kingdom of the soul and the mind, yet that curtain is enough to create a barrier between our little self and the glorious Universal Self. A seeker yearns to tear that veil away. He or she tries more meditation, more prayer, more selfless service, more study, and more purification—but nothing really seems to work. As the longing and frustration mount, there comes a desperate cry from the soul, which spontaneously results in self-surrender.

Self-surrender means surrendering all your actions and their fruits to the Divine. You still continue to do your practice, but you no longer feel that you are the doer of the practice. Now the internal conditions of the practice are totally different: at this stage you feel that the practice is being done by the divine being who dwells within you, and that you are simply witnessing it. You no longer have the feeling that you are working hard to penetrate the veil that stands between you and the Divine; rather, it's the grace of the Divine that lifts the veil. At that instant, the lover and the Beloved become one. The experience of this union is ecstasy. After attaining this state of ecstasy, there is nothing else to be achieved. Here the process of meditation is transformed into a state of meditation, and the meditator remains in that meditative state even while living in the world.

Q As meditation deepens, does the role of letting go and witnessing change?

The witnessing aspect remains the same, although the depth and complexity deepen as meditation deepens. However, the process of letting go does change somewhat. In the early stages of meditation, when the mind is not yet well-trained, witnessing is a simple process of keeping your mind focused on your mantra or other object of meditation. When you notice another thought running in the back of your mind, simply let it go. If that thought becomes so overwhelming you cannot ignore it, then witness it without involving yourself with it: simply observe the undesirable thoughts passively.

Later on, when your meditation deepens, trivial thoughts no longer flash in your mind. Instead thoughts, concerns, and issues that you never knew you had begin to surface from your unconscious. To deal with this deep-rooted unconscious material you must develop a more profound and methodical practice of witnessing. You cannot just witness those unconscious contents; they are too powerful, and the deeper they have been stored in the unconscious, the more powerful they are. They forcibly capture your attention and stir your entire being, demanding resolution.

You must recognize the unconscious contents for what they are and use the power of non-attachment to disentangle yourself from them. If you are still bothered by them, then resort to the highest technique of all: surrender them to God. This whole process is called "witnessing." It is a dynamic internal process in which the mind is actively involved with the object of meditation, with periodic interruptions for contemplation and prayer, and this makes it possible to surrender this powerful material to God. This is what the scriptures call the action of an inactive mind. As meditation continues to deepen, the process of witnessing is further refined.

In the highest stages of meditation you are witnessing the object of your meditation. There is no longer anything else to witness. You witness the object of your meditation effortlessly because it is already there. You simply allow yourself to be in the presence of your mantra: the mantra is there; you are also there. Because the process of witnessing the mantra is totally effortless, you are meditating and yet you are not meditating. In other words, you meditate in a manner in which you don't exist any more as a meditator—rather, you become the process of meditation.

At some point the process of witnessing the object of your meditation becomes so profound and subtle that you are neither the meditator nor the process of meditation; rather, you are the object being meditated upon. By this time, the mind has transcended all its modifications and merged into atman (pure consciousness). Consciousness stands behind the curtain of all thinking and knowing. The intrinsic functioning of the soul is witnessing. Atman is not the doer but the pure witness. It remains uninvolved, unentangled, untainted through birth, death, and all that occurs in between. By the time you reach the state of awareness where the witness alone is left, you have attained pure *samadhi.*

Q **I know that the path of spirituality I'm following is perfect for me; I know that it will lead me to the highest goal—yet my motivation for practice fades. Why do I become distracted and forget my goal?**

You seem to already have the first prerequisite: a firm conviction that the path of spirituality you have decided to follow is the best one for you. The next step is to make a firm resolution to commit yourself to following that path. The best way to avoid becoming distracted and forgetting your goal is to practice regularly and sincerely, with love and reverence.

Often in life we know what ought to be done, but our habit patterns drive us in the opposite direction. Such habit patterns can be conquered only by other habit patterns, which are equally or more powerful. Habit patterns are created through our repeated actions. A meditative habit created by undertaking the practice voluntarily and consciously can counteract the effects of unconscious habit patterns. That's why the *Yoga Sutra* recommends that we continue our practice sincerely and respectfully for a long period of time without interruption.

Doing so helps form a new habit related to the practice itself. Because old habits are constantly getting in our way and we are not yet fully devoted to our practice, we find many reasons to interrupt our practice, postpone it, or drop it altogether. If we do not know how important the practice is, we'll have very little interest in doing it. If we undertake a practice out of mere curiosity, we can't sustain it for long.

Sometimes people come to me for practices with the attitude "Oh well, I'll try this thing," although they are not really convinced it will be beneficial. When you have such a dubious attitude, you begin to count the minutes while doing the practice, wondering how many minutes you have been sitting and what benefit you are getting. This is a businessman's attitude: counting the time and assessing the fruits. Because you see no immediate tangible result, you get discouraged. But spirituality is not a short-term investment. How much time are you willing to invest? One lifetime? Several lifetimes?

We make all kinds of risky investments that are short-term and temporary. By the time some investments are about to mature, we may have to leave everything behind. Everything in this world is full of risk, because everything in the external world is temporary and transitory. Spirituality is the only investment that does not involve any risk, because it is eternal. Even when the body is dropped, our spiritual evolution continues, and we continue to reap the fruit of our so-called investment.

Because there is nothing more profound and valuable than finding spiritual meaning in life, the practice leading to the unfoldment of that spiritual meaning is very precious, too. However, to remain inspired and to avoid becoming complacent, start with a small goal—perhaps you want to be healthy, or to learn a particular technique, or to work with certain habits or tendencies of the mind. Achieving these minute goals will let you know that you are making progress.

But as far as your overall spiritual practice is concerned, don't confine yourself to these paltry objectives. Rather, know that spiritual practice is a lifelong pursuit, and thus develop respect for it. Whether you notice any results or not, keep practicing and find delight in the practice itself. Whether you get anything out of it or not doesn't matter; just train your mind to find some delight in the fact that you are doing the practice.

You need to have more respect and reverence for your practice than for anything else in the world. Practice to your fullest capacity, according to your best grasp of the concepts, and even if you have a bad teacher, or have not understood properly, you will find that something valuable manifests from the practice itself. This happens because the Truth is within you, and if your goal is the Truth, you are bound to reach it.

If you do the practice respectfully, for an unbroken and prolonged period, that practice becomes a powerful guiding and protective force and will draw the Truth toward you. That's why regularity is important. You may say, "I don't have time to practice, I have too much work to do." This statement shows that you have not yet understood that the practice is never less important than any work you are doing. You need to get to a point where you know that life is a complete waste—meaningless and useless—unless the higher purpose of that life is accomplished. Once you realize that nothing is more important than your practice, you will find that you have lots of time for it.

Reserve time for meditation, contemplation, and study. Regular study of genuine spiritual texts will remind you of your goal and inspire you to stay on the path, especially during those periods when you are just about to slip.

Q **I long for spiritual bliss when I'm surrounded by pain, misery, and grief, but once the conditions in my world become better, I lose my spiritual fervor. How can I keep it alive?**

To keep your spiritual fervor alive, you must be skillful. This is also part of *sadhana*—to kindle your desire and keep making it stronger and stronger.

The company of like-minded people is a driving force in your practice. Those of us who are not yet perfect can easily be influenced by the company we keep: in the company of saints we behave like saints, but in negative company our animal tendencies manifest quite easily. We do not intend to drop our spiritual quest and get caught in the concerns of the mundane world, but until our desire for spiritual advancement becomes strong, people and objects can easily distract us. Think of how affected you are by your friends and family. How often do you delay or miss your meditation practice to entertain and please the people who are closest to you?

Friends bring forth in you desires that are similar to theirs. You have to be careful, even in a spiritual environment. Through introspection, analyze your thoughts, speech, and actions, and try to understand to what degree they are affected by your environment. This self-study and self-analysis will minimize the negative effect of company and help you keep your spiritual desire kindled.

Also try to discover methods of expanding your capacity. This entails growing emotionally, intellectually, and spiritually by cultivating fortitude, forbearance, forgiveness, kindness, patience, sincerity, openness, and a deeper understanding of life itself. An ever-increasing physical, mental, and spiritual capacity brings stability in practice. A stable practice is what pushes us toward the goal and acts as a magnet to pull the goal toward us. Create an environment in which you can maintain a constant awareness of your spiritual life. This will keep your spiritual fervor high. Practically speaking, self-analysis, self-observation, self-study, regularity of practice, and right company are the key factors in helping you maintain a constant awareness of your inner life. Without them, the help you receive from books and teachers is of little use.

In addition, try to create and nurture a sense of connection with the greatest source of strength: divine grace. No matter how satisfying or unsatisfying your practice is, be aware of the Lord of Life within. The awareness that the true guide is within will help when you become discouraged, doubtful, or frustrated. The power of surrender supersedes all other powers, because it draws forth divine grace. The effort that you put into your practice is like a budding flower, and grace is like the fragrance of that flower. If you cultivate this flower and wait patiently until it blossoms, you will receive its fragrance.

Q I try to be both disciplined and systematic in my practice and so have been following a systematic method of breathing, relaxation, and concentration on the mantra for many years. Yet my mind still wanders here and there instead of resting on the mantra, and my meditation practice has borne no fruit. Why?

You are working in the subtle realm with intangible tools, and yet you are expecting a tangible result. This is self-contradictory and self-defeating. We are conditioned to experiences in the gross realm of physical existence. In the external world, we work with tangible tools and see a tangible result: here is the cause—here is the effect. When we bring this conditioning and these expectations to the subtle realm we meet with disappointment.

That is one problem. The other is that your mind is still not under your control. It is not fully convinced that by doing this meditation practice it is really going to achieve something wonderful. The mind has not found the joy that is within you because the mind is not fully convinced that the joy is there. The mind thinks, "The mantra is still just a sound. What's the big deal?"

The mind has not understood that there is something infinitely more valuable than whatever it is searching for in the external world. That is why it keeps experimenting with thoughts and objects even when you are sitting and attempting to concentrate on your mantra. What you need is to bring the Divine into the realm of your practice. Let your practice be fully accompanied by love for the Lord. Once you fall in love with the Divine and experience that the Lord of Life is right here, then your mind will no longer be interested in wasting its time anymore.

Q That's a tall order. How do I go about falling in love with something as intangible as the Divine?

Imagine that the mantra is like God himself in the form of sound. Or if you don't believe in it, forget the mantra. You must have some kind of image or symbol of God. For purposes of illustration, let's say it is the cross and that the cross itself is the focal point of your meditation. If you are fully convinced that the cross is a living symbol of God, then the mind will not have any interest in running elsewhere. The problem is that the mind is not convinced that this shape really means anything. There are many actors and actresses more beautiful than this symbol. A breathtaking landscape is more captivating than this symbol. What is so great about this symbol?

From the standpoint of the mind there is no divine awareness involved in the symbol of the cross. You may be offended when someone else criticizes this symbol, but when it comes to adoring the cross in your heart, when you sit down and concentrate on it, you do not find yourself in a blissful state. This symbol is not able to generate a state of ecstasy. Although you may believe that this a great symbol, somehow it has less power over your mind than many of your possessions. Even your car seems to be more precious and impressive than this cross. Think about it for a few minutes in an honest manner. When somebody steals your wallet or purse, you become frantic. Or if you park your car in a large parking lot and can't find it because you don't remember exactly where you parked it, you panic and run around thinking "Where's my car? Oh my God—it must have been stolen. I need to call the police!" That car has so much importance that misplacing it has an enormous effect on you.

But do you ever become frantic about forgetting your awareness of the cross? Or your mantra? When you realize that you are not remembering your mantra, you don't feel bad, and this means you have not really understood what the mantra is. Why? Because the mind is not fully convinced that it is a privilege to be in the presence of the mantra, the cross, the name of God, or whatever your object of meditation is. But if you bring awareness, spiritual awareness, to your meditation—"My mind is not fully convinced that the Lord of Life has entered my heart. This is a blessed moment; let me simply be in the company of the Lord, everything else can wait until I finish my period of meditation"—then you will see improvement.

Q I feel fiery all the time and tend to snap at people. But at the same time I feel tired and sluggish and easily dissolve into tears. What can I do?

If my understanding of your problem is correct, your fire element is low, and that is why you feel tired and sluggish, and why at the same time you can't stop snapping at people. So do not worry about having a fiery nature. In fact, you do not have a lot of fire; you have very little fire, and even that is not under control.

In your case fire in the form of anger is more like a firecracker than a volcanic eruption; you don't have enough fire in your system to turn into a fiery volcano. Your anger is more like that of a tiny firecracker which briefly explodes and then quickly lapses into a dense darkness of sadness and depression. People who have low fire, or let's say a weak constitution, usually experience these symptoms.

According to the observations of yogis, such people have weakness in the area of the first three chakras, where the energy is usually low and stagnant. Practices such as *ashvini mudra, mula-bandha,* and the abdominal lift will help you immensely. (If you have had surgery in this area, and if you feel that it is still not completely healed, be careful and get the advice of a healthcare practitioner.)

A variation of *agni sara* that involves contracting and lifting the abdominal muscles while exhaling—and relaxing and releasing these same muscles while inhaling—is particularly helpful for this. In this variation of agni sara the energies of the first two lower chakras are activated and forced to flow upward to the navel center.

Tiredness, sloth, inertia, heaviness, dullness, fear, and sadness caused by failure and loss are associated with the first chakra, called *muladhara.* Practices such as *ashvini mudra* and *mula-bandha* have a direct effect on this chakra. Like the base of a fire bowl, the *muladhara* is where the fire of kundalini shakti resides. Anatomically situated at the base of the tailbone, this area is rich in nerve endings. According to yoga, this is the area which governs our most primitive urges—fear and self-preservation. By activating the energy at this center and moving it upward, we transcend our animal tendencies.

Desire, sensuality, frustration, and anger are associated with the second chakra, *svadhishthana.* This chakra is extremely subtle; physiologically it is hidden deep in the interior of the pelvic region. Gaining access to the second chakra and activating it is extremely difficult. With the help of agni sara, however, we can unblock its energy, and move it up to the navel center, as we did with the energy of the first chakra.

The navel center, the *manipura,* is the center of the fire element. When the forces of the first and second chakras are offered into the fire of the third chakra all physical, emotional, and biological energies come under control. It is the fire at the navel center that enables us to attain mastery over ourselves.

Q **Does dreaming deplete the storehouse of energy that might otherwise be used to nourish other aspects of life, most importantly the spiritual disciplines? What disciplines can an aspirant practice to curtail this involuntary expenditure of energy?**

According to yogis, dreams are a waste of time. However, dreaming is necessary and therapeutic for most people. This is because through dreams the mind attempts to satisfy those desires which due to some limitations or constraints could not be fulfilled during the waking state.

During sleep, when the conscious mind relaxes, the unconscious takes over. It gently triggers the conscious mind to the point where, although the conscious mind still remains relaxed to some degree, it begins to reassociate itself with the objects of its unfulfilled desires. During this time the conscious mind, without disturbing its rest, tries to embrace its phantom lady, but fails because this phantom lady does not exist in the conscious mind. So the unconscious comes up with a substitute and, in the process, some of the memories that are still lodged in the conscious mind combine with the contents of the unconscious and a dream is created. This is why most of our dreams are a mixture of fact and fantasy.

If the dream is intense, the neuromuscular responses to the activity of dreaming are almost the same as they would be if these events were occurring during the waking state. When we wake up from such dreams we find we are exhausted. According to yogis, dreaming is the childish mind's attempt to satisfy its hunger by sucking on a pacifier. Just as a pacifier satisfies a child for a while without providing nourishment, a dream pacifies the mind momentarily, although the gain is illusory and energy is lost in the process.

Yoga nidra (yogic sleep) is the practice that yogis prescribe to curtail dreaming. Before you can begin to learn this practice, you must learn how to relax properly. Systematic relaxation enables you to overcome your fatigue and sloth. More importantly, it counteracts the stress caused by trivial, day-to-day concerns. This method of relaxation incorporates elements of meditation, which helps you free your mind from thoughts, worries, and anxieties. In fact, systematic relaxation alone can markedly improve the quality of your sleep. The better the quality of your sleep, the fewer dreams you will have. The first step in the actual practice of yoga nidra is mental preparation. This consists of learning how to switch your mind on and off at will. You must train your mind to remember only what you want to remember and to forget what you decide to forget. This training entails cultivating the yogic habit of working hard but taking it lightly. The sense of indifference toward all worldly matters is indispensable for the practice of yoga nidra. You can do this practice successfully only if you are fully convinced that the world will not fall apart if you do not attend to it during the practice. Decide to attend to the concerns and issues of the world only after the practice is over.

Once you have trained your mind to harbor only those thoughts that you choose to harbor, the next step is to make a firm decision to go to sleep without losing conscious awareness of your waking state. You must learn to sleep while remaining aware of yourself. This awareness will prevent you from dreaming, and this conscious sleep will enable you to provide your body with the rest it needs. Furthermore, before you begin the practice you must decide that you will stay in that state for a specific period of time—such as twenty minutes—and you must not use an alarm clock to come out of yoga nidra promptly. In the beginning your anxiety about waking up at the precise time may cause your practice to become shallow. However, with continuous, uninterrupted practice for a prolonged period, the mind will develop its own alarm clock and you will be able to go into yogic sleep and come out, as you wish.

Because our minds are not properly trained, it is very hard to keep the mind free from all objects. For this reason the yogis have designed a method of yogic sleep that provides an object for the mind to focus on effortlessly, allowing it to get the maximum rest. Several of these methods are described in books, but because we practice them with the same old untrained mind, none of them seem to grant all the promised results. Therefore avoid the temptation to rush out and find a detailed description of how to do this practice. First prepare yourself. Proper preparation for yoga nidra is even more important than the practice itself.

Q How can I prepare myself to practice yoga, beyond working with the body and breath?

It has to be done systematically. Begin by observing where you stand in worldly and spiritual life. Notice how strong you are physically and emotionally. How fulfilling or dissatisfying do you find the world around you? How entangled are you with your physical complaints, biological urges, emotional issues, and worldly duties and obligations? This analysis will guide you in determining how much emphasis to put on postures, breathing exercises, and basic relaxation and concentration techniques.

Don't forget to analyze the role that the four basic urges—food, sleep, sex, and the desire for self-preservation—play in your life. Working with these urges is an important part of any yoga practice. If they are not properly regulated, they can undermine the positive effects of your practice. Therefore, know to what extent you are controlled by these urges and learn how to regulate them.

How can I prepare myself to do advanced pranayama?

Many texts say that a student should practice pranayama only after achieving mastery of the asanas, but attaining perfection in asana is not a simple task. The purpose of asana is to create enough flexibility and strength in the body so that the body itself does not become an obstacle in meditation. This takes considerable time, and while you are doing it you can also work with the breath by using simple practices, such as deep diaphragmatic breathing and alternate nostril breathing. These will benefit anyone who practices them. There are breathing practices, such as *bhastrika, kapalabhati,* and *ujjayi,* which fall between asana and pure pranayama practices. They can be done daily, even if you have not yet attained mastery over your sitting posture. Meanwhile, keep refining your postures and preparing yourself for the practice of advanced pranayama.

I know several people who have been practicing meditation for a number of years. They seem to be sincere about their practice, and yet they all display unspiritual qualities: one has an enormous ego that shows no signs of shrinking, another is obsessed with money and possessions, and so on. I don't understand how this is possible. At some point, shouldn't the effects of meditation begin to be apparent in our lives?

Yes, meditation will trigger a process of transformation if it is real meditation undertaken with a spiritual purpose. However, it often happens that meditation is treated as a mental exercise, not as a spiritual practice. In order to make meditation spiritual, the practitioner has to infuse it with spiritual fervor. When people practice sincerely yet fail to experience spiritual unfoldment, it is usually because they are caught up with the process of concentration, and concentration alone cannot help us transform ourselves.

Meditation is like a bird: it needs two wings to fly, and both of those wings need to be equally strong. One wing is a one-pointed mind, the other is constant awareness of the higher goal of life. One-pointedness is developed by practicing concentration; constant awareness comes through the practice of contemplation. Meditators who simply concentrate on the object of their meditation may develop a relatively one-pointed state of mind, but without spiritual awareness there can be no inner transformation, and thus no transformation in our behavior.

PILGRIMAGE AND RITUAL

Q Does making a pilgrimage to a holy shrine have any value in our spiritual development?

The answer is both "yes" and "no." Holy sites are like mirrors—they reflect what we have inside. If we know our motivation for visiting these places, if this motivation is spiritual, and if we have learned the proper method of seeking, then making a pilgrimage to these sites will certainly be conducive to our spiritual growth.

To visit these places as a tourist or to earn religious merit has no spiritual value. Tourists find satisfaction in stopping by because they find it entertaining to visit places mentioned in the guidebooks. Faithful pilgrims believe they gather merit by visiting such places, and so they find joy in making the trip. But those who understand the spiritual significance of shrines and the relationship of these shrines with specific practices they have undertaken visit a holy site for a precise reason. Often they make a temporary dwelling in the vicinity, do their practices as prescribed by the scriptures or by a teacher, and find joy when they experience how the energy of the shrine accelerates their practice.

To take full advantage of the spiritual energy of a shrine, you must know the history of that place, the exact spiritual tradition associated with it, and the spiritual laws that uphold the sanctity of the site. You can benefit from these holy places even more when you understand that these shrines are not necessarily associated with a particular religious or ethnic group, but rather are the living abodes of divine energy, which makes no distinction among various groups of humans or between humans and other living beings. Regardless of background or religious orientation, if you visit these places in the right frame of mind and undertake the practices compatible with the characteristics of the shrine, you will certainly experience a deepening in your practice.

Q If you don't approach a shrine in the proper frame of mind, is it possible to have a negative experience instead of a positive one?

Yes. If your attitude is not correct and if the practices that you have been doing are not in conformity with the energy of the shrine, then you may have an unpleasant experience. The experience of a spiritual leader from the United States who took a group to Gangotri, a holy place deep in the Himalayas, illustrates this point.

It was this teacher's first visit, and he and the group of students accompanying him were fascinated by the idea of spending a few nights and doing their practices in the famous cave of the Pandavas at Patangana, half a mile from the main shrine. Tents were erected outside the cave for the group members, but the teacher asked the tour guide to fix a place for him in the cave itself. The guide told him that it was not appropriate to disturb the cave, but the teacher insisted, and in the evening he retired to the cave to meditate. When night fell and everyone else had fallen asleep, the teacher began to have frightening visions—he heard strange, disturbing sounds, and fearful images flashed through his mind. Convinced that the cave was haunted, he ran out and joined his wife in her tent.

According to the tradition to which I belong, this cave is very special. It is where Arjuna and his four brothers did their meditation several thousand years ago, and since that time it has been favored by the Himalayan adepts as a place to do their practice. I could not understand how the cave could be haunted. How could anyone be fearful or restless there? When I asked one of the saints about it, he explained that this cave is for those who meditate, not for those who worship ghosts and spirits, as was customary in the tradition of that particular teacher. Furthermore, the teacher was trying to impress his students by spending the night in the cave—a practice of sheer hypocrisy. The powerful spiritual energy of that cave does not permit such misbehavior.

Q Why are some shrines compatible with particular practices and incompatible with others?

The answer to this question lies in understanding the dynamics of the energy involved in the formation of these shrines. Today we assume, incorrectly, that a shrine has to be associated with a particular god or goddess.

In ancient times holy men, intent on intensifying their practice without interruption and achieving their desired goal, retreated to a secluded place, either singly or with groups of aspirants, where they could do their practices without attracting attention. These places offered only the bare necessities, and so they attracted only those who were fully committed to *sadhana*—the austere environment repelled those who were less sincere. And here, in isolation, sincere seekers were free to experiment with practices that would have been difficult to do elsewhere. In time the energy generated by their intense and prolonged practices became so concentrated that these remote sites began to exhibit their own life, and subsequent aspirants—even novice seekers—were able to feel the powerful energy supporting their practice.

After the original adepts left their bodies, their faithful followers came to regard these remote places as shrines, living abodes of the spiritual energy of their masters. In honor of the adepts of their lineage, or the aspect of divinity that had enabled these adepts to reach high levels of realization, the disciples and followers erected monuments to them, many of which were later modified into temples.

As the decades rolled by, people gradually forgot the history of the adepts who had founded the shrines and the nature of their practices, although they still regarded the site with reverence. Visitors usually focused their attention on the monument itself, or on the temple, or on an altar or statue that it housed, but the truth of the matter is that the actual shrine is the entire locale where the adepts lived and practiced—a stretch of riverbank, a hilltop, an entire mountain valley, or a sizable tract of forest. Pilgrims, unfamiliar with the dynamics of the energy that vibrates throughout the locale at a subtle level, pay homage to a monument or to the deity in the temple, but knowledgeable spiritual aspirants bask in the energy, taking it in by living in the vicinity of the shrine and undertaking a prolonged practice there.

Some of these shrines have traditionally been occupied by a group of spiritual seekers who undertook the same or a similar practice, while at other sites adepts and their students may have experimented with a variety of practices of varying intensities and with different goals. As a result, the energy of a shrine and its adepts is so well-polarized that if we undertake a compatible practice while living in the vicinity we are naturally immersed in that stream of energy and glide toward the goal almost without effort, whereas if our practice is not compatible with the energy of the site we will confront formidable obstacles.

Let me give an example. At the northern tip of the Vindhya Range in central India is a site known as Chittrakut, for centuries the abode of masters and aspirants alike. Situated on a bank of the Mandakini River, the ashram of Sage Atri and Mother Anasuya is as vibrant today as it was thousands of years ago. A group of sadhus known as *vairagi* dominate this site, and for untold ages the saints of this tradition, through their practices, have so charged a hill in the area that it is known as Kamad Giri—the wish-yielding mountain. The nature of the practices performed here has been such that through the millennia this mountain has become an embodiment of love, compassion, kindness, and complete surrender. If a practice undertaken here is not in conformity with these characteristics, you will feel uncomfortable doing it. Those seeking name, fame, or the acquisition of *siddhis* (spiritual powers) feel intensely bored, frustrated, and lonely while doing their practices here.

Not far away there is another shrine, called Maihar. It has a totally different flavor. Maihar is a site of miracles. Aspirants intent on cultivating healing power and creativity in the fine arts find their practices thriving at this shrine, but saints seeking divine love and surrender to God feel bored, frustrated, and lonely here.

Q **I have been doing a daily two-hour ritual worship for two years, but I don't feel any closer to God or my inner self than I did before I began. Why?**

Certain schools of yoga prescribe ritual worship as a means to come closer to God, but this is effective only if you understand the meaning and spiritual significance of those rituals. If understood properly, rituals can create such a devotional atmosphere that it will be easy for you to withdraw your mind from the external world and turn it inward. But if rituals do not help you make your mind flow inward, then they are merely a superficial exercise.

In my long experience I have seen that most people involved in ritual worship switch their devotion from one form of God to another and from one set of rituals to another. These are the kind of people who keep going from one temple to another and from one guru to another—and find no satisfaction anywhere.

"Know thyself"—this dictum is at the root of all the great traditions. Who are you? What is your place in this vast universe? How are you related to the eternal truth? The answers to these questions must come from within. No book, no teacher, no temple, no prophet can give you a permanently satisfying answer.

Becoming closer to God requires training, training that includes practices that help you demolish the wall of duality that stands between you and God. Rituals normally do not help demolish this wall, for they stand on the ground of duality. But if you have the right attitude, if you have a contemplative mind, and if you are well-versed in deciphering the inner meaning of the rituals, then they can help you see God's reflection in this world of duality. That is a great achievement. But even so, sooner or later you must go beyond rituals and see the truth directly, rather than through their reflection. When performed with the right understanding, rituals are a stepping-stone to the next level of your spiritual practice.

I've heard about a powerful practice called *rudra yaga*. How can it help me and how can it help the world?

"Rudra" normally refers to Lord Shiva, who according to popular belief is the god of destruction. In the Vedic tradition, however, "rudra" has another meaning: Rudra is the divine being whose eyes are filled with tears of compassion. When Rudra sees people suffering, these tears spontaneously drop from his eyes and manifest in the form of the scriptures which embody the techniques for overcoming pain and misery. Those same tears also manifest in the form of saints and sages, herbs, and the healing sciences. That is why not only the scriptures but also the science of ayurveda—physicians, saints and sages, and herbs—are said to be living forms of Rudra.

Eight different aspects of nature are the direct manifestations of Rudra: earth, water, fire, air, space, the Sun, the Moon, and the life-force. Gaining knowledge of Rudra, cultivating proper respect for all of his manifestations, and serving Rudra by serving these manifestations is called rudra yaga. Anything good and auspicious, anything that keeps us healthy and happy, and anything that helps us attain freedom from pain and misery is Rudra, and worshipping that Rudra is called rudra yaga.

Here "worship" does not mean just performing rituals or participating in some sort of ceremony. In Sanskrit "yaga" means "to give, to serve, to contribute, to share, to sacrifice, to become part of." Therefore "rudra yaga" means that you contribute to the well-being of nature—the direct manifestation of Rudra. By serving nature's forces you serve yourself, you serve creation, and you serve the Creator. This requires self-sacrifice—which is why rudra yaga and other highly evolved practices are called "sacrifices."

The recitation of mantras and the fire offering are the core of this practice. The set of mantras recited during the rudra yaga are called "Shata Rudri." Recitation of even one single mantra with full understanding and with the appropriate discipline is enough to initiate an everlasting transformation, both within us and in the world around us. However, if you do not understand the meaning of the mantras, this practice can easily be mistaken for a Hindu ritual or a form of Shiva worship.

This practice was first done as part of a twelve-year-long group practice that the sages did long ago to restore and honor natural law, to restore the harmony and balance in the planet's ecology. That practice was known as the *ashva medha,* the horse sacrifice. Symbolically it means sacrificing one's personal pleasure and comfort for the welfare of all creation. In this context, "horse" refers to the mind and senses; therefore it also means attaining mastery over oneself; gaining control over one's thought, speech, and action; and using the forces of body, breath, and mind to attain self-realization. This is the highest and most ambitious of all practices.

This practice can be done in several steps. The practice of rudra yaga is something all of us can do. If we are proficient in the knowledge of Sanskrit, the Vedas, and tantras, that is good—but if not, we can still do this practice. It is a group practice, which means that participants of varying degrees of spiritual development can join this practice and benefit from it personally while contributing to the peace and prosperity of the world. Many of the mantras recited in the rudra yaga clearly state that this practice is an absolute necessity for those who have a body and therefore eat, drink, sleep, and are interested in living a healthy, happy, peaceful life.

Q I don't understand these mantras or know their meaning. So what purpose does it serve for me to stand around and watch the fire ceremony and listen to these mantras being recited? How does it help me, and how does it help the world?

Just standing around watching the fire ceremony and listening to the mantras will not help you much. But if you connect with the practice, it will certainly help. Even if you know nothing about electricity and nothing about electrical appliances or the dynamics of light and sound, when you plug your lamp into the electrical socket and turn it on, the lamp will be lit. Similarly, these practices will bring light to the world whether you understand them or not. However, if you understand the dynamics of rudra yaga and take an active part in it, then not only will you receive this energy, but you will be instrumental in broadcasting it. Furthermore, restoration and propagation of this kind of knowledge is our spiritual obligation.

You plug into the rudra yaga by following the basic rules of this practice, such as maintaining cleanliness in thought, speech, and action for the period of time this practice continues; waking up before dawn; saying a prayer or doing a meditation practice; and participating in the fire offering, which involves the recitation of mantras. Even if you do not know the mantras, the group knows it, and therefore you automatically reap the benefit of that group knowledge. The power of rituals, mantra recitation, the promise of the sages, the efficacy of time and place, and your intention—together these forces will carry the energy of rudra yaga to the various aspects of nature. All living beings, including yourself, who are dependent on these aspects of nature—which are manifestations of Rudra—will be nourished by this energy.

Q But what kind of practice will fill my personal life with peace and harmony and contribute to the peace and harmony of the world?

For your personal peace, undertake the practices of self-study, mantra japa, and prayer. For the peace and harmony of the world, make a strong resolution not to hurt others and, most importantly, not to hurt nature. This resolution and the commitment to carry it out is a great practice in itself. During both of these practices, maintain a positive attitude toward yourself and toward others. Stop searching for faults in others. Don't pollute your mind by cataloguing the bad behavior and unwholesome activities of others. Don't waste your time in distinguishing the virtuous from the non-virtuous or in deciding who is holy and who is a sinner. Simply mind your own business. Just as you have been trying to surrender both your vices and virtues to God, let others surrender theirs. If they don't, it is not your problem.

THE DAWNING OF ENLIGHTENMENT

Q These days bookstores and magazines that deal with spiritual subjects trumpet the claims of people who say that they're enlightened. Is it possible to somehow gauge the degree of enlightenment in ourselves and others? Are there signs of enlightenment, and if so, what are they?

First, it is important to be clear about what we mean when we use the word "enlightenment." Enlightenment means self-realization, inner illumination of the self, illumination from the inside out. In the light of self-realization you begin to see things the way they really are. Your personal prejudices and preoccupations regarding yourself and others vanish, and in this enlightened state you become realistic. You no longer have any false expectations of yourself or others. Thus you attain that state of happiness which cannot be altered by anything.

Purity of mind is a sure sign that enlightenment is dawning, and it is only through purity of mind that we come to know ourselves and our place in creation. The mind is a tool, a vehicle for experiencing the glory and greatness of the Divine. It is the perfect tool for experiencing the beauty that pervades every aspect of creation, every aspect of life. The purer the mind, the more clearly we see the world as the manifest form of the Divine abundant, beautiful, full of mystery and surprises.

Anyone who claims to be enlightened and yet has no love for Nature is confused, for those who have had a glimpse of the Divine automatically become lovers of Nature. Nature is an extension of the Divine. Just as God resides in each individual heart—hidden deep, invisible to us—so is the Divine present in every blade of grass, in dancing streams, in the shining stars. If your heart does not respond to the call of the birds, the wind in the trees, the Moon slipping behind a cloud, you have not understood that the Divine manifests in every form of Nature. And when you find yourself responding to the beauty of Nature—when you begin to see beauty even in dust storms, floods, hail, the sparseness of the desert, as well as in a lush rainforest—the divine being within you is awakening. That in itself begins to purify your mind—it becomes more and more transparent, more and more joyful. Such a mind is no longer able to cast a veil over the light that shines within. This is a sure sign that enlightenment is dawning.

Then is serving Nature the same as serving the Divine?

Anyone who is dedicated to serving Nature, to preserving her beauty, and to protecting the integrity of the environment is a spiritual person. Even those who are not engaged in a recognizable form of spiritual practice, even those who say they have no interest in spiritual matters—somewhere deep down they are spiritual people. Their life itself is a spiritual practice because they are contributing to God's creation, serving Nature herself. When such people die, they leave a great legacy for others because their efforts have enhanced the purity of the air, the water, or the soil. If someone plants trees, for example, that person is automatically contributing to the health, joy, and well-being of others. Those trees will produce oxygen, give shade, provide homes for the birds long after the one who planted them is gone. This a high form of service.

Is service to Nature the highest form of service?

The highest form is contributing to the field of knowledge. And the highest form of knowledge is that which brings about a qualitative transformation in human life—in other words, spiritual knowledge. This knowledge is not associated with ritualistic practices or visiting temples, mosques, or churches. The value of such activities is limited. True spiritual knowledge allows you to reflect on the meaning and purpose of life—how to find it, how to hold on to it, and how to figure out what is right and what is not right—without being dependent on others. The highest form of spiritual knowledge helps you understand what is the best way of living in the world and attaining the higher goals of life while contributing to the peace and happiness of others.

From time to time, for example, people have interpreted the ancient wisdom so that it can be understood in modern times. When we contribute to that kind of endeavor, we are serving God and humanity on a large scale. That is the best method of helping ourselves and others, because by doing so we create the means to acquire the knowledge that helps us gain access to ourselves. Without it we remain dependent on external advice: we go to this pandit, that priest, this teacher, that therapist, consult this book, listen to that tape. And even after seeking advice from all quarters, some degree of doubt and fear remains. It is only when we gain knowledge from within that we are completely free from our own doubts and fears. This is the knowledge that helps us gain access to ourselves, shows us how to purify our mind and heart, and teaches us how to bring about a qualitative transformation in our own life. That is the highest form of knowledge. Contributing to the expansion of that kind of knowledge is the best way to serve ourselves and others, to please ourselves and please God. That is how we attain true enlightenment.

Q **When the mind is enlightened—when it has merged with the soul—what kind of experience is left? Does the mind continue to have experiences after enlightenment?**

An enlightened mind sees everything in the light of the soul. Its experiences become pure and objective. Mind merged with soul becomes *drashta* (the seer) rather than *bhokta* (the victim of experiences). Similarly, the action of an enlightened person becomes spontaneous and effortless, and the fruits of action do not bind the performer, because the true performer—mind merged with soul—does not identify itself with the action, nor does it cling to the fruit of the action. In fact, the experiences you have after enlightenment are the only valid ones. Before that, any experience you have is tainted by the prejudices and preoccupations of your impure mind, your habit patterns, and the clinging of your senses. Merging with atman does not mean that you lose your mind; rather, you get the best form of mind you can imagine. This mind is as limitless and transparent as the soul itself.

It is known as the perfect mind.

An enlightened person doesn't become inert, useless, or dull. Quite the contrary: such a person becomes sharp, quick, fast. They will also exhibit the following five qualities:

Shraddha: Faith. An enlightened person becomes endowed with faith—faith which is not contaminated by the slightest trace of doubt.

Virya: An indomitable will. Once an enlightened person decides to do something, nothing can stop them.

Smriti: Memory. Once something enters the mind of an enlightened person, it stays there. Memory becomes so powerful that they never forget what they said, what they decided to do, or what is the goal of their life.

Prajña: The flash of intuition that comes with clarity of mind. An enlightened person comes to know things they never thought they knew. As soon as the question flashes, the answer is there—coming from some deeper field of intuitive wisdom where the ordinary mind can't reach.

Samadhi: The state in which all questions are answered. This state is beyond language, yet the person is fully conscious, fully aware. All memories are present, but the mind is so stable that those memories aren't constantly pouring in to the field of conscious awareness. When an enlightened person needs to remember something, they remember it. Otherwise, the mind is free from memories.

These five qualities unfold as enlightenment dawns. And the more you cultivate these qualities through constant practice, self-study, and self-reflection, the closer you are to enlightenment, the clearer your mind becomes, and the more these virtues begin to grow automatically.

the Journey's end

The longing of the soul sets us on the path and keeps us there until we realize our true identity. We may occasionally get sidetracked, our pace may slow to a crawl, but even so we remain curious about who we are, where we have come from, and where we will go after we die. It doesn't matter whether we are atheists or theists; all of us are under the influence of an invisible inner force that will not let us rest until we have unveiled the mysteries of life and attained a state of spiritual revelation which frees us forever from fear, anguish, and loneliness. It is the longing for this freedom that impels us to undertake the spiritual journey and that will not let us rest until we know ourselves on every level.

We can reach the goal only if we broaden our understanding of life and stubbornly refuse to settle for anything less than spiritual revelation. We must understand the difference between developing psychic powers and attaining spiritual wisdom, and strive for the latter even at the cost of the former. As we have seen in the preceding pages, we must not ignore our body and mind, but it is folly to focus on these to the exclusion of the more subtle aspects of our being. Gaining access to our true self requires penetrating the outer layers of our being, one after the other, but while doing this, we must take care not to become ensnared by the charms and temptations of the external world or by our own multi-level personalities.

Finding a Focus

Success in spiritual endeavors requires a one-pointed mind. But before cultivating the skill of one-pointedness, we must be sure we have our sights set on the highest Truth. Spiritual revelation comes only from samadhi, or spiritual absorption. Samadhi requires a spiritual object into which the mind can be absorbed. Selection of this object is all-important. A mind absorbed in a non-spiritual object may gain great powers of concentration and may even exhibit miraculous powers, but it cannot open our heart and connect it with the Divine. Such practices and the experiences they induce have nothing to do with spirituality. This point is clarified by the following story, versions of which appear throughout the scriptures:

Long ago there was a potter who lived near the main gate of a great city. He had nothing in the world but his potter's wheel, a donkey to transport clay, a kiln to fire the pots, and his skillful hands. All day long he sat in front of the rotating wheel giving shape to pots. He looked up from his work only when the king and his retinue came riding by with their chariots and well-bred horses. Once the riders were gone, his concentration returned to the pot forming between his hands. Every now and then the memory of the strength and beauty of the king's horses flickered through his mind.

This potter had one great quality: a remarkably one-pointed mind. He gained this one-pointedness by concentrating his attention on the center of his rotating wheel. Even when he was not actually making pots, just thinking of the center of the wheel allowed him to ward off all other thoughts and to attain such a deep state of mental absorption that awareness of time and space were left behind. People thought that he was a great meditator. They believed that by virtue of having such a one-pointed mind, he must have attained inner wisdom. Eventually he became so famous for having mastered his mind that he was summoned to the royal palace. The king made a public declaration that if the potter could demonstrate his ability to withdraw his mind from all external affairs, turn it inward, and maintain this state of inner absorption for a prolonged period, he would honor the potter with any gift he desired.

The potter was delighted. He asked for the gift of a horse, and the king took him to the stable to select one. The potter was a good judge of horses and chose the best one in the stable, the magnificent red stallion that was the king's favorite mount. The party then returned to the king's audience hall, and the potter sat down in the center of the room, surrounded by the king and his courtiers. The potter closed his eyes, withdrew his mind from all directions, and focused it on the image of his wheel.

Strangely, he found it hard to concentrate. His mind kept returning to the image of the red horse. His fear that he would lose the bet created anxiety. But he was smart—he switched his object of concentration from his potter's wheel to the red horse. It worked. He began meditating on the horse. Soon he lost his external awareness and no longer remembered that he was sitting in front of the king, surrounded by courtiers. However, he was still fully aware of the process of meditation, himself as a meditator, and the horse as an object of meditation.

He went deeper. The trinity of meditation, meditator, and object of meditation gradually dissolved into a homogeneous unity. In that state, however, the thought of the horse remained as the prominent stream of awareness. Thus in a sense the potter's awareness of meditation as a process and himself as a meditator merged into the object of meditation—the horse.

The potter's absorption deepened further. Slowly the horse, with its discrete body, color, and shape, dissolved; only the idea of "horse" remained. The mind was totally absorbed in pure unalloyed horse-consciousness.

As his mind merged into pure horse-consciousness, the potter transcended the realm of time and space. Hours passed. Days passed. Months and years passed. Eventually, the magnificent red horse died. Then the king died and the prince assumed the throne. All the while, the potter remained absorbed in deep meditation. Throughout the kingdom people spoke of the potter's greatness, regretting that when he had lived among them they were too ignorant to recognize it. Now the assembly hall was reserved for the potter's samadhi. People came and bowed to him silently from a respectful distance.

Decades elapsed. Eventually the potter's consciousness began to descend from the highest unitary state—he again became aware of the horse as an entity with distinct limbs and features. He gradually became aware of himself as a meditator, the horse as an object of meditation, and the process of meditation. Next he became aware of the bet, then the now-dead king, and the assembly hall where he was sitting. Finally he became aware of the whole scenario. He opened his eyes and cried, "Your majesty, where is my red horse? Where is my red horse?"

People had expected that he would come back with some great spiritual revelation received in his deep meditation. They were shocked and disappointed to discover that he brought back only the horse, a mundane and transient object.

As this story shows, no matter which path we follow, no matter which discipline we practice, it is a spiritual pursuit only if it helps us gain access to our true self. A practice is spiritual only if it helps us penetrate the layers of our inner being, ultimately reaching that domain where the soul dwells in its perfect glory and bliss.

Traveling in Stages

As part of this systematic journey, we must discover the hidden wealth in our body. The body is the vehicle in which we undertake the spiritual journey. Even when it is bogged down in experiences of pleasure and pain, the body is a key to finding our lost treasure. We must learn how to enjoy the gift of the body while using it to serve the purpose of the soul. To discover our hidden wealth we have to learn to stop crippling the extraordinary abilities of the body and recapture and restore what we have lost. Understanding the principles of a healthy diet, how to keep the body strong and flexible, and how to breathe properly are all indispensable to our spiritual unfoldment. Making sure that we do not turn the living shrine of the body into a landfill is an integral part of our spiritual practice.

The next stage of the journey requires us to pay attention to the pranic sheath, the subtle body that is made of pure vital energy. This vital energy, known in yogic literature as the pranic force, stands between the body and mind and regulates the activities of both. Other traditions call this force *chi* or *hara*. It not only sustains the body and mind but also maintains a harmonious balance between them. If this energy is deranged, the health and well-being of both the body and mind are jeopardized. According to the masters, therefore, a system of spiritual practice will be incomplete and ineffective if it does not include techniques for working with this force.

Having gained some proficiency with the body and breath, the spiritual aspirant next seeks to free the forces of the mind. The mind can be the cause of bondage or of liberation. As we come to understand the workings of the mind, we begin to notice how an unstable mind disturbs the harmony of both the physical and pranic bodies, as well as the environment around us. We acquire firsthand experience of how useless thoughts and emotions prevent us from plumbing the depths of our inner self. At this stage the spiritual journey consists of practicing disciplines that help us discover and overcome problems embedded in our totally personal world: the world of our mind. A well-designed meditation practice is the vehicle for understanding the dynamics of the mind, as well as the causes of mental tranquility and mental turmoil. Such a practice gradually trains the mind to turn inward, and as it does, the practitioner begins to notice how the concentrated force of the mind penetrates its own sheath and unveils its own mystery.

Eventually we discover something even more subtle than the ordinary mind: our own personal realm of intelligence. As we journey inward, we notice that the powers of discrimination, self-trust, self-confidence, and determination flow from the center of our own intelligence. Because we have not gained access to this realm we are dependent on the shallow aspects of the mind, which know only how to argue, doubt, and be confused. A sincere seeker goes beyond the mysteries of the body, pranic sheath, and mind, reaching the domain of pure intelligence. Here we lift the veil and experience the brilliance of higher intelligence in its full glory.

The key to completing this stage of the journey successfully lies in refusing to be distracted by the bogus advice of the lower mind. We must turn away from the charms and temptations of the conscious mind, and refuse to be frightened by the contents of the unconscious mind. We must heed our inner voice. Firmness of conviction is a sure sign that we have reached the realm of our intelligence. Here our experiences become so clear and so satisfying that we have no need to verify their validity. Glimpses of pure bliss, known as intuitive flashes, begin to occur spontaneously. They are so intoxicating that we no longer care about the previous rules governing our journey. We rush headlong toward the center of bliss.

When this happens, worldly people may call us insane; others may call us mystics. Driven by this spiritual insanity, we cannot rest until we pierce the thin wall of duality veiling the boundless bliss. Having penetrated this mystery, we understand how those who have not done so cling helplessly to mortal life, while those who are fully enlightened go beyond and attain immortal, infinite bliss. Thus the journey ends.

Here at the summit, differences between Universal Consciousness and individual consciousness vanish. The aspirant becomes an adept. Secular and sacred, human and divine become one. The mystery of birth and death, the law of karma, and the dynamics of reincarnation stand revealed. Inebriated with the Love Divine, the child of infinity lives in the world and yet remains above it. For such a blessed one, success and failure, loss and gain, honor and insult, pleasure and pain, birth and death have no meaning. Far above such distinctions, the realized being builds a dwelling and disperses the light of love and knowledge to all those still trapped by the narrow confines of caste, creed, nationality, and cultish religious values. Such beings are the true light in the world, for darkness cannot stand against their brilliance. These realized souls enter and leave this world at will.

Although this is where the journey ends, those who have reached the goal may continue on the path as a means of helping and guiding others. They are the true givers, for they have found everything and need nothing.

Glossary

Advaita. Non-duality.

Agni sara. The essence of fire. A specific exercise to activate the navel center and unfold prana, the vital energy,

Asana. The physical postures of hatha yoga.

Atman. The pure self, pure consciousness. The atman is the real self, which is eternal. Its essential nature is truth, consciousness, and bliss, and it permeates the states of waking, dreaming, and sleeping. It remains above all mundane pains and pleasures, as opposed to the petty ego, which identifies itself with the objects of the world.

Ayurveda. The ancient Indian medical science that promotes a long, healthy life.

Bandhas. Special techniques of hatha yoga consisting of postures and breathing exercises; in English, such practices are roughly translated as "locks."

Bhastrika. A pranayama practice in which both the inhalation and exhalation are activated by the muscles of the lower abdomen and are vigorous and forceful.

Bija. Seed; root of all knowledge.

Bija mantra. A seed syllable; a phoneme, which in the science of mantra is the focus of divine powers.

Brahman. All-pervading, eternal, and absolute Truth.

Chakras. Centers of consciousness. There are seven centers: at the base of the spine, the pelvic center, the navel center, the heart center, the throat center, the center between the eyebrows, and the crown center.

Dvaita. Duality.

Guru. One who dispels the darkness of ignorance; a spiritual preceptor or guide.

Gurudeva. A way of referring to the guru with honor and respect; literally, "a bright being who dispels the darkness of ignorance."

Ishta Devata. The name and form of God which is most suitable to an aspirant; the completely personal concept of God.

Japa. Remembering a mantra; the practice of repeating a mantra at each bead of the *mala.*

Jñana. Knowledge; awareness; observation.

Kapalabhati. A yogic cleansing practice in which the exhalation is forceful and the inhalation is passive.

Kapha. In ayurveda, one the three *doshas,* or humors, of the body; the water dosha.

Karma. Action. It includes the law of cause and effect, actions and reactions, the driving forces of one's present and future.

Karma yoga. The yoga of action; the practice of performing one's actions selflessly, lovingly, and skillfully.

Kundalini shakti. The primordial force that remains dormant at the base of the spine; the coiled-up energy.

Mala. A string of 108 beads used for keeping track of the number of times a mantra is repeated.

Mantra. A set of divine syllables, sounds, or words revealed to the sages and used by a meditator as an object of meditation.

Mantra shastra. The literature pertaining to mantras and mantra *sadhana.*

Mudra. An advanced posture accompanied by pranayama used for attaining greater control over body and mind; in tantra yoga, a mudra is a hand gesture.

Muladhara. The first, most basic center of consciousness; according to kundalini yoga, it is located at the perineum.

Nadis. Energy channels; the pathways of the pranic force.

Nadi shodhanam. Energy-channel purification; a pranayama practice.

Nauli. A yogic technique for activating the solar plexus.

Niyamas. The five restraints that are the foundation of yoga practice: cleanliness, contentment, austerities, self-study, and surrender to God.

Pitta. In ayurveda, one the three *doshas,* or humors, of the body; the fire dosha.

Prakriti. Primordial nature; the cause of this manifest world.

Prana. The vital force that nourishes both body and mind; the energy that keeps body and mind together and thus keeps beings alive.

Pranayama. Control over and expansion of the vital force; yogic breathing exercises.

Pranic sheath. The body made of pranic energy; the connecting link between the subtle body and the physical body.

Purash charana. The practice of completing a specific number of repetitions of a mantra within a designated period of time; literally, "the first step toward the divine experience."

Raja yoga. "The royal path"; the eightfold path of yoga as described by Patanjali in the *Yoga Sutra.*

Ramayana. The tale of Rama; historically, the first scripture of the Sanskrit language.

Sadhana. Spiritual practice.

Samadhi. Spiritual absorption; the tranquil state of mind in which fluctuations of the mind no longer arise.

Samskaras. Mental impressions created by past actions.

Sankhya. The most ancient among all systems of Indian philosophy; it stands as the backbone of yoga practices.

Sattvic. Illuminating, uplifting energy; the force which is a prerequisite for spiritual unfoldment.

Shakta. Relating to Shakti, the Divine Mother.

Shakti. The Divine Mother; primordial energy; the eternal pulsation of consciousness.

Shaktipata. The descent or transmission of spiritual energy.

Shiva. The auspicious one; pure consciousness; the lord of yogis.

So hum. "I am that." A sound that flows with the breath and which can be used as a focal point during meditation.

Tapas. That which generates heat; austerities including practices which perfect the body, mind, and senses, and give rise to the power of determination; the second of the five observances that are the basis of spiritual practice.

Upanishads. The last portions of the Veda; a group of scriptures which expound the philosophy of non-dualism and yogic practices.

Vasanas. Subtle impressions of past deeds that influence the actions we perform in the present; habit patterns; innate tendencies of mind; subtle personality traits

Vata. In ayurveda, one the three *doshas*, or humors, of the body; the air dosha.

Veda. The world's most ancient scriptures, which contain the wisdom of the ancient sages. According to yogic tradition, every word of the Veda is divinely revealed wisdom.

Yamas. The five observances that regulate an aspirant's relationship with other beings: non-violence, truthfulness, non-stealing, discipline of senses, and non-possessiveness.

Yantra. A geometrical diagram that imparts a visual understanding of invisible forces of nature; a geometric figure laden with symbolic meanings, often used as an object of concentration.

Yoga. The Indian philosophy systematized and codified by the sage Patanjali; also, the practical aspect of any philosophy, particularly Sankhya. Literally, "yoke," referring to the uniting of the individual self and the Universal Self.

Yoga mudra. An advanced practice of breath retention done in the lotus posture.

Yoga Sutra. The collection of 196 aphorisms formulated by Patanjali to systematize and organize the ancient science of yoga.

Yogi. Practitioner of yoga; one who is adept in the practice of yoga.

of related Interest

FROM THE HIMALAYAN INSTITUTE PRESS

Books

From Death to Birth: Understanding Karma and Reincarnation
by Pandit Rajmani Tigunait, Ph.D.
The Power of Mantra and the Mystery of Initiation
by Pandit Rajmani Tigunait, Ph.D.
Tantra Unveiled by Pandit Rajmani Tigunait, Ph.D.
Meditation and Its Practice by Swami Rama
Path of Fire and Light, Volumes 1 and 2 by Swami Rama
A Practical Guide to Holistic Health by Swami Rama
The Royal Path: Practical Lessons on Yoga by Swami Rama
Science of Breath: A Practical Guide by Swami Rama et al.
Yoga: Mastering the Basics by Sandra Anderson and Rolf Sovik, Psy.D.
Meditation Is Boring? Putting Life in Your Spiritual Practice
by Linda Johnsen
Common Sense About Uncommon Wisdom by Dhruv S. Kaji
Choosing a Path by Swami Rama
Freedom from the Bondage of Karma by Swami Rama
Spirituality: Transformation Within and Without by Swami Rama
Yoga and Psychotherapy: The Evolution of Consciousness
by Swami Rama et al.

Tapes

Eight Steps to Self-Transformation by Pandit Rajmani Tigunait, Ph.D.
Nine Steps to Disarming the Mind by Pandit Rajmani Tigunait, Ph.D.
Guided Meditation for Beginners by Swami Rama
Learn to Meditate by Rolf Sovik, Psy.D.

About the author

The spiritual head of the Himalayan Institute, Pandit Rajmani Tigunait, Ph.D. is the successor of Swami Rama of the Himalayas. Lecturing and teaching worldwide for more than a quarter of a century, he is a regular contributor to *Yoga International* magazine, and the author of eleven books, including his classic work, *At the Eleventh Hour. The Biography of Swami Rama* of the Himalayas.

Pandit Tigunait holds two doctorates: one in Sanskrit from the University of Allahabad in India, and another in Oriental Studies from the University of Pennsylvania. Family tradition gave Pandit Tigunait access to a vast range of spiritual wisdom preserved in both the written and oral traditions. Before meeting his master, Pandit Tigunait studied Sanskrit, the language of the ancient scriptures of India; Pali, the language of Buddhist scriptures; Prakrit, the language of Jaina scriptures; and Zend-Avesta, the language of the Zorastrian tradition. In 1976, Swami Rama ordained Pandit Tigunait into the 5,000-year-old lineage of the Himalayan masters.

While living in the world with his wife and two children, Pandit Tigunait walks in the footsteps of his master — he writes, teaches, guides and administers the work and mission of the Himalayan Institute, a multi-national organization, while joyfully maintaining his personal commitment to his spiritual pursuits. He is thus an example of the core teachings of Swami Rama and the Himalayan sages: "Live in the world, and yet remain above it; find a balance between the sacred and mundane, and between worldly success and inner fulfillment."

the Himalayan institute

The main building of the Institute headquarters, near Honesdale, Pennsylvania

Founded in 1971 by Swami Rama, the Himalayan Institute has been dedicated to helping people grow physically, mentally, and spiritually by combining the best knowledge of both the East and the West.

Our International headquarters is located on a beautiful 400-acre campus in the rolling hills of the Pocono Mountains of northeastern Pennsylvania. The atmosphere here is one to foster growth, increased inner awareness, and calm. Our grounds provide a wonderfully peaceful and healthy setting for our seminars and extended programs. Students from around the world join us here to attend programs in such diverse areas as hatha yoga, meditation, stress reduction, ayurveda, nutrition, Eastern philosophy, psychology, and other subjects. Whether the programs are for weekend meditation retreats, week-long seminars on spirituality, months-long residential programs, or holistic health services, the attempt here is to provide an environment of gentle inner progress. We invite you to join with us in the ongoing process of personal growth and development.

The Institute is a nonprofit organization. Your membership in the Institute helps to support its programs. Please call or write for information on becoming a member.

programs, services and facilities

Institute programs share an emphasis on conscious holistic living and personal self-development, including:

- Special weekend or extended seminars to teach skills and techniques for increasing your ability to be healthy and enjoy life
- Meditation retreats and advanced meditation and philosophical instruction
- Vegetarian cooking and nutritional training
- Hatha yoga workshops
- Hatha yoga teachers training
- Residential programs for self-development
- Holistic health services, and Ayurvedic Rejuvenation and Pancha Karma Programs through the Institute's Center for Health and Healing.

A Quarterly Guide to Programs and Other Offerings is free within the USA. To request a copy, or for further information, call 800-822-4547 or 570-253-5551, fax 570-253-9078, email bqinfo @HimalayanInstitute.org, write the Himalayan Institute, RR 1 Box 1127, Honesdale, PA 18431-9706 USA, or visit our website at www.HimalayanInstitute.org.